Greek For All Ages

An Introduction to New Testament Greek

Greek For All Ages

An Introduction to New Testament Greek

Ann F. Castro

Word Association Publishers
www.wordassociation.com

Cover Design: Codex Sinaiticus
© British Library Board. All Rights Reserved (ADD 43725 f244v f245)

Greek font: Graeca UBS (Laser Greek II)
Used by permission of Linguist's Software, Inc. P.O. Box 580, Edmonds, WA 98020

Printed in the United States of America.

ISBN 13: 978-1-59571-204-2
Library of Congress Control Number: 2007934469

Word Association Publishers
205 5th Avenue
Tarentum, PA 15084
www.wordassociation.com

For all my students

σπούδασον σεαυτὸν δόκιμον παραστῆσαι τῷ θεῷ, ἐργάτην ἀνεπαίσχυντον, ὀρθοτομοῦντα τὸν λόγον τῆς ἀληθείας. (2 Timothy 2:15)

Πάτερ ἡμῶν ὁ ἐν τοῖς οὐρανοῖς
    ἁγιασθήτω τὸ ὄνομά σου·
    ἐλθέτω ἡ βασιλεία σου·
    γενηθήτω τὸ θέλημά σου,
        ὡς ἐν οὐρανῷ καὶ ἐπὶ γῆς·
    τὸν ἄρτον ἡμῶν τὸν ἐπιούσιον δὸς ἡμῖν σήμερον·
    καὶ ἄφες ἡμῖν τὰ ὀφειλήματα ἡμῶν,
        ὡς καὶ ἡμεῖς ἀφήκαμεν τοῖς ὀφειλέταις ἡμῶν·
    καὶ μὴ εἰσενέγκῃς ἡμᾶς εἰς πειρασμόν,
        ἀλλὰ ῥῦσαι ἡμᾶς ἀπὸ τοῦ πονηροῦ. [ἀμήν.]

Table of Contents

Preface 11

Works Cited 15

Chapter 1
The Alphabet / Accents / Breathing Marks / Diphthongs / The Lord's Prayer. . . 16

Chapter 2
The Verb: Present Active Indicative / Nu-movable / Negation / Proclitics / Conjunctions / Aspect 19

Chapter 3
The Noun and Article: Nominative and Accusative Cases (Second Declension Masculine) / Subject / Direct Object / Prepositions with the Accusative Case / Noun Accent / Word Order 23

Chapter 4
The Verb: Imperfect Active Indicative / Verb Accent / Postpositives 27

Chapter 5
The Noun and Article: Genitive and Dative Cases (Second Declension Masculine) / Genitive of Possession / Indirect Object / Prepositions with the Genitive Case / Prepositions with the Dative Case 31

Chapter 6
The Verb: Future Active Indicative / Principal Parts of a Verb / The Particles μέν and δέ / Elision / Genitive Direct Object / Dative Direct Object 36

Chapter 7
The Noun and Article: First Declension Feminine (Nominative Singular Ending in Eta) 41

Chapter 8
The Noun and Article: First Declension Feminine (Nominative Singular Ending in Alpha) / Prepositions with the Genitive or Accusative Case 43

Chapter 9
The Verb: Aorist Active Indicative / First and Second Aorist / Third Principal Part 46

Chapter 10
The Verb εἰμί: Present and Imperfect Indicative / Enclitics / Predicate Nominative 52

Chapter 11
Compound Verbs / First Class Conditions 56

Chapter 12
The Noun and Article: Second Declension Neuter / The Definite Article as a
Substantive with a Genitive or Prepositional Phrase / Numbers from One to
Ten / Objective Genitive / Adverbial καί 59

Chapter 13
Deponent Verbs: Present M/P and Future Middle Indicative / Deponent
Futures / Dative of Destination / Dative of Association 63

Chapter 14
Adjectives (First and Second Declension) / Agreement of Adjectives /
Position of Adjectives / Adjectives as Substantives 68

Chapter 15
Deponent Verbs: Imperfect M/P and Aorist Middle Indicative /
Subordinate Causal Clauses 73

Chapter 16
First Declension Masculine Nouns / Second Declension Feminine Nouns /
Nouns with Contracted Endings / Second Class Conditions / Preposition
with Genitive, Dative, or Accusative Case 76

Chapter 17
The Passive Voice: Both a Form and a Concept 81

Chapter 18
The Middle Voice: Both a Form and a Concept 84

Chapter 19
Personal Pronouns / Intensive Pronoun / Reflexive Pronouns /
Dative of Means / Punctuation 92

Chapter 20
Epsilon Contract Verbs / Indirect Statement (Indirect Discourse) 99

Chapter 21
Demonstrative Pronouns / Possessive Pronouns / Reciprocal Pronoun /
Dative of Time 104

Chapter 22
Alpha Contract Verbs / Omicron Contract Verbs / Regular Formation
of Adverbs 108

Chapter 23
*Interrogative Pronouns and Adverbs / Indefinite Pronoun and Adverbs /
Partitive Genitive (Genitive of the Whole) / Historical Present* 112

Chapter 24
*Third Declension Masculine and Feminine Nouns / Vocative Case /
Genitive of Time / The Preposition εἰς to Express Purpose* 118

Chapter 25
*Contract Futures / Liquid Stem Verbs / Aorist Active Indicative of
γινώσκω / Indirect Question* 125

Chapter 26
*Relative Pronoun / Indefinite Relative Pronoun / Relative Adjectives /
Relative Particles and Conjunctions* 129

Chapter 27
*Third Declension Neuter Nouns / Adjectives and Numbers with Third
Declension Forms / Comparative Adjectives / Genitive of Comparison* . . . 136

Chapter 28
*The Verb: Perfect Active Indicative / Pluperfect Active Indicative / Fourth
Principal Part* 145

Chapter 29
*The Verb: Perfect M/P Indicative / Pluperfect M/P Indicative / Fifth
Principal Part / Perfect M/P Participle / Periphrastic Constructions* 152

Chapter 30
*The Verb: Aorist Passive Indicative / Future Passive Indicative / Sixth
Principal Part / Overview of the Indicative* 159

Chapter 31
-μι Verbs 165

Chapter 32
Participles: General Introduction / Participle Forms 176

Chapter 33
Participle Uses 194

Chapter 34
*The Subjunctive Mood: General Introduction / Subjunctive Forms /
Uses of the Subjunctive (Part 1: ἵνα Clauses)* 208

Chapter 35
Uses of the Subjunctive (Part 2) 111

Chapter 36
*Infinitives: General Introduction / Accusative Subject of the Infinitive /
Infinitive Forms / Uses of the Infinitive (Part 1) / Accusative of Measure
(or Extent of Time)* 226

Chapter 37
Uses of the Infinitive (Part 2) 233

Chapter 38
The Imperative Mood: General Introduction / Forms and Uses 237

Appendix A: Principal Parts List 243

Appendix B: Accents and Breathing Marks That Matter 248

Appendix C: Guide to Unaugmented Aorist Stems 251

Appendix D: The Optative Mood 253

Text Vocabulary 256

Vocabulary Supplement 267

Index 271

Preface

Welcome to the study of New Testament Greek. While I know that some of you have been eagerly anticipating this opportunity to acquire a valuable tool for your study of Scripture, I also know that there is a fair amount of trepidation surrounding the study of Greek. I hope that in the days and weeks to come you will return to this introduction, because some of it won't make much sense to you until you actually work with Greek and learn what it is like. Two things above all I want you to remember: Greek is hard and Greek is worthwhile. I am confident that each and every one of you can do the work involved in learning New Testament Greek, but it will take effort and cooperation. Some of you may have had bad experiences with language learning in the past. My hope is that you will put that behind you and prepare for a different kind of learning experience. The materials which I have created for your study are designed to help you along the way, but there are several things you need to know from the start.

Greek is not English. You know that, of course, and yet there is always the temptation to hope that, apart from a different alphabet and some different vocabulary, Greek is some kind of "code" for English. There are, of course, some similarities: a subject is still a subject, a prepositional phrase is still a prepositional phrase, etc. But basically you must accept Greek on its own terms.

One of the main ways in which Greek is different from English is that there are many more forms to learn. Take a basic verb like "swim." In English we can use the subject "I" or "you" or "we" or "they" with this same form. The only change necessary is that, if the subject is "he" or "she," we must say "swims." In Greek, however, the form of the verb changes to correspond to each of the different subjects. We will meet these forms in due course, but in general there are a couple of things to remember. (1) Greek likes to "re-cycle" word endings, so that when you learn something in one context you will likely see it again in another. Make this work for you! (2) It is more important to be able to recognize given forms when you see them than to be able to rattle off lists. The best way to accomplish this is to make good use of your homework exercises. By the time you are done with the work for a given chapter, if you have done it properly, you should know most of the material without the tedious memorizing of lists. Nevertheless, memorization is important and it is better to do it thoroughly at first than to do it half way and then keep playing "catch up."

A very important facet of Greek study, and one of the harder ones to get used to, is the need to be simultaneously precise and flexible. Let me explain. When you are deciding how to translate a given word, you must be precise about identifying the exact form and knowing the vocabulary root. But then you must be flexible, because the form may convey a variety of concepts and you must decide which one applies. Likewise the vocabulary root may represent a number of different English ideas, and again you must choose. There are also times when Greek conveys information in subtle ways which may not come across in translation. And there are times when, although you must choose one word for translation, the other possible meanings may color your understanding of a passage. All of this, by the way, is what people mean when they talk about things "getting lost in translation." Any translation you read represents someone else's choices, and all the other possible choices are no longer available to you unless you have access to the original language. Some of this will become apparent very quickly and some will not apply until later, but it is a good idea to have an awareness from the start that translation is, in many ways, more of an art than a science.

This text is part of a set of materials designed to facilitate the teaching and the learning of New Testament Greek. It is intended to serve as a long-term reference tool. It is not a complete grammar book in that it does not include every possible use of various noun and verb forms. But it does set forth the basics. In addition to this text, the materials also include a workbook and study guide with answer keys and a CD for teachers and those who are working on their own. Both of these include their own separate introductions, so I will not repeat here what is said there. The title reflects my hope that these materials will be used in a wide range of settings: the traditional classroom at various levels, home schooling, review for clergy and classes within their parishes, and individual study.

The material has been developed in accordance with two standard reference texts. While these are generally more complicated than is helpful for beginning students, you will see them referenced occasionally. They are *Greek Grammar Beyond the Basics* by Daniel B. Wallace and *A Greek-English Lexicon of the New Testament and Other Early Christian Literature*, 3rd edition, revised and edited by Frederick William Danker. Much of the terminology has been chosen to agree with the Wallace grammar book in order to provide a smooth transition to upper level work. Eventually you will probably want to acquire these reference works for yourself.

At the beginning of the course, you will find that chapters alternate between verb chapters and noun chapters. This allows you to begin immediately to work with short sentences. As we move on, other parts of speech are gradually added. At the very end of the course, you will find chapters dealing with the most complex material: participles, the subjunctive mood, infinitives, and the imperative mood. Each chapter includes a section entitled "preparing for the quiz" or "preparing for the exam." This gives a summary of the important points to be remembered from the chapter, but it is not a substitute for reading each chapter thoroughly and learning the new material. I always suggest to my students that, before doing the workbook exercises, they re-read the chapter carefully. Especially in a regular classroom setting, it is impossible to pick up all the points in the chapter the first time around.

Throughout the text, you will find boxes enclosing various paradigms: the full forms of the new material to be learned. Rather than repeating all of these at the end of the text, I have provided a comprehensive index which includes references to forms. The table of contents also lists the material covered in each chapter. The combination of the index and the table of contents should enable you to quickly access any information you need.

The text, along with the accompanying workbook and study guide, represents my attempt to provide as clear explanatory material as possible. You will often find me saying, "Do this!" or "Don't do that!" I have tried to point out those places which often cause difficulty and I have tried, as much as possible, to offer explanations in easy to understand language, though some technical terminology is necessary. I sometimes describe myself as a guide who has been over the territory many times and knows where all the potholes and road blocks are. My intent is to guide you through and around these to an understanding of how the Greek language works. As you have already seen in this introduction, I often address you, the student, directly, rather than speaking in impersonal terms.

Finally, I would like to point out a couple of details about the text itself. (1) There are several appendices in the back. Your teacher (or the teacher's manual, if you are working alone) will point these out at the appropriate time and tell you how to make the best use of them. (2) Several years ago I made the decision to "frontload" the vocabulary. What this means is that the great majority of the vocabulary you are asked to learn appears in Chapters 1-27. After that point, most chapters do not have more than five or six new words to learn, and some have none at all. This is so that, as we move into the more complicated material and you are being asked to learn new verbal forms, you are not also being asked to add a lot of new words.

I really do owe this project to all my students. I began by creating additional exercises for them and just kept going. I especially thank all those who gave me the encouragement and gentle prodding to get the project published, especially Travis Hines who finally pushed me to get it done. It would take too long to list everyone and I'm sure I would miss someone. To anyone who provided any kind of encouragement, constructive criticism, challenge, or inspiration – thanks!

As the project has neared completion, there have been several who have made special contributions. Again, thanks go to Travis for all the time spent critiquing and proofreading the materials. I should also mention those whose sharp eyes helped catch and correct the many errors in the text, especially Gerry Clemmons, Roman Roldan, Martha Chambers, Larry Noyes, Kathleen Bushyager, and Kyle Tomlin. Thanks also to Lauren Larkin who provided a second set of eyes in correcting the proofs. And finally there is the small group who gave suggestions on the presentation of the material: Travis Hines, Martha Chambers, Larry Noyes, and Tara Jernigan.

Then there are a few individuals who made unique contributions: Tara Jernigan and her son Isaac who have been using the materials for home schooling, my colleague Rod Whitacre who has offered encouragement and suggestions, my college professor Ruth Pavlantos who put me started on the journey, and my husband Dwight who has been with me all the way.

Finally, I would like to thank Tom Costello and Word Association for helping me take the last step on the journey to publication.

I have enjoyed producing these materials over the years and my students claim that they have enjoyed using them to learn Greek. I hope that you will "complete our joy" by making good use of them and by making your own discovery of the adventure of New Testament Greek.

$$\tau\hat{\omega}\ \theta\epsilon\hat{\omega}\ \mu\acute{o}\nu\omega\ \dot{\eta}\ \delta\acute{o}\xi\alpha$$

Ann F. Castro

Works Cited

Berry
A Dictionary of New Testament Greek Synonyms, George Berry (Grand Rapids, MI: Zondervan, 1979)

Bowne
Paradigms and Principal Parts for the Greek New Testament, Dale Russell Bowne (Lanham, MD and London: University Press of America, 1987)

Danker
A Greek-English Lexicon of the New Testament and Other Early Christian Literature, 3rd edition, revised and edited by Frederick William Danker (Chicago and London: University of Chicago Press, 2000)

GNT
Greek New Testament, 4th revised edition, edited by Barbara Aland, Kurt Aland, Johannes Karavidopoulos, Carlo M. Martini, and Bruce M. Metzger (Stuttgart: United Bible Societies, 1994)

Hewett
New Testament Greek: A Beginning and Intermediate Grammar, James Allen Hewett (Peabody, MA: Hendrickson, 1986)

Metzger
Lexical Aids for Students of New Testament Greek, Bruce Metzger (Published by Author: Distributed by Theological Book Agency, Princeton, NJ, 1983)

NASB
New American Standard Bible (Glendale, CA: Regal Books, 1973)

Robertson
A Grammar of the Greek New Testament in the Light of Historical Research, 4th edition, A.T. Robertson (New York: Hodder & Stoughton, Stoughton, 1923)

RSV
The Holy Bible: Revised Standard Version (New York: American Bible Society, 1973, 1980)

Smyth
Greek Grammar, Herbert Weir Smyth, revised by Gordon M. Messing (Cambridge, MA: Harvard University Press, 1963)

Vance
Greek Verbs in the New Testament and Their Principal Parts, Laurence M. Vance (Pensacola, FL: Vance Publications, 2006)

Wallace
Greek Grammar Beyond the Basics: An Exegetical Syntax of the New Testament, Daniel B. Wallace (Grand Rapids, MI: Zondervan, 1996)

Young
Intermediate New Testament Greek: A Linguistic and Exegetical Approach, Richard A. Young (Nashville: Broadman & Holman, 1994)

Chapter 1
The Alphabet / Accents / Breathing Marks / Diphthongs / The Lord's Prayer

THE ALPHABET: The Greek alphabet consists of twenty-four characters. Some of them correspond very closely to our alphabet and will be recognizable to you; others are quite different. You will need to be able to **recognize** both capital (uncial) and small (minuscule) letters. You will also need to be able to **write** the small letters. You should know the letters and their names in alphabetical order, since eventually you will have to use a lexicon. Make it a practice from the beginning to name the letters by their Greek names.

One difference which you will notice immediately between English and Greek is that the majority of Greek sentences do not start with a capital letter. Capital letters will appear in the GNT (Greek New Testament) under the following circumstances:

    1) The beginning of a paragraph.
    2) Proper names.
    3) Quotations and direct speech.
    4) The beginning of a sentence which, in the opinion of the editors, starts a
       new thought.

ACCENTS: On each of the Greek words which follow you will see an accent mark: acute (´), grave (`), or circumflex (^). Originally the accent was a pitch accent, indicating the raising or lowering of the voice. It is customary today to treat the accent as a stress accent, stressing the accented syllable. Generally there is one accent per word, although some small words have no accent and certain situations occur when a word has two accents. Rules for accent placement will be discussed in subsequent chapters. Accent marks are always placed on a vowel or diphthong. In the case of diphthongs, the accent is placed on the second of the two letters. If the first letter of a word is a capital letter, the accent mark will be placed in front of that letter.

BREATHING MARKS: A word which begins with a vowel, a diphthong, or the letter *rho* has a breathing mark on the first syllable. a smooth breathing mark (') or a rough breathing mark ('). This mark goes above a small letter and in front of a capital letter. Breathing marks, like accents, go on the second letter of a diphthong. A smooth breathing mark has no effect on pronunciation. A rough breathing puts an "h" sound in front of the vowel, diphthong, or *rho*. It is possible for the same letter to have both an accent and a breathing mark.

Name	Uncial	Miniscule	English =	Pronunciation
alpha	A	α	a	f<u>a</u>ther / $\delta\rho\hat{\alpha}\mu\alpha$
beta	B	β	b	<u>b</u>oy / $\beta\iota\beta\lambda\acute{\iota}o\nu$
gamma	Γ	γ	g	<u>g</u>o / $\dot{\alpha}\gamma\alpha\theta\acute{o}\varsigma$
		$\gamma\gamma$	ng	si<u>ng</u> / $\ddot{\alpha}\gamma\gamma\epsilon\lambda o\varsigma$
		$\gamma\kappa$	ngk	sli<u>nk</u> / $\ddot{\eta}\nu\epsilon\gamma\kappa\alpha$
delta	Δ	δ	d	<u>d</u>awn / $\delta\acute{\epsilon}\kappa\alpha$
epsilon	E	ϵ	e	b<u>e</u>d / $\theta\epsilon\acute{o}\varsigma$
zeta	Z	ζ	z	<u>z</u>ero / $\zeta\omega\acute{\eta}$
			dz	a<u>dz</u>e / $\beta\alpha\pi\tau\acute{\iota}\zeta\omega$
eta	H	η	e	th<u>ey</u> / $\phi\omega\nu\acute{\eta}$
theta	Θ	θ	th	<u>th</u>eology / $\theta\epsilon\acute{o}\varsigma$
iota	I	ι	i	b<u>i</u>t / $\pi\acute{\iota}\sigma\tau\iota\varsigma$
				mach<u>i</u>ne / $\pi\acute{\iota}\nu\omega$
			y [j]	<u>y</u>ellow / $'I\eta\sigma o\hat{\upsilon}\varsigma$
kappa	K	κ	k	<u>k</u>eep / $\dot{\alpha}\kappa o\acute{\upsilon}\omega$
lambda	Λ	λ	l	<u>l</u>etter / $\lambda\acute{o}\gamma o\varsigma$
mu	M	μ	m	<u>m</u>ine / $\nu\acute{o}\mu o\varsigma$
nu	N	ν	n	<u>n</u>ow / $\nu\acute{o}\mu o\varsigma$
xi	Ξ	ξ	x	a<u>x</u> / $\ddot{\epsilon}\xi$
omicron	O	o	o	f<u>o</u>g / $\lambda\acute{o}\gamma o\varsigma$
pi	Π	π	p	<u>p</u>at / $\pi\iota\sigma\tau\epsilon\acute{\upsilon}\omega$
rho	P	ρ	r	<u>r</u>ow / $\theta\eta\sigma\alpha\upsilon\rho\acute{o}\varsigma$
sigma	Σ	σ,ς	s	<u>s</u>ettle / $\kappa\acute{o}\sigma\mu o\varsigma$
tau	T	τ	t	<u>t</u>own / $\tau\alpha\hat{\upsilon}\rho o\varsigma$
upsilon	Υ	υ	u [y]	French u, German ü / $\nu\hat{\upsilon}\nu$
phi	Φ	ϕ	ph	<u>ph</u>ilosophy / $\phi\acute{\iota}\lambda o\varsigma$
chi	X	χ	ch	lo<u>ch</u> / $\psi\upsilon\chi\acute{\eta}$
psi	Ψ	ψ	ps	hi<u>ps</u> / $\psi\upsilon\chi\acute{\eta}$
omega	Ω	ω	o	wr<u>o</u>te / $\lambda\acute{\upsilon}\omega$

DIPHTHONGS: Certain combinations of vowels produce a single sound unit. These combinations are called diphthongs. The following diphthongs occur in Greek. (Any other vowel combinations need to be pronounced as separate sounds.)

αι	aisle / παῖς
ει	fr<u>ei</u>ght / εἰμί
οι	b<u>oi</u>l / φίλοι
υι	q<u>ue</u>en / υἱός
αυ	n<u>ow</u> / θησαυρός
ευ, ηυ	f<u>eu</u>d / θεραπεύω
ου	s<u>ou</u>p / ἀκούω

THE LORD'S PRAYER: From now on, you should begin each day's class or study time with the Lord's Prayer (Matthew 6:9b-13) in Greek. You will find it at the beginning of the book facing the Table of Contents. You can begin immediately to name the letters and to practice pronouncing the words.

PREPARING FOR THE QUIZ:

(1) You should be able to *recognize and identify by name* both the uncial (capital) and miniscule (small) letters.

(2) You should know the *sounds* of the letters and be able to pronounce them in words.

(3) You should be able to say and write the Greek alphabet in *Greek alphabetical order*.

(4) You should be able to *write the miniscule Greek letters* in such a way that they can be recognized for what they are.

Chapter 2
The Verb: Present Active Indicative / Nu-movable /
Negation / Proclitics / Conjunctions / Aspect

PRESENT ACTIVE INDICATIVE: One of the first things to be learned about verbs is the language grammarians use to describe them. (This is actually quite a complicated topic, but for now we will keep it as straightforward as possible.) Three words of this grammatical language appear in the chapter title: *present, active,* and *indicative. Present* refers to the *tense* of the verb. Verbs in the present tense refer to something going on in the present time (from the viewpoint of the speaker or writer) or something which is always happening or true. *Active* refers to the *voice* of the verb. When the voice is active the subject of the verb is doing / does the action of the verb. *Indicative* refers to the *mood* of the verb. Verbs in the indicative mood describe an action or state of being as real or actual. All the verbs in this chapter are present active indicative.

The Greek verb is *inflected.* This means that it has different forms (or more specifically different endings) corresponding to the personal pronoun subjects.

In English a complete *conjugation* (listing of forms) of a regular verb includes the personal pronouns and shows very little change in form.

EXAMPLE: I hear   we hear
              you (s.) hear   you (pl.) hear
              he/she/it hear<u>s</u>   they hear

Two additional terms used in verb identification are *person (first, second,* and *third)* and *number (singular* and *plural).*

> First person singular is "I." / First person plural is "we."
> Second person is always "you."
> Third person singular is "he/she/it." / Third person plural is "they."

Because Greek has a different form for each of these six possibilities, it is possible to omit the personal pronouns. [They do exist; we will learn them later.] The present active indicative has a *stem* which remains constant and gives the root meaning of the word and six *personal endings* which correspond to the pronouns.

Using the stem λυ–, which has as one of its meanings "free," we can write the *present active indicative conjugation* thus:

	Singular			Plural	
1st person	λύω	I free		λύομεν	we free
2nd person	λύεις	you (s.) free		λύετε	you (pl.) free
3rd person	λύει	he/she/it frees		λύουσι(ν)	they free

NU-MOVABLE: The third person plural adds a *nu* to the end of the verb if the verb comes at the end of a sentence or the next word begins with a vowel. The so-called ***nu-movable*** is also *sometimes* added when the next word begins with a consonant. Be prepared to recognize the third person plural either with or without the *nu*.

ACCENT: In all of these forms there is an ***acute accent*** on the syllable immediately preceding the personal ending. Be sure to include the accent when you are doing your homework exercises. The placement in this paradigm is easy to learn. Further accent rules will be explained as needed.

VERY IMPORTANT NOTE: In addition to "free" (the English simple present), the Greek present tense can also be translated with the English present progressive ("we are freeing"). Much less frequently, it is also possible to use the emphatic present ("they do free"). Context is generally the determining factor. Furthermore, "free" is not the only meaning conveyed by the stem λυ–. Among the other possibilities are "release," "untie," "break," and "loose." Again context will help in making the choice. The result of all this is the combination of precision and flexibility which was mentioned in the introduction. In terms of precision, λύομεν is always present active indicative first person plural. In terms of flexibility, it could be translated: "we release," "we are breaking," "we free," "we are untying," etc.

NEGATION: Negation in Greek is expressed by the word οὐ before a word beginning with a consonant and οὐκ before a word beginning with a vowel. The negation word is generally placed in front of the word it negates (most often the verb), though it can be placed elsewhere for some kind of emphasis.

οὐ πιστεύω.   I do not believe.
οὐκ ἀκούει.   He does not hear. / She is not listening.

PROCLITICS: Note that οὐ and οὐκ do not have an accent, only a breathing mark. Words such as this are considered to be so closely connected to what follows that they are not accented separately. These words are called "proclitics."

CONJUNCTIONS: A conjunction is a word that connects two or more words, phrases, or clauses. Two common Greek conjunctions are καί ("and") and ἀλλά ("but"). When these words appear in a vocabulary list they have an acute accent. When they are followed immediately (i.e., with no intervening punctuation) in a sentence by another word, the accent is changed to a **grave** accent. This is true not only for these two words but for any word with an acute accent on the last (or only) syllable.

ἐσθίουσι καὶ πίνουσιν.   They are eating and drinking.

ASPECT / TYPE OF ACTION: In Greek, the tense of a verb gives more information than just time. In fact, absolute time is only a part of the verb tense in the indicative mood. In addition, the tense indicates something about the nature of the action or how the writer views the action (or wants the reader to view it). The present tense describes an action as on-going or continuous (though the duration may be very brief) or it describes something which is always happening or true. It sees the action in progress. On the one hand, the present tense is used for specific situations: "The cat is chasing a mouse." / "I hear you." On the other hand, it can also be used for general statements: "Cats chase mice." Statements of the latter type sometimes have the characteristic of being maxims or general truths: "God loves us." The question of "aspect" or "type of action" should never be ignored when dealing with Greek verbs.

VOCABULARY

The words given in brackets following some vocabulary entries are English **derivatives** from the Greek words. These are not usually the same as a definition for the Greek word, though occasionally they are, but they can serve as memory aids for vocabulary learning (and for expanding your English vocabulary!).

λύω – loose, untie; free, set free, release; break, annul; destroy [analysis]
δοξάζω – glorify [doxology]
κωλύω – hinder, prevent
ἀκούω – hear, listen (to) [acoustics]
λέγω – say, speak, tell
ἔχω – have, possess, hold

ἐσθίω – eat

σῴζω – save (The mark under the *omega* is called an *iota subscript*. It is part of
the spelling, but does not affect pronunciation. We will see more
examples of this later.)

πίνω – drink

πέμπω – send

βαπτίζω – baptize [baptize]

ἀγοράζω – buy

ἐλπίζω – hope, hope (for)

οὐ, οὐκ – not [utopia]

καί – and

ἀλλά – but

PREPARING FOR THE QUIZ:

(1) You should understand what is meant by the terms: *present*, *active*, and
indicative.

(2) You should have *memorized the vocabulary* given in the chapter. [This is
true for each chapter and will not be specifically mentioned again.]

3) You should *recognize immediately* the six personal endings and be able to
connect them to the correct English pronoun subject.

(4) You should be comfortable with the fact that a given Greek word may be
translated into English in *more than one way*. This applies to both vocabulary
choice and ways to express the present tense.

Chapter 3

The Noun and Article: Nominative and Accusative Cases (Second Declension Masculine) / Subject / Direct Object / Prepositions with the Accusative Case / Noun Accent / Word Order

THE NOMINATIVE AND ACCUSATIVE CASES: Like the verbs, Greek nouns have different endings, depending on how they are used in a sentence. Noun forms are identified by *case* and *number*. There are four major cases in use in Greek, along with a fifth one of more limited use. In this chapter we will look at two of the cases: the *nominative case* and the *accusative case*. In Chapter 5 we will add the genitive and dative cases. The fifth case, called the vocative, will be added considerably later (Chapter 24). It is important to note from the beginning that *each of the four main cases can be used in more than one way in a sentence*. A two step process is involved here: (1) identify the noun form by *case* and *number* and (2) determine the noun *function* or *use* in the sentence. In this chapter we will look at one use for the nominative case (*subject*) and two uses for the accusative case (*direct object* and *object of certain prepositions*). The subject of a sentence with an active verb is the "doer" of the verbal action. The direct object is the person or thing to whom / which the verbal action is done. In the English sentence "The friends are buying bread," the subject is "friends" and the direct object is "bread."

As with the verbs, there is a *stem* that remains constant and *endings* that change. Using the stem ἀδελφ– (root meaning "brother"), we add the nominative singular (–ος) and accusative singular (–ον) endings.

>   ὁ ἀδελφὸς λέγει.   The brother is speaking. *(subject)*
>   ἀδελφὸν ἔχει.   He/she has a brother. *(direct object)*

Notice that in the first example the noun replaces the third person singular subject "he/she/it."

To get the plural forms, we add –οι (nominative) and –ους (accusative).

>   οἱ ἀδελφοὶ λέγουσιν.   The brothers are speaking.
>   ἀδελφοὺς ἔχει.   He/she has brothers.

This gives four forms (i.e., endings) to be learned so far. The genitive and dative forms are included in brackets in this paradigm and the next one to illustrate the traditional order. You do not need to concern yourself with them until Chapter 5.

```
* * * * * * * * * * * * * * * * * * * * * * * * *
*                  Singular              Plural          *
*                                                         
*   Nominative     ἀδελφός              ἀδελφοί          *
+   [Genitive      ἀδελφου              ἀδελφῶν]
*   [Dative        ἀδελφῷ               ἀδελφοῖς]         *
*   Accusative     ἀδελφόν              ἀδελφούς         *
*                                                         *
* * * * * * * * * * * * * * * * * * * * * * * * *
```

DEFINITE ARTICLE: The Greek *definite article* has a wide variety of uses and nuances. It is frequently translated with the English definite article "the," although we will see from the start that there are times when Greek uses a definite article and English does not and vice versa. There is no Greek word which corresponds to the English indefinite article "a" / "an." You will need to add an indefinite article to your translations where appropriate. For example, Greek says, "He/she has brother." This is not good English, so we add the indefinite article: "He/she has a brother."

Greek often uses a definite article with proper nouns (e.g. ὁ Ἰησοῦς) and the word "God" (ὁ θεός). ὁ οὐρανός can be translated as "the sky" or "heaven."

The forms of the definite article correspond to those of the noun. The nominative forms of the article are proclitics, like οὐ and οὐκ, and so have no accent of their own. The accusative forms are treated like any other word with an accent on the last (or only) syllable.

```
* * * * * * * * * * * * * * * * * * * * * *
*                                              *
*              λόγος – word                    *
*                                              *
*       Singular              Plural           *
*                                              *
*   N.  ὁ λόγος           οἱ λόγοι             *
*   [G.  τοῦ λόγου         τῶν λόγων]           *
*   [D.  τῷ λόγῳ           τοῖς λόγοις]         *
*   A.  τὸν λόγον          τοὺς λόγους          *
*                                              *
* * * * * * * * * * * * * * * * * * * * * *
```

PREPOSITIONS: A preposition is a word which introduces a phrase (a group of words without a verb). The word which follows the preposition is called the *object of the preposition*. Some Greek prepositions are followed by an object in the accusative case. Two such prepositions are πρός ("to," "toward") and εἰς ("into").

πρὸς τὸν ναόν   to the temple
εἰς τὸν οὐρανόν   into the sky / into heaven

NOUN ACCENT: The noun accent has several possible placements in the word. The starting position must be observed when learning the form given in the vocabulary list (i.e., the nominative singular). If possible, the accent will remain on the same syllable for all forms of a given noun. For this reason, the term "persistent" is used to describe the noun accent. The nouns in this chapter illustrate two *accent patterns*. In one pattern the accent is on the last syllable (e.g., ἀδελφός). In the nominative and accusative cases this accent is acute, but changes to a grave when another word follows immediately (like καί and ἀλλά). In the other pattern the accent is on the next to the last syllable (e.g., λόγος). An acute accent in this position remains the same throughout the different forms. *Note*: Three terms often used when talking about word accents are *ultima* (the last syllable), *penult* (the next to the last syllable), and *antepenult* (the syllable before the penult). These three syllables are the only ones which can have the word accent.

WORD ORDER: Since Greek nouns are inflected (i.e., have distinctive endings to designate the case), and since word function is indicated by the *form* of the word rather than its position in the sentence, word order in Greek can be much more flexible than in English. The typical English word order of subject / verb / direct object will be found in *some* Greek sentences also. But, as the sentences in the exercises will show, considerable variety is possible. Greek writers frequently made use of this flexibility to emphasize a word or phrase or to connect ideas in ways that are not possible in English and sometimes cannot even be brought into English. When you do translation work, you should put your sentences in English word order, keeping in mind, however, that even in English a direct object or prepositional phrase may sometimes be placed first in the sentence for emphasis.

<u>VOCABULARY</u>

ἀδελφός – brother [Philadelphia]
υἱός – son

θεός   God [theist]

καρπός – fruit

οὐρανός   sky; heaven [uranium]

θησαυρός – treasure; treasury [thesaurus]

λαός   people; nation (The word "people" here is a collective noun; its plural would be "peoples.") [laity]

ναός – temple, sanctuary (This word is usually used to refer to the shrine itself, the holy place and the holy of holies. It is also used to refer to the person in whom the Holy Spirit dwells. There is another word which we will meet later which refers to the entire sacred enclosure, the temple precinct with all its building, courts, etc.)

νόμος – law [Deuteronomy]

κόσμος – world [cosmic]

φίλος – friend [philanthropy]

λόγος – word; Word [logic]

ἄρτος – bread (*plural*: loaves of bread)

ὄχλος – crowd [ochlocracy]

πρός – to, toward [proselyte]

εἰς – into [eisegesis]

PREPARING FOR THE QUIZ:

(1) You should know *the names of the two cases* introduced in this chapter and be able to identify the forms *on sight.*

(2) You should know *one use for the nominative case* and *two for the accusative case* and be comfortable with the terminology: *subject, direct object, object of the preposition.*

(3) You should be thoroughly comfortable with the fact that *word order is flexible.* You *must* look at the noun endings in order to determine the word function. You cannot depend on word order as in English.

Chapter 4
The Verb: Imperfect Active Indicative / Verb Accent / Postpositives

THE IMPERFECT TENSE: While still using the *active voice* and the *indicative mood*, we will now begin to look at some of the other verb *tenses*. The first of these other tenses is called the *imperfect*. The aspect of the imperfect tense is the same as that of the present: it describes an action as *continuous* or *on-going*. It sees the *action in progress*, looking at the *internal make-up of the action*. With the imperfect tense, however, the action is in the past (from the standpoint of the speaker or writer). Note carefully, however, that you should always label this tense with the correct term ("imperfect"), not just "past," since there are other tenses which also describe past actions.

There are several different ways to translate the imperfect tense and all of them should be kept in mind and used where appropriate. We will use the verb "teach" (διδάσκω) to illustrate them. The most common one is "was / were teaching." Others include "used to teach," "kept teaching," "began teaching," and occasionally, if the context suggests it, "was / were trying to teach."

The *same stem* which was used to form the present tense is used to form the imperfect. (When analyzing a verb form, you must always note very carefully *which stem* is used.) Different endings are used for *some* forms, and an *augment* is added at the beginning. When the stem begins with a consonant, the augment is *epsilon (ἐ – διδασκ – ον).*

```
* * * * * * * * * * * * * * * * * * * * * * * * * * * *
*            Imperfect Active Indicative of διδάσκω        *
*                                                          *
*                    Singular              Plural          *
*                                                          *
*   1st person    ἐδίδασκον          ἐδιδάσκομεν    *
*   2nd person    ἐδίδασκες          ἐδιδάσκετε     *
*   3rd person    ἐδίδασκε(ν)        ἐδίδασκον      *
*                                                          *
* * * * * * * * * * * * * * * * * * * * * * * * * * * *
```

NOTES:

(1) The first person singular and the third person plural are identical. Context must be used to make the distinction. When identifying this form *out of context*, write or say "first person singular (1 s.) / third person plural (3 pl.)."

(2) The personal endings of the first person plural and second person plural are the same as the present tense. The augment is the distinguishing factor between present and imperfect.

When the verb stem begins with a vowel rather than a consonant, a different type of augment is used. (It is called a *temporal augment,* whereas the other is called a *syllabic augment.*) The initial vowel is changed (the correct grammatical term is "lengthened"): *alpha* or *epsilon* lengthening to *eta,* and *omicron* lengthening to *omega.* The diphthong ευ sometimes lengthens to ηυ and sometimes does not.

$$\mathring{\alpha}κούω - \mathring{\eta}κουον \qquad\qquad εὑρίσκω \quad εὕρισκον / ηὕρισκον$$

In the case of the verb ἔχω, the *epsilon* does not lengthen to *eta* but to the diphthong ει. This is an exception to the general pattern. (Note that *eta* and ει have the same sound. The spoken language precedes the written one.)

```
* * * * * * * * * * * * * * * * * *
*      Imperfect Active Indicative of ἔχω      *
*                                              *
*           Singular        Plural             *
*                                              *
*      1st    εἶχον         εἴχομεν            *
*      2nd    εἶχες         εἴχετε             *
*      3rd    εἶχε(ν)       εἶχον              *
*                                              *
* * * * * * * * * * * * * * * * * *
```

The verb ἔχω by nature expresses a *continuing situation,* not a single action. For this reason the translation "I had" is often acceptable for the imperfect rather than "I was having." In general, however, one should **avoid the English simple past when translating the Greek imperfect.**

VERB ACCENT: The rule for verb accents is very easy to learn and applies in almost all situations. It is based on the length of the last syllable (the ultima). If this syllable is long (i.e., contains a long vowel or diphthong) the second syllable from the end (the penult) has an acute accent.

$$ἀκούεις \qquad κωλύω \qquad πιστεύει$$

If, however, the last syllable contains a short vowel, the accent is on the third syllable from the end (the antepenult).

$$ἔλυον \qquad ἤκουε \qquad ἐλέγομεν \qquad ἐσθίετε$$

The verb accent is a circumflex if the verb has two syllables, the first being long and the second short: $\epsilon\hat{\iota}\chi o\nu$.

The term **recessive** is used to describe the verb accent, since it "recedes" from the end of the word toward the beginning.

POSTPOSITIVES: There are some little words in Greek which *never appear first* in a sentence, though they are often translated first in English. These words are called **postpositives**. They usually are placed after the first word in the sentence, even if this is the definite article. (Thus they are allowed to separate an article from the noun it goes with.) Two very frequently used postpositives are γάρ ("for") and οὖν ("therefore").

> ὁ γὰρ ὄχλος οὐκ ἤκουε τὸν λόγον.   For the crowd was not
>   listening to the word.
> τὸν οὖν θεὸν ἐδοξάζομεν.   Therefore we began glorifying God.

SPELLING CHANGE: When the following word has a rough breathing mark on the first syllable, the negative οὐκ becomes οὐχ. This spelling change, like others we will encounter, simply reflects what happens automatically in speaking.

> οὐχ εὑρίσκει   he/she is not finding

VOCABULARY

κελεύω – order, command
πιστεύω – believe; believe (in), trust (When one wants to say "believe in,"
        πιστεύω is combined with the preposition εἰς.)
θεραπεύω – heal [therapeutic]
γινώσκω – know, come to know [gnostic]
διδάσκω – teach [didactic]
εὑρίσκω – find [heuristic]
πειράζω – try; tempt; test
κηρύσσω – proclaim, preach [kerygma]
φυλάσσω – guard; keep; protect [phylactery]
πράσσω – do, accomplish [praxis]
γάρ – for
οὖν – therefore

PREPARING FOR THE QUIZ:

(1) You should know the *augment rules* and the *personal endings* for the imperfect active indicative.

(2) You should be aware of the *aspect / kind of action* which the imperfect tense represents and the *variety of ways* in which the Greek imperfect can be translated into English.

(3) You should know what is meant by the term *"postpositive"* and be able to identify two Greek postpositives.

Chapter 5

The Noun and Article: Genitive and Dative Cases (Second Declension Masculine) / Genitive of Possession / Indirect Object / Prepositions with the Genitive Case / Prepositions with the Dative Case

THE GENITIVE AND DATIVE CASES: Chapter 3 introduced the nominative and accusative cases of the noun along with some basic uses of those two cases. This chapter takes up the other two main cases: the **genitive** and the **dative**.

GENITIVE: There are *many possible uses* for the genitive case. We will look at two of them in this chapter and add others later on. In many of the uses, the noun in the genitive case is modifying another noun (called the "head noun"). This means that it gives some sort of information about the head noun which specifies or limits it in some way. Many of these uses can be translated into English with the preposition "of," e.g., "man of sorrows," "half of my kingdom," and "jar of wine." In order to identify the specific genitive use, the translator or exegete must consider *what kind of modifying information the noun in the genitive case conveys*. Another way to say this is that one must consider *the relationship of one noun to the other*. One of the most common uses of the genitive case is the **genitive of possession** (also called the **possessive genitive**); the noun (or pronoun) in the genitive case "possesses" the head noun. The possessive genitive answer the question "Whose?" in regard to the head noun.

The genitive singular ending is –ου. The genitive plural ending is –ων.

> ὁ οἶκος τοῦ φίλου   the house <u>of the friend</u> / <u>the friend's</u> house
> τὸν οἶκον τῶν φίλων   the house <u>of the friends</u> / <u>the friends'</u> house

NOTES:

(1) When a noun referring to a person or a part of the body is modified by a word in the genitive case, the idea of possession is not strictly literal. One does not "possess" one's foot or one's friend. For this reason, grammarians sometimes subdivide this category in various ways. Such situations, however, are still under the broad umbrella category of the possessive genitive and are best identified as such (at least for now).

(2) Be sure you know where the apostrophe goes in English possessives!

(3) A very common word arrangement in Greek is to put modifying information, in this case the genitive noun, between the noun it modifies and that noun's article. This does not change the translation and does not appear to have any particular significance, although it can help a writer make completely clear which noun a given genitive modifies.

αἱ τοῦ ἀδελφοῦ φίλαι   ὁ τοῦ θεοῦ υἱός

DATIVE: The dative case also has *many possible functions.* One of the most common is to express the ***indirect object*** of the verb, i.e., the indirect recipient or beneficiary of the action of the verb, the one in whose interest the action of the verb is performed. This is often translated with the English "to" or "for": "He gave the book to me." It is also possible to translate the indirect object without the "to" or "for": "He gave me the book." In the latter example, one must distinguish carefully between what is actually given (the book) and the one who benefits from the action (me).

The dative singular ending is –ῳ. The dative plural ending is –οις.

> λέγει τῷ φίλῳ.   He is speaking <u>to his friend</u>.
> ἄρτον ἀγοράζομεν τοῖς ὄχλοις.   We are buying bread <u>for the crowds</u>.

NOTES:

(1) Both the noun and the article in the dative singular have an ***iota subscript*** under the *omega.* Remember that this is part of the correct word spelling, though it does not affect pronunciation.

(2) With the verb λέγω either the indirect object dative or the preposition πρός (with its object in the accusative case) can be used. The indirect object dative is more common. A direct object of some kind ("words," "thoughts," etc.) is generally understood but frequently not expressed with λέγω.

(3) The "of" which is sometimes used to translate the genitive case and the "to" and "for" used to translate the dative are *added by the translator to express the ideas conveyed by these cases.* When asked to identify such nouns, you should say "genitive of possession" / "possessive genitive" or "indirect object." ***Only identify the noun as "object of the preposition" if there is a Greek preposition involved.*** This means that when you are asked for the function of nouns you must look at the Greek, not at your English translation.

DECLENSION: Whereas a listing of verb forms in a certain order is called a verb ***conjugation***, a listing of noun forms in a certain order is called a noun ***declension***. (We "conjugate" verbs and "decline" nouns.) We now have eight possible forms for the nouns learned so far. Here is the standard arrangement (declension) of these noun forms and the corresponding definite articles.

```
* * * * * * * * * * * * * * * * * * * * * * * * * * * * * * * *
*        Singular      Plural            Singular      Plural          *
*                                                                      *
*   N.   ὁ υἱός         οἱ υἱοί           ὁ λόγος       οἱ λόγοι        *
*   G.   τοῦ υἱοῦ       τῶν υἱῶν          τοῦ λόγου     τῶν λόγων       *
*   D.   τῷ υἱῷ         τοῖς υἱοῖς        τῷ λόγῳ       τοῖς λόγοις     *
*   A.   τὸν υἱόν       τοὺς υἱούς        τὸν λόγον     τοὺς λόγους     *
*                                                                      *
* * * * * * * * * * * * * * * * * * * * * * * * * * * * * * * *
```

Nouns that share *identical or similar endings* are grouped together for identification purposes. All the nouns in this chapter and Chapter 3 belong to the noun category called **second declension masculine**. The question of noun gender will be further considered in Chapter 7.

ACCENT PATTERNS: There are *four accent patterns* displayed by second declension masculine nouns. The easiest one is the one illustrated by λόγος. In this pattern the acute accent stays on the same syllable in all eight forms. In the pattern represented by υἱός the accent stays on the same syllable (the ultima), but changes to a circumflex in the genitive and dative. In the other two patterns changes regarding the accent are based on the length of the last syllable. In the so-called "κύριος pattern" there is an acute accent on the third syllable from the end (antepenult) when the last syllable is short and on the second syllable from the end (penult) when this syllable is long. (Although diphthongs are normally regarded as long, the –οι of the nominative plural is considered short for determining accent placement.) In the "δοῦλος pattern" the accent is always on the same syllable (the penult), but it is a circumflex if the last syllable is short and acute when that syllable is long.

```
* * * * * * * * * * * * * * * * * * * * * * * * * * * * * * * *
*        κύριος – master, lord              δοῦλος – slave             *
*                                                                      *
*        Singular      Plural            Singular      Plural          *
*                                                                      *
*   N.   ὁ κύριος       οἱ κύριοι         ὁ δοῦλος      οἱ δοῦλοι       *
*   G.   τοῦ κυρίου     τῶν κυρίων        τοῦ δούλου    τῶν δούλων      *
*   D.   τῷ κυρίῳ       τοῖς κυρίοις      τῷ δούλῳ      τοῖς δούλοις    *
*   A.   τὸν κύριον     τοὺς κυρίους      τὸν δοῦλον    τοὺς δούλους    *
*                                                                      *
* * * * * * * * * * * * * * * * * * * * * * * * * * * * * * * *
```

NOTE: With the exception of the nominative forms, which are proclitics, the definite article follows the accent pattern of a noun with the accent on the last syllable.

PREPOSITIONS: Just as some Greek prepositions are followed by an object in the accusative case, others are followed by an object in the genitive case. Two such prepositions are ἀπό ("from," "away from") and ἐκ ("from," "out of").

> ἀπὸ τοῦ οἴκου   from / away from the house
> ἐκ τοῦ οὐρανοῦ   from / out of the sky / heaven

Note that ἐκ has an alternate form ἐξ which is used when the following word begins with a vowel.

Still other prepositions are followed by an object in the dative case. Two of the most common are ἐν ("in") and σύν ("with").

> ἐν τῷ ναῷ   in the temple
> σὺν τοῖς διακόνοις   with the servants

NOTE: The correct identification of the noun following *any **Greek** preposition* is "object of the preposition." (Later on we will see prepositional phrases used to express ideas which can also be expressed by the case alone. At that time, correct identifications will be explained.)

VOCABULARY

When nouns are listed in a lexicon, the following three items are given: (1) the full form of the nominative singular, (2) the *ending* of the genitive singular, and (3) some indication of the gender (in this case the letter "m."). The reason for listing all three of these items will become more obvious as we learn more about nouns.

ἄνθρωπος, -ου, m. – person, man, mankind [anthropology]
θάνατος, -ου, m. – death [thanatopsis]
κύριος, -ου, m. – lord, master; Lord
ἥλιος, -ου, m. – sun [heliocentric]
διάκονος, -ου, m. – servant, minister; deacon [deacon]
διδάσκαλος, -ου, m. – teacher [didactic]
οἶκος, -ου, m. – house [economy]

οἶνος, -ου, m. – wine [oenophile]

δοῦλος, -ου, m. – slave, servant

ἀπό (preposition with genitive) – from, away from [apotropaic]

ἐκ / ἐξ (preposition with genitive) – from, out of [exodus]

ἐν (preposition with dative) – in [energy] (Also appears in compounds as "em,"
    e.g. empathy.)

σύν (preposition with dative) – with [synchronize] (Also "sym" [symphony] or
    "syl" [syllogism].)

VOCABULARY NOTES:

(1) The noun ἄνθρωπος in the singular can refer to a specific "man" or "person"
or it can be translated as "man" meaning "mankind" or "humanity," as in the
phrase ὁ υἱὸς τοῦ ἀνθρώπου – "the Son of Man." In the plural it is best translated as "people" or "men."

(2) When the definite article appears with ***abstract nouns*** such as θάνατος, it is
sometimes translated and sometimes not. When the reference is to a specific
death, the article is usually translated (e.g., "the death of our friend"). When the
reference is to the concept in general, the article is not used in English (e.g., "fear
of death").

PREPARING FOR THE QUIZ:

(1) You should know the ***names of the two new cases*** and ***two ways in which
each can be used***.

(2) You should know all the ***correct terminology*** for identifying case uses.

(3) You should consider ***starting lists*** to keep track of case uses and cases used as
the objects of prepositions.

(4) You should be aware of certain ***characteristics of Greek*** in terms of specific
vocabulary definitions and uses of the definite article.

(5) Remember that since this is a "noun chapter," your verb information to date
stays the same (present and imperfect active indicative).

Chapter 6

The Verb: Future Active Indicative / Principal Parts of a Verb / The Particles μέν and δέ / Elision / Genitive Direct Object / Dative Direct Object

THE FUTURE TENSE: The future tense of the verb talks about something that will take place in the future and is translated into English with "will..." or "shall...." (Note that English no longer makes much distinction between "will" and "shall" in the future tense.) The aspect or type of action of the future indicative is not the same as that of the present and imperfect. Rather the future tense looks at the action from the outside and describes the action *as a whole* or *unit*. It simply says that something will take place, without any comment about whether or not the action will be continuous or repeated. This type of action, therefore, is referred to as "unitary," or "summary." Do *not* translate the future tense with "will be –ing." (There is a way to say that, but we will not meet it for a long time.)

The future tense form in Greek makes use of a ***different verb stem***. There are several possible ways to arrive at the future stem. (1) A regular verb whose present tense stem ends in a long vowel or diphthong forms the future stem by *adding sigma to the present stem*. The personal endings are *the same as those of the present tense*. This means that one must be very careful to look at the entire stem preceding the ending, not just the first few letters.

```
* * * * * * * * * * * * * * * * * * * *
*          Future Active Indicative of ἀκούω      *
*                                                 *
*            Singular              Plural         *
*                                                 *
*    1st     ἀκούσω         ἀκούσομεν              *
*    2nd     ἀκούσεις       ἀκούσετε               *
*    3rd     ἀκούσει        ἀκούσουσι(ν)           *
*                                                 *
* * * * * * * * * * * * * * * * * * * *
```

(2) When the verb stem ends in a consonant, the future tense stem is often formed by combining *sigma* with that consonant. These are the usual combinations:

Labials (consonants formed with the lips: π, β, φ) combine with σ to become ψ.

Palatals (consonants formed in the throat: κ, γ, χ) combine with σ to become ξ.

Dentals (consonants formed with the teeth: τ, δ, θ) and often, but not always, ζ drop out, leaving the σ alone.

The combinations σκ and σσ usually combine with σ to become ξ.

Examples: πέμπω – πέμψω   πειράζω – πειράσω
          ἄγω ("lead") – ἄξω   διδάσκω – διδάξω
          πείθω ("persuade") – πείσω φυλάσσω – φυλάξω

The preceding two ways to form the future stem are considered regular (i.e., predictable) changes.

(3) There are, however, some verbs which have a future stem which is not predictable. These future tense stems **must be memorized** along with the vocabulary. Examples of verbs with an irregular future stem are:

          εὑρίσκω – εὑρήσω   κλαίω ("weep") – κλαύσω
          ἔχω – ἕξω   κράζω ("cry out") – κράξω

PRINCIPAL PARTS: Note that any irregularities in forming the future tense involve the stem, not the endings. In fact, verb stems are so crucial to form identification that grammarians organize Greek verb stems by what they call the "principal parts" of the verb. The principal parts are a sequence of *six indicative verb forms* (though many verbs lack one or more of them for various reasons) which provide the stems for *all* verbal forms (including participles, subjunctives, infinitives, and imperatives). The present active [or M/P (Chapter 13)] is the *first principal part*. The imperfect is not considered a principal part because it uses the *same stem* as the present. The future active [or middle (Chapter 13)], because it uses a different stem, is considered the *second principal part*. The principal parts are listed with the first person singular ending, but it is the *stems* which are the crucial element.

PARTICLES: Greek has a number of small words which express shades of meaning or emphasis in ways which are often untranslatable into English. Koine Greek (the language of the New Testament) has a greatly reduced number of such particles, but it does have some. One of the most common is δέ. δέ is used frequently and is sometimes, though much less often, paired with another particle: μέν. Study the following examples for the uses of these particles.

(1) By far the most common use for δέ is as a rather weak connective, generally translated as "and" or "but," depending on the context. It appears as a postpositive, i.e., the second word in its clause. δέ is so common in the GNT that it is sometimes omitted by translators.

> ὁ δὲ δοῦλος οὐ μένει ἐν τῇ οἰκία (= τῷ οἴκῳ) εἰς τὸν αἰῶνα
> But the slave does not remain in the house forever. (John 8:35)

> πάλιν δὲ εἶπεν ἡμῖν...   And again he said to us

(2) The next most common use of δέ is to indicate a change of subject. This can be done within a sentence or in separate sentences (especially in dialogue situations). To do this the δέ is paired with an appropriate definite article (not translated as "the" in this situation).

> ὁ κύριος τοὺς ὄχλους ἐδίδασκεν, <u>οἱ δὲ</u> οὐκ ἤκουον.   The master was teaching the crowds, <u>but they</u> were not listening.

> ὁ Ἰησοῦς εἶπεν τῷ Πέτρῳ. <u>ὁ δὲ</u> εἶπεν τῷ ἀδελφῷ.   Jesus spoke to Peter. <u>And he</u> (i.e., Peter) spoke to his brother.

(3) δέ is sometimes paired with μέν to express some kind of comparison or contrast. The two words are placed close to the words they are highlighting. The μέν is generally *not* translated.

> τὸν μὲν δοῦλον πέμψω, τὸν δὲ υἱὸν οὔ.   I shall send my slave, but not my son. [The οὐ acquired an accent here because it is the last word in the sentence. Notice that in comparison / contrast situations some words may be omitted from the second part of the sentence and must be understood from the first.]

> ὁ μὲν διδάσκαλος διδάσκει, ὁ δὲ διάκονος ἀκούει.   The teacher is teaching, and his (the) servant is listening.

NOTE: Occasionally, if the contrast is seen as particularly strong, the translations "on the one hand"…"on the other hand" may be used.

ELISION: Sometimes a short vowel at the end of a word is dropped if the next word begins with a vowel. This is quite common with ἀλλά and prepositions. The elision is marked, as in English, with an apostrophe.

> οἱ φίλοι οὐκ ἔλεγον ἀλλ᾽ ἤκουον τοὺς λόγους τοῦ διδασκάλου.   The friends were not speaking but were listening to the teacher's words.

GENITIVE DIRECT OBJECT: Although the accusative case is the one regularly used for the direct object of a verbal action, there are some verbs which have their direct object in the genitive case instead. One such verb is ἄρχω ("rule"). Make note of this information at the same time you learn the vocabulary. It would be a good idea to keep a running list of verbs which take their direct object in the genitive case. Identify this usage as "genitive direct object" to distinguish it from the more common accusative direct object. Note that this is your *third* possible use for the genitive case.

> οἱ κύριοι ἄρχουσι τῶν δούλων.   The masters rule their (the) slaves.

The familiar verb ἀκούω should also be added to this list, since it *sometimes* takes a genitive direct object. The usage is not one hundred percent consistent, but in general it seems to be the case that words referring to what is actually heard ("voice," "word," "speech," etc.) are put in the accusative case, whereas the source of the sound, usually a person, is put in the genitive case.

> τὸν τοῦ κυρίου λόγον ἠκούομεν.   We were listening to the word of
>   the Lord.

> ἀκούουσι τῶν ἀδελφῶν.   They are listening to their (the) brothers.

DATIVE DIRECT OBJECT: There are also some Greek verbs which have their direct object in the dative case. One example is πιστεύω when it has the meaning "believe" or "trust" rather than "believe *in*." (It is worth noting that verbs followed by a dative direct object generally imply a personal relationship of some kind, e.g., "trust," "serve," "worship," "follow," "obey," etc.) You should also have a place to keep track of verbs with their direct object in the dative case. This is your *third* possible use for the dative case.

> τῷ διδασκάλῳ πιστεύω.   I believe my (the) teacher.

VOCABULARY

Your text and workbook both include a master list of all the verbs covered in the introductory course (*Appendix A*). Use that list to keep track of verb principal parts. The list in the workbook has space between the words where you can write definitions or other information you need to remember. Lexicons will normally list irregular principal parts, but they will not list those that are formed regularly. Some of the verbs which you have learned have future forms which you are not yet prepared to deal with. Do not concern yourself at this point with any verb whose second principal part ends in –ῶ or –ομαι.

βλέπω, βλέψω – look (on / at); see

γράφω, γράψω – write [graphics]

στρέφω (No future active forms in the GNT.) – turn (*transitive*[1]) [apostrophe]

διώκω, διώξω – persecute; pursue, seek after

ἄγω, ἄξω – lead, bring [synagogue]

ἄρχω, ἄρξω – rule (*genitive direct object*) [patriarch]

πείθω, πείσω – persuade, convince

ἑτοιμάζω, ἑτοιμάσω – prepare, make ready

σκανδαλίζω (No future active forms in the GNT.) – cause (someone) to sin, cause (someone) to give up his faith; offend, shock [scandalize]

κλαίω, κλαύσω – weep, weep for

κράζω, κράξω – call out, cry out

μέν / δέ – particles with various uses (See examples.)

*A *transitive* verb is one which can, and usually does, have a direct object. An *intransitive* verb does not have a direct object. Certain Greek verbs are transitive in some forms and intransitive in others; στρέφω is one of them.

NOTE: Some verbs (e.g., στρέφω) have one or more principal parts which only appear in the Greek New Testament in compounds. Such principal parts will not be listed when these verbs are introduced, but they are included in brackets on the master verb list. For other verbs (e.g., σκανδαλίζω), either the principal part (in this case the future) does not exist or it does not appear at all in the GNT.

PREPARING FOR THE QUIZ:

(1) You should understand the *aspect of the future tense* and the *appropriate way to translate it*.

(2) You should know the rules for *regular formation of the future tense stem*.

(3) You should know what is meant by the term *"principal parts"* and what the first two principal parts of the Greek verb are

(4) You should be aware of the ways the particles μέν and δέ can be used in a sentence.

(5) You should start *two more lists*: verbs which take a genitive direct object and verbs which take a dative direct object.

Chapter 7

The Noun and Article: First Declension Feminine
(Nominative Singular Ending in Eta)

FIRST DECLENSION FEMININE NOUNS: In Chapter 5 the concept of classifying nouns by declension was introduced. To review, this means the grouping together for identification purposes of nouns with *identical or very similar endings*. Another concept used to identify and classify nouns is **gender**. Although some masculine nouns do refer to male persons (e.g., υἱός and ἀδελφός) and some feminine nouns to female persons (e.g., ἀδελφή – "sister" and μήτηρ – "mother"), the concept of gender in Greek is essentially a grammatical one; like declension, gender is used to identify nouns according to their endings. The nouns in Chapters 3 and 5 were all **second declension masculine**. The nouns in this chapter and Chapter 8 are all **first declension feminine**. Here are the declensions of two first declension feminine nouns and the feminine definite article:

* *

	φωνή – voice		νεφέλη – cloud	
	Singular	*Plural*	*Singular*	*Plural*
N.	ἡ φωνή	αἱ φωναί	ἡ νεφέλη	αἱ νεφέλαι
G.	τῆς φωνῆς	τῶν φωνῶν	τῆς νεφέλης	τῶν νεφελῶν
D.	τῇ φωνῇ	ταῖς φωναῖς	τῇ νεφέλῃ	ταῖς νεφέλαις
A.	τὴν φωνήν	τὰς φωνάς	τὴν νεφέλην	τὰς νεφέλας

* *

When learning new forms it is useful to find the points of similarity and difference between the new forms and those you already know. What are the similarities and differences between these forms and the second declension masculine nouns?

NOTE: The gender of a noun does not affect the way it is used in the sentence. These new noun *forms* will be used in exactly the same way as the nouns you already know: subject, possessive, indirect object, etc.

ACCENT: These two nouns follow the accent patterns used for ἀδελφός (and υἱός) and λόγος. All first declension nouns have a circumflex accent on the last syllable (ultima) of the genitive plural, regardless of which accent pattern they are otherwise following. All endings of the first declension feminine nouns in this chapter are long except for the nominative plural. (Although it is a diphthong and technically should be considered long, the –αι, like the οι of the second declension masculine nouns, is considered short for the purposes of accent placement.) If the next to the last syllable (penult) has the word accent *and* includes a long vowel or diphthong, it will turn to a circumflex on just this one form. Example: λύπη   λύπῃ.

VOCABULARY

φωνή, -ῆς, f. – voice; sound [phonograph]

ψυχή, -ῆς, f. – soul, life; one's inner being, self [psychiatrist]

ἀρχή, -ῆς, f. – beginning; ruling power, authority, ruler ("an authority figure
    who initiates activity or process," Danker, p. 138) [archaic]

κεφαλή, -ῆς, f. – head [encephalograph]

ὀργή, -ῆς, f. – anger, wrath

ζωή, -ῆς, f. – life [Zoe]

ἐντολή, -ῆς, f. – command, commandment

ἀγάπη, -ης, f. – love

εἰρήνη, -ης, f. – peace [irenic, Irene]

νεφέλη, -ης, f. – cloud [nephelometer]

δικαιοσύνη, -ης, f. – righteousness; justice

λύπη, -ης, f. – grief, pain

VOCABULARY NOTE: Remember that abstract nouns (e.g., ἀγάπη, εἰρήνη, etc.) when used in a general sense often have a definite article in Greek but not in English. If they are specific, the definite article will be translated (e.g., "the love of God"). In some prepositional phrases, however, the opposite situation occurs: the preposition is not there in Greek, but needs to be supplied in English (ἐν ἀρχῇ – in the beginning).

PREPARING FOR THE QUIZ:

(1) You should be aware of the new classification concept: *gender*.

(2) You should know the new set of endings and the new definite article which are used for *first declension feminine*.

Chapter 8

The Noun and Article: First Declension Feminine (Nominative Singular Ending in Alpha) / Prepositions with the Genitive or Accusative Case

ADDITIONAL FIRST DECLENSION FEMININE NOUNS: Remember that the term "declension" is used to group together nouns with identical or *similar* endings. Also (along with those from Chapter 7) classified as *first declension feminine* are nouns with a nominative singular ending in either a long or short *alpha*. *All first declension feminine nouns have the same plural endings as the nouns learned in Chapter 7, so we are only concerned here with variations in the singular forms.*

(1) The most common pattern for nouns with a nominative singular ending in *alpha* is to have a long *alpha* in all the singular forms (just substitute the *alpha* for the previously learned *eta).*

```
* * * * * * * * * * * * * * * * * * * *
*                                      *
*              ἡ ἡμέρα – day           *
*                                      *
*         Singular        Plural       *
*                                      *
*   N.    ἡ ἡμέρα       αἱ ἡμέραι      *
*   G.    τῆς ἡμέρας    τῶν ἡμερῶν     *
*   D.    τῇ ἡμέρᾳ      ταῖς ἡμέραις   *
*   A.    τὴν ἡμέραν    τὰς ἡμέρας     *
*                                      *
* * * * * * * * * * * * * * * * * * * *
```

(2) A few first declension feminine nouns have a *short alpha* in the nominative and accusative singular. The genitive and dative singular revert to either an *eta* or a *long alpha.* (**Note:** You don't really hear any difference between a long and short *alpha*, but the accent placement is affected.)

```
* * * * * * * * * * * * * * * * * * * * * * * * * * * * * * *
*     ἡ δόξα – glory            ἡ ἀσθένεια – sickness         *
*                                                            *
*    Singular     Plural       Singular        Plural        *
*                                                            *
* N. ἡ δόξα      αἱ δόξαι      ἡ ἀσθένεια     αἱ ἀσθένειαι   *
* G. τῆς δόξης   τῶν δοξῶν     τῆς ἀσθενείας  τῶν ἀσθενειῶν  *
* D. τῇ δόξῃ     ταῖς δόξαις   τῇ ἀσθενείᾳ    ταῖς ἀσθενείαις *
* A. τὴν δόξαν   τὰς δόξας     τὴν ἀσθένειαν  τὰς ἀσθενείας  *
*                                                            *
* * * * * * * * * * * * * * * * * * * * * * * * * * * * * * *
```

OBSERVATIONS:

(1) The singular article remains the same regardless of whether the noun forms have *eta* or *alpha*. This is very good news, but it does mean that the noun and article don't always "match."

(2) If *alpha* is used throughout the declension, there will be **duplicate forms** in the *genitive singular* and *accusative plural*. If the definite article is present, you can easily distinguish one form from the other. Otherwise you will have to rely on context.

(3) Since a lexicon entry includes the ending of the genitive singular, one can easily tell to which category a noun belongs. Keep in mind, though, that *your* only concern is being able to recognize the form in context and you should be able to do that regardless of whether the ending has an *eta* or an *alpha*.

PREPOSITION: Some Greek prepositions may have an object in **either the genitive or the accusative case.** **The meaning of the preposition will differ depending on the case of the object.** One such preposition is κατά. Although κατά, like most prepositions, has a wide variety of meanings, we will concentrate on just a few. When the object is in the *genitive* case, use the translation "against." When the object is in the *accusative* case, use the translation "according to" / "in accordance with."

> κατὰ τοῦ διδασκάλου   against the teacher
> κατὰ τῆς ἀληθείας   against the truth / against truth
> κατὰ Μᾶρκον   according to Mark
> κατὰ τοὺς νόμους   according to / in accordance with the laws

In addition to these meanings, it is possible to use κατά with the accusative case in what is called the "distributive" sense: house by house, year by year, etc. Thus the phrase καθ᾽ ἡμέραν would be translated "day by day," "daily," or "every day."

CONSONANT CHANGE: We have already seen that a short vowel at the end of a word may be elided when the next word begins with a vowel. When the following word has a rough breathing, in addition to dropping the short vowel the consonant preceding the vowel is modified.

> ἀπ᾽ becomes ἀφ᾽   κατ᾽ becomes καθ᾽

VOCABULARY

ἡμέρα, -ας, f. – day [ephemeral]
ὥρα, -ας, f. – hour [horoscope]
χώρα, -ας, f. – country, region [chorography]
ἀγορά, -ᾶς, f. – market place [agoraphobia]
καρδία, -ας, f. – heart [cardiology]
σοφία, -ας, f. – wisdom [philosophy]
ἁμαρτία, -ας, f. – sin
θύρα, -ας, f. – door
ἀδικία, -ας, f. – wrongdoing; wickedness, unrighteousness, injustice (**Note**:
    The *alpha* on the beginning of this word is a negating prefix.)
βασιλεία, -ας, f. – kingdom
θάλασσα, -ης, f. – sea [thalassocracy]
δόξα, -ης, f. – glory [doxology]
ἀλήθεια, -ας, f. – truth
ἀσθένεια, -ας, f. – sickness; weakness [myasthenia]
κατά (preposition with genitive) – against [cataclysm]
    (preposition with accusative) – according to, in accordance with

PREPARING FOR THE QUIZ:

(1) Make sure you understand that the nouns from both Chapter 7 and Chapter 8 are *first declension feminine*. This means that the category "first declension feminine" has two sub-groups in it.

(2) You should be clear on what is going on with the preposition κατά and add κατά to the list of prepositions with the genitive *and* the list of prepositions with the accusative.

Chapter 9

THE AORIST TENSE: Our fourth verb tense, the aorist, has the same aspect or type of action as the future, but this time the action is in the past (from the standpoint of the speaker or writer). The aorist tense looks at the verbal action from the outside and describes the action as a whole. It simply says that *something happened*, without any comment about whether or not the action continued or was repeated (it may have, but that is not how the aorist portrays it). This type of action is referred to as "unitary," "summary," or "undefined." (The Greek word ἀόριστος means "indefinite" or "indeterminate.") This is most often translated into English with the English simple past, though there are exceptions. Keep in mind that this gives us *two* Greek verb tenses which talk about actions in the past. Greek writers were generally quite careful about choosing between these two and you must also be careful in your translations, e.g. "he was teaching" (imperfect) / "he taught" (aorist), "we were preparing (imperfect) / "we prepared" (aorist).

FIRST AORIST: A distinction is made in *form only* between what we call *first aorist* and *second aorist*. Remember that this is a distinction regarding form only; the translation is the same for both.

First aorist forms *usually* occur in verbs for which all or most of the principal parts are regular, i.e., they can be determined or predicted from the first principal part by following certain rules of formation. This is roughly analogous to adding "–ed" to an English verb: e.g., heal / healed.

When the stem of the first principal part ends in a long vowel or a diphthong, the formation of the first aorist is as follows:

> (1) Prefix an augment according to the same rules learned for the
>   imperfect (Chapter 4).
> (2) Add *sigma* to the stem as was done for the future (Chapter 6).
> (3) Add the personal endings for first aorist.

We can illustrate this by using the verb θεραπεύω: ἐ – θεραπευ – σ – α (translation: "I healed").

```
* * * * * * * * * * * * * * * * * * * * * * *
*        First Aorist Active Indicative of θεραπεύω   *
*                                                     *
*              Singular              Plural           *
*                                                     *
*   1st   ἐθεράπευσα          ἐθεραπεύσαμεν            *
*   2nd   ἐθεράπευσας         ἐθεραπεύσατε             *
*   3rd   ἐθεράπευσε(ν)       ἐθεράπευσαν              *
*                                                     *
* * * * * * * * * * * * * * * * * * * * * * *
```

When the verb stem ends in certain consonants or consonant combinations, the same formations occur as in the regular future tense formations.

πέμπω, πέμψω, ἔπεμψα   ἑτοιμάζω, ἑτοιμάσω, ἡτοίμασα
διώκω, διώξω, ἐδίωξα   φυλάσσω, φυλάξω, ἐφύλαξα
πείθω, πείσω, ἔπεισα

NOTES:

(1) In verbs with this kind of regular formation, the future and first aorist have the same stem, although they have different endings and presence / absence of augment.

(2) There are some verbs which have first aorists which are not formed in this predictable way. Do *not* make the common (but incorrect) assumption that all first aorists will have a *sigma* or *sigma combination* at the end of the stem. *Any aorist active indicative first person singular which ends in alpha is considered a first aorist.*

(3) For the most part, verbs have *either* a first or second aorist, not both. (There are exceptions to this, but you do not need to worry about them now.)

SECOND AORIST: Verbs with a second aorist are analogous in principle to English words such as "sing," "eat," and "speak." The present tense stem is not altered in any regular way, but rather a new stem is created: "sang," "ate," and "spoke." Usually one can see some relationship between the two stems, but there is no way of predicting from looking at the present what the aorist will be. For this reason, second aorist stems *must be memorized* at the time new vocabulary is learned. The endings are the same as those of the imperfect. Therefore one must look very carefully at the stem. *The aorist active [or middle (Chapter 15)] is the third principal part of the Greek verb.*

```
* * * * * * * * * * * * * * * * * *
*        Second Aorist Active Indicative of        *
*        λαμβάνω – take / ἔλαβον   took            *
*                                                   *
*            Singular            Plural             *
*                                                   *
*    1ˢᵗ    ἔλαβον            ἐλάβομεν              *
*    2ⁿᵈ    ἔλαβες            ἐλάβετε               *
*    3ʳᵈ    ἔλαβε(ν)          ἔλαβον                *
*                                                   *
* * * * * * * * * * * * * * * * * *
```

ADDITIONAL INFORMATION:

(1) There are two very common second aorists which you should learn at this time, even though you do not yet know their first principal parts.

$$εἶδον – \text{saw} \qquad ἦλθον – \text{came}$$

(2) If there are any irregularities in the principal parts of a verb, these forms will be listed in a lexicon. If only the first principal part is listed, one may assume that all existing principal parts are formed regularly.

(3) The time put in learning the second aorist stems will eventually be well rewarded. For one thing, when we move beyond the indicative, most of the verbs encountered will be either present or aorist. Furthermore, we see the importance of the aorist stem in those situations where English derivatives and/or other Greek words are related to it rather than to the present stem. An example of the former is the stem φαγ– (the aorist of ἐσθίω). English derivatives such as esophagus and sarcophagus come from this stem. An example of the latter is the stem μαθ– (the aorist of μανθάνω) which we will meet later in the word μαθητής ("disciple"). In fact, we sometimes find that the present stem is actually the "odd man out," as is the case with εὑρίσκω. The stem used in forming all the other tenses is the second aorist εὑρ–.

CONJUNCTIONS: The Greek conjunction ἤ has the meaning "or." When doubled in a sentence the meaning is "either"… "or." Likewise καί when used twice may mean "both"…"and" (although there are times when two or more καί's are all translated as "and").

ἢ οἱ φίλοι ἢ οἱ ἀδελφοί   either the friends or the brothers
καὶ οἱ ἀδελφοὶ καὶ οἱ υἱοί   both the brothers and the sons

VOCABULARY

The completely new vocabulary in this chapters consists of the new conjunction, seven new verbs for six of which only the present (and imperfect) and second aorist can be learned at this time, and the two additional second aorists εἶδον and ἦλθον. In addition, the aorists of most of the previously learned verbs can now be added. (See the complete list beginning on the next page.)

ἤ   – or
ἤ...ἤ   – either...or
καί...καί – both ...and
ἁμαρτάνω, ἁμαρτήσω, ἥμαρτον – sin
βάλλω, [βαλῶ], ἔβαλον – throw [ballistics]
λαμβάνω, [λήμψομαι], ἔλαβον – take; receive [epilepsy]
μανθάνω, ---, ἔμαθον – learn [mathematics]
πάσχω, ---, ἔπαθον – suffer (Again, note that the English derivatives come
        from the aorist stem rather than from the present stem.) [sympathy,
        empathy]
πίπτω, [πεσοῦμαι], ἔπεσον – fall, fall down
φεύγω, [φεύξομαι], ἔφυγον – flee [fugitive]
εἶδον – saw
ἦλθον – came

NOTES:

(1) The letter *eta* with a smooth breathing mark and an acute accent (ἤ) is the first of a number of examples where the accent and/or breathing mark is the only difference between two (or, in this instance, more than two) words, i.e., the actual letters are the same. We have already seen *eta* with a rough breathing mark and no accent (ἡ) as the nominative singular feminine definite article. There is a list of such words in *Appendix B: Accents and Breathing Marks That Matter* and the same list appears in the workbook. Use the list in the workbook to check off or highlight these words as we come to them.

(2) The forms given in brackets are forms which you do not need to worry about just now. They are included in the list just so that you may know that they are there. Do not mark them yet on the master principal parts list.

(1) Verbs which have a *first* aorist:

First Principal Part (Present)	Second Principal Part (Future)	Third Principal Part (Aorist)
λύω	---	ἔλυσα
κωλύω	---	ἐκώλυσα
ἀκούω	ἀκούσω / |ἀκούσομαι|	ἤκουσα
κελεύω	---	ἐκέλευσα
πιστεύω	πιστεύσω	ἐπίστευσα
θεραπεύω	θεραπεύσω	ἐθεράπευσα
πέμπω	πέμψω	ἔπεμψα
βλέπω	βλέψω	ἔβλεψα
γράφω	γράψω	ἔγραψα
στρέφω	---	ἔστρεψα
διώκω	διώξω	ἐδίωξα
ἄρχω	ἄρξω	ἦρξα
πείθω	πείσω	ἔπεισα
δοξάζω	δοξάσω	ἐδόξασα
σῴζω	σώσω	ἔσωσα
βαπτίζω	βαπτίσω	ἐβάπτισα
ἀγοράζω	---	ἠγόρασα
πειράζω	πειράσω	ἐπείρασα
ἑτοιμάζω	ἑτοιμάσω	ἡτοίμασα
σκανδαλίζω	---	ἐσκανδάλισα
διδάσκω	διδάξω	ἐδίδαξα
κηρύσσω	κηρύξω	ἐκήρυξα
φυλάσσω	φυλάξω	ἐφύλαξα
πράσσω	πράξω	ἔπραξα
κράζω	κράξω	ἔκραξα
κλαίω	κλαύσω	ἔκλαυσα
ἐλπίζω	|ἐλπιῶ|	ἤλπισα

(2) Verbs which have a *second* aorist:

ἄγω	ἄξω	ἤγαγον
εὑρίσκω	εὑρήσω	εὗρον
ἔχω	ἕξω	ἔσχον

ἁμαρτάνω	ἁμαρτήσω	ἥμαρτον
λαμβάνω	[λήμψομαι]	ἔλαβον
μανθάνω	---	ἔμαθον
φεύγω	[φεύξομαι]	ἔφυγον
πάσχω	---	ἔπαθον
ἐσθίω	[φάγομαι]	ἔφαγον
λέγω	[ἐρῶ]	εἶπον
πίνω	[πίομαι]	ἔπιον
βάλλω	[βαλῶ]	ἔβαλον
πίπτω	[πεσοῦμαι]	ἔπεσον
[ὁράω]	[ὄψομαι]	εἶδον
[ἔρχομαι]	[ἐλεύσομαι]	ἦλθον
γινώσκω	[γνώσομαι]	[ἔγνων]

NOTES:

(1) Remember that the imperfect, while a separate tense, is not considered a separate principal part, because it is formed from the present tense stem.

(2) It is obvious that in a few situations some of the principal parts have no similarity whatsoever, e.g., λέγω and εἶπον, ἐσθίω and ἔφαγον. What has happened is that there were originally two or more words with the same or very similar meaning. Over time some of the principal parts of each dropped out and the remaining principal parts came to be associated with each other. Fortunately, there are not many of these. Unfortunately, they are among the more common verbs.

PREPARING FOR THE EXAM:

(1) **Review** the previous chapters thoroughly, including all the "Preparing for the Quiz" sections.

(2) Know the distinction in **form** between first and second aorist active.

(3) Learn the **new endings** for first aorist and **memorize the second aorists**.

(4) Be sure you know how to keep the **translations** separate for the imperfect and the aorist tenses.

(5) Use the list in this chapter to update your **master verb list**. Do not to mark any verb which is in brackets; these are forms you are not yet prepared to learn.

Chapter 10

The Verb εἰμί: Present and Imperfect Indicative /
Enclitics / Predicate Nominative

THE VERB εἰμί: The verb "to be" in Greek, as in many other languages, is irregular. The stem ἐσ– appears in modified form in the present tense.

```
* * * * * * * * * * * * * * * * * * * * * * * * * *
*              Present (Active) Indicative of εἰμί          *
*                                                          *
*         Singular                    Plural               *
*                                                          *
*   1st   εἰμί   I am            ἐσμέν   we are            *
*   2nd   εἶ    you are          ἐστέ   you are            *
*   3rd   ἐστί(ν)  he/she/it is,  εἰσί(ν)  they are,       *
*              there is               there are            *
*                                                          *
* * * * * * * * * * * * * * * * * * * * * * * * * *
```

NOTES ON εἰμί:

(1) Note carefully the possible translations "there is" (3 s.) and "there are" (3 pl.).

(2) Technically εἰμί represents a state of being rather than an action. Nevertheless, since the *form* is active, when you are identifying the present and imperfect forms, you may put *active* in the *voice* column. Note, however, that some grammar books omit the voice entirely.

ENCLITICS: With the exception of the second person singular, these forms are *enclitics*. An enclitic is a word which is accented together with the *preceding word*. The accents shown in the paradigm above are modified in actual usage as follows:

(1) When the preceding word is accented on the ultima, the enclitic *loses its accent and an acute accent on the preceding word remains acute.*

   ἀδελφοί ἐσμεν.   We are brothers.

(2) When the preceding word has an acute accent on the penult, *a two syllable enclitic keeps its accent.*

   φίλοι ἐστέ.   You (pl.) are friends.

(3) When the preceding word has an acute accent on the antepenult or a circumflex on penult, *the enclitic loses its accent **and** the preceding word gets a second accent on the ultima.*

> διδάσκαλός ἐστιν.   He is a teacher.
> δοῦλοί εἰσιν.   They are slaves.

Sometimes you will see the third person singular with an accent on the first syllable. This is most likely to occur when:

(1) It is the first word in the sentence or it has the meaning "exists."

(2) It follows οὐκ, ἀλλά, or καί.

In any other situation, if an enclitic follows a proclitic, the proclitic will acquire an accent which it would not otherwise have (see Chapter 2 for proclitics).

> οὔκ ἐσμεν δοῦλοι.   We are not slaves.

NOTE: These accent rules ***do not affect translation*** – just be aware that sometimes strange accent patterns will occur and enclitics are usually involved.

IMPERFECT: The imperfect of εἰμί is also irregular, but it is *not* an enclitic. The forms in parentheses only appear in a few passages; you do not need to learn them now.

```
* * * * * * * * * * * * * * * * * * * * * * * * *
*              Imperfect (Active) Indicative of εἰμί          *
*                                                             *
*              Singular                 Plural                *
*                                                             *
*   1st   ἤμην (ἦν) I was        ἦμεν (ἤμεθα) we were         *
*   2nd   ἦς (ἦσθα) you were     ἦτε you were                 *
*   3rd   ἦν he/she/it was,      ἦσαν they were,              *
*              there was                there were            *
*                                                             *
* * * * * * * * * * * * * * * * * * * * * * * * *
```

PREDICATE NOMINATIVE: The verb εἰμί is followed in thought ***not by a direct object***, but by a ***predicate nominative***. The predicate nominative gives information or makes an assertion about the subject. One of two possible relationships may exist between the subject and predicate nominative.

(1) The two are equal and interchangeable.

> Ἰησοῦς ἐστιν ὁ Χριστός.   Jesus Is the Christ / Messiah.

(2) The predicate nominative describes the class to which the subject belongs or qualifies the subject. The two are not interchangeable.

> Παῦλος ἀπόστολός ἐστιν.   Paul is an apostle.

Since Greek word order is flexible, it cannot be relied upon to distinguish the subject from the predicate nominative. Various rules, therefore, have been devised to assist in making this distinction.

(1) The first rule applies when **only one** of the two nominatives fits into certain categories. This one is definite and is having something asserted about it. It will be the subject and the predicate nominative will *not* be equal and interchangeable. The three categories are:

> (a) A pronoun (except for the interrogative pronoun), written or contained in the verb ending.
>
>> δοῦλοι ἦτε τῆς ἁμαρτίας.   You were slaves of sin. (Rom. 6:20)

> (b) A noun with a definite article.
>
>> θεὸς ἦν ὁ λόγος.   The Word was God. (John 1:1)

> (c) A proper noun.
>
>> Πέτρος ἦν μαθητής   Peter was a disciple.

(2) The second rule applies if *both* the subject and predicate nominative fit into one of these categories. Then the two are considered equal and interchangeable. So which will be the subject?

> (a) A pronoun has priority.
>
>> ὁ υἱὸς τοῦ θεοῦ ἦν οὗτος. [οὗτος is a demonstrative pronoun.]
>> This man was the Son of God.

(b) Nouns with an article and proper nouns seem to have equal priority. Word order will generally be the deciding factor.

ʽΟ πατὴρ ἡμῶν ᾽Αβραάμ ἐστιν. Our father is Abraham. (John 8:39a) [The first word is capitalized because it begins a direct quotation. The letter "a" indicates the first part of the verse, ending with a period.]

NOTE: This is your *second use of the nominative case*. Note that it is restricted to use with certain "state of being" or "linking" verbs. In this beginning material, the only two such verbs are εἰμί and γίνομαι (Chapter 13). There is another verb, ὑπάρχω, which also means "to be" and would be associated with a predicate nominative. These three verbs will *not* have a direct object. They are your indicator ("contextual clue") to look for a predicate nominative.

PREPARING FOR THE QUIZ:

(1) Memorize the *irregular conjugations* for the present and imperfect of εἰμί and be sure you know the correct translations for them.

(2) Add *predicate nominative* to your list of uses for the nominative case. Be sure you know what is meant by the term *predicate nominative* and the circumstances under which you can expect to see one.

(3) Be sure you know how to decide which word in a sentence is the *subject* and which is the *predicate nominative*.

Chapter 11
Compound Verbs / First Class Conditions

COMPOUND VERBS: Compound verbs are *extremely common* in Greek. A compound verb is created by putting a prepositional prefix onto another verb. The principal parts of the compound are the same as those of the basic verb. Sometimes there is virtually no difference in meaning between the basic verb and the compound (e.g., *θνῄσκω* and *ἀποθνῄσκω* both mean "die"), though the prefix on the compound may have an intensifying force. Frequently the meaning of the compound can be figured out logically by knowing the meaning of both parts (e.g., *ἐκ* + *βάλλω* – "throw out"). Occasionally the meaning of the compound is not immediately obvious and must be learned as a separate vocabulary word.

When forming the imperfect and aorist of compound verbs, the augment goes on the **basic verb stem, not on the prepositional prefix**. In other words, it goes *between* the prefix and the stem.

present: *ἀπολύω* – I release
imperfect: *ἀπέλυον* – I was releasing
future: *ἀπολύσω* – I will release
aorist: *ἀπέλυσα* – I released

present: *παραλαμβάνω* – I receive
imperfect: *παρελάμβανον* – I was receiving
future: [*παραλήμψομαι*] – I will receive
aorist: *παρέλαβον* – I received

Notice that when the prefix ends in a vowel this is usually dropped in front of the augment.

CONDITIONS: A conditional sentence has two parts: an "if" part and a "then" part. The technical name for the "if" part is **protasis**; for the "then" part the name is **apodosis**. The "if" part of a conditional sentence is our first example of a **subordinate clause**. (A clause is the smallest *complete* unit of thought. A clause must have a verb, even if this is an unwritten form of *εἰμί*. A noun with other modifying information is just a *phrase*.) Conjunctions such as *καί* and *ἀλλά* connect two or more clauses on an equal footing. These are called **coordinating conjunctions**. The conjunction used to introduce the "if" clause of a conditional sentence is *εἰ*. It is called a **subordinating conjunction**.

Grammarians use a variety of systems to name and classify conditions in Greek. One of the most widely used systems calls them first class conditions, second class conditions, etc. The different kinds of conditions can be recognized in context by the conjunction introducing the "if clause," the tense and mood of the verbs in both parts, and the presence or absence of the particle ἄν.

FIRST CLASS CONDITIONS: First class conditions use εἰ and *any tense of the indicative mood* in the protasis and *any tense / any mood* in the apodosis. These conditions assume, for the sake of argument, that the "if" clause is true. (Note that this does not mean it actually *is* true, only that it is assumed to be true for the sake of argument.) First class conditions are easy to translate; just translate each verb as you usually would.

εἰ φίλος ἡμῶν εἶ, σώσεις ἡμᾶς.
If you are our friend [and we assume that you are], you will save us.

εἰ οἱ κύριοι ἐδίωξαν τοὺς δούλους, οἱ δοῦλοι ἔφυγον.
If the masters persecuted the slaves [and we assume that they did], the slaves fled.

VOCABULARY

Since several of these verbs have their own idiosyncrasies, this chapter employs a "narrative" vocabulary list. Comments are made on the individual words as they are presented. Although not usually listed with the principal parts, the imperfect forms are given in parentheses so that the augment may be observed. ***Be sure to note which verbs have a first aorist and which have a second aorist.***

(1) φέρω (ἔφερον), οἴσω, ἤνεγκα – bring, carry; bear, endure [Christopher]
(2) προσφέρω (προσέφερον), ---, προσήνεγκα – bring to; offer, present

> As is the case with several other verbs, the principal parts of φέρω and its compounds come from separate verbs. Note that the aorist is a first aorist, although it is not a regular formation. The *gamma* is sounded as ng.

(3) ἀνοίγω (ἀνέῳγον), ἀνοίξω, ἀνέῳξα – open

> This is, in fact, a compound verb (ἀνά + οἴγω), but the basic verb, which also meant "open," was no longer in use during the Koine period. Note the unusual double augment (both an *epsilon* and a lengthened vowel: *omicron* to *omega* and the *iota* becomes an *iota* subscript).

[θνήσκω]

(4) ἀποθνήσκω (ἀπέθνησκον), [ἀποθανοῦμαι], ἀπέθανον – die

> The basic verb need not be learned at this time as only the aortist tense appears in the GNT.

(5) λείπω (ἔλειπον), ---, ἔλιπον – leave
(6) καταλείπω (κατέλειπον), καταλείψω, κατέλιπον – leave, leave behind
(7) τάσσω (ἔτασσον), ---, ἔταξα – arrange; order, appoint [tactics]
(8) ὑποτάσσω (ὑπέτασσον), ---, ὑπέταξα – subject, subordinate [hypotaxis]

> The following compound verbs are formed from verbs which you already know. Remember that principal parts stay the same.

(9) ἀπολύω (ἀπέλυον), ἀπολύσω, ἀπέλυσα – release, set free; send away
(10) συνάγω (συνῆγον), συνάξω, συνήγαγον – gather, bring together
> (**transitive verb** / Note that the verb accent cannot precede the augment.) [synagogue]
(11) παραλαμβάνω (παρελάμβανον), [παραλήμψομαι], παρέλαβον – receive, accept; take with, take along (usually with a person or people as direct object)
(12) ἐκβάλλω (ἐξέβαλλον), [ἐκβαλῶ], ἐξέβαλον – cast out, drive out; send out, take out (without the connotation of force)   Note that the ἐκ changes to ἐξ in front of the augment.

εἰ – if (This word appears on the *Accents and Breathing Marks That Matter* list because it is spelled the same as the second person singular present form of εἰμί.)

PREPARING FOR THE QUIZ:

(1) Learn the rule for *augmenting compound verbs*.

(2) Pay particular attention to the *formation of the different tenses* of the new vocabulary. These tend to be more difficult to deal with than they might first appear. Practice with them until they are familiar.

(3) Learn to recognize and translate *first class conditions*.

Chapter 12

*The Noun and Article: Second Declension Neuter / The Definite Article as a
Substantiver with a Genitive or Prepositional Phrase / Numbers from One to
Ten / Objective Genitive / Adverbial καί*

SECOND DECLENSION NEUTER NOUNS: In addition to the masculine
nouns already learned, the *second declension* also includes nouns which are
classified as *neuter*. A look at the case endings will show that *in the genitive and
dative cases the second declension neuter nouns are identical to the second
declension masculine nouns.* The underlined forms in the paradigm below are the
only new ones to be learned. Also note the new articles for the nominative and
accusative singular and plural.

```
* * * * * * * * * * * * * * * * * * *
*            τὸ ἱερόν – temple            *
*                                         *
*         Singular         Plural         *
*                                         *
*    N.   τὸ ἱερόν        τὰ ἱερά         *
*    G.   τοῦ ἱεροῦ       τῶν ἱερῶν       *
*    D.   τῷ ἱερῷ         τοῖς ἱεροῖς     *
*    A.   τὸ ἱερόν        τὰ ἱερά         *
*                                         *
* * * * * * * * * * * * * * * * * * *
```

The accent patterns for second declension neuter nouns parallel those for second
declension masculine nouns (see Chapter 5). Examples:

  τὸ ἱερόν ("temple") = ὁ υἱός
  τὸ ἔργον ("work") = ὁ λόγος
  τὸ δαιμόνιον ("demon") = ὁ κύριος
  τὸ πλοῖον ("boat") = ὁ δοῦλος

The *alpha* ending of the nominative and accusative plural is short, hence: τὰ
δαιμόνια and τὰ πλοῖα.

EXTREMELY IMPORTANT INFORMATION:

(1) It is characteristic of neuter nouns, pronouns, and adjectives that the
nominative and accusative singular are identical, as are the nominative and
accusative plural. This means that the same form can serve as the subject or the
direct object (as well as predicate nominative and object of certain prepositions)

in many sentences. Therefore you must look for contextual or logical clues in making such decisions.

(2) Under most circumstances a plural noun subject requires a third person plural verb. This is known as "agreement", the noun and verb "agree." Very often, however, *a neuter plural subject has a third person singular verb*. This generally occurs when the plural subject is thought of as a group rather than as individuals: τὰ δένδρα φέρει καρπόν. The trees are bearing fruit.

DEFINITE ARTICLE: With this chapter you have the last new forms of the definite article. Here is a summary of these forms. These will be paired by gender with nouns of any declension.

	Masculine		Feminine		Neuter	
	Sing.	*Pl.*	*Sing.*	*Pl.*	*Sing.*	*Pl.*
N.	ὁ	οἱ	ἡ	αἱ	τό	τά
G.	τοῦ	τῶν	τῆς	τῶν	τοῦ	τῶν
D.	τῷ	τοῖς	τῇ	ταῖς	τῷ	τοῖς
A.	τόν	τούς	τήν	τάς	τό	τά

THERE ARE FIVE ADDITIONAL POINTS IN THIS CHAPTER:

(1) The definite article can be used to turn various types of phrases and parts of speech other than nouns into *substantives*. Nouns are called substantives, as are words or phrases which are *functioning as nouns* in a sentence. We will see this done in Chapter 14 with adjectives and again in Chapter 33 with participles. It can also be done with a genitive word or phrase and with a prepositional phrase. The *gender and number* of the substantive are indicated by the gender and number of the article. The *case of the article* depends on how the substantive is functioning in the sentence.

> οἱ ἐν τῷ οἴκῳ   those in the house, the people in the house, those (who
> are / were) in the house

> τὰ Καίσαρος...τὰ τοῦ θεοῦ   the things of Caesar / which are
>   Caesar's...the things of God / which are God's (Matthew 22:21b)
>   [***Note:*** Καίσαρος is a genitive singular third declension noun.]

(2) Numbers from one to ten are as follows:

εἷς, μία, ἕν – one	ἕξ – six
δύο – two	ἑπτά – seven
τρεῖς, τρία – three	ὀκτώ – eight
τέσσαρες, τέσσαρα – four	ἐννέα – nine
πέντε – five	δέκα – ten

Do not worry about the numbers one, three, and four for right now. They have different forms for the different cases and genders and some of these forms are third declension (the final Greek noun declension, introduced in Chapter 24). The other numbers, however, do not change form and so can be used with nouns of any case and gender (obviously they are plural). They should be learned at this time. [Note that εἷς, ἕν, and ἕξ appear on the *Accents and Breathing Marks That Matter* list.]

(3) Like *κατά,* the preposition *μετά* has different meanings depending on whether its object is *genitive or accusative.*

> μετὰ τῶν υἱῶν   with the sons
> μετὰ δύο ἡμέρας   after two days

(4) ***Objective genitive***: Phrases such as ἡ ἀγάπη τῆς δικαιοσύνης represent a use of the genitive case known as the ***objective genitive***. The head noun is a noun with a verbal idea, in this case "love." The relationship of the head noun to the noun in the genitive case is that of a verb to its direct object, hence the term "objective" genitive. There are many verbal nouns which could be followed by an objective genitive. Just a few examples are: fear (the fear of death: ὁ φόβος τοῦ θανάτου), hope (hope of / for glory), and judgment (judgment of this world). [The opposite of an objective genitive is a ***subjective genitive***: the noun in the genitive case is the *subject* of the verbal idea in the head noun. The phrase "the love of God" is an interesting example. If it means "someone loves God," then "God" is an objective genitive. If it means "God loves someone," "God" is a subjective genitive. You do not need to add subjective genitive to your list right now, but you should add objective genitive.]

(5) The word καί can be used as an adverb as well as a conjunction. When used adverbially the translation is "also" or "even."

τὸ εὐαγγέλιον κηρύξομεν καὶ τοῖς ἔθνεσιν [ἔθνεσι(ν) is another third declension noun].   We shall proclaim the Gospel to the Gentiles also. / …even to the Gentiles.

VOCABULARY

ἱερόν, -οῦ, n. – temple (This word is generally used to refer to the temple in Jerusalem, including everything within the temple precinct, though it can also be used of pagan temples.) [hierarchy]

ἔργον, -ου, n. – work, deed   [ergonomic]

τέκνον, -ου, n. – child

δένδρον, -ου, n. – tree   [philodendron]

βιβλίον, -ου, n. – book   [bibliophile]

πλοῖον, -ου, n. – boat

δῶρον, -ου, n. – gift   [Theodore]

σημεῖον, -ου, n. – sign; miraculous sign, miracle   [semiotic]

πρόσωπον, -ου, n. – face   [prosopography]

ἱμάτιον, -ου, n. – coat, robe (outer garment); garment, clothing

δαιμόνιον, -ου, n. – demon   [demon]

εὐαγγέλιον, -ου, n. – good news, gospel   [evangelize]

μετά (preposition with genitive) – with, among
        (preposition with accusative) – after   [metaphysics]

καί (adverbial) – also, even

PREPARING FOR THE QUIZ:

(1) You should know how the **second declension neuter nouns** fit into the overall second declension framework. Note especially the similarities and differences between these and the second declension masculine nouns.

(2) Make a special note of the fact that **neuter plural subjects often have third person singular verbs**.

(3) Learn the five additional points in this chapter. This **adds to your lists** another use for the genitive case (**objective genitive**) and another preposition with one meaning when the object is in the genitive case and another meaning when the object is in the accusative case (**μετά**). It also adds another idiomatic use of the language (the definite article with a prepositional phrase or a genitive phrase to create a **substantive**), some **numbers**, and the **adverbial use of καί**.

Chapter 13
Deponent Verbs: Present M/P and Future Middle Indicative /
Deponent Futures / Dative of Association / Dative of Destination

DEPONENT VERBS: In this chapter and Chapter 15 we will look at a *different set of personal endings* for the present, imperfect, future, and aorist tenses. In this chapter we will focus on three things:

(1) One new set of endings.
(2) The correct terminology for identifying these endings.
(3) **One** use for these endings.

Up to this point the identification of a verb *form* has provided enough information to translate that verb. This is because all the verbs we have seen so far are in the form labeled "active" (all the verbs in Chapters 2, 4, 6, 9, and 11). When a verb form is labeled "active," the translation of that verb is automatically active. With the new endings introduced in this chapter we encounter a different situation. These endings have *several different functions.* **One begins by identifying the form of the verb, but then, in order to translate that form, one must know more about the particular verb involved.**

Here are the new endings for this chapter:

	Singular	*Plural*
1st	–ομαι	–όμεθα
2nd	–η	–εσθε
3rd	–εται	–ονται

For **all verbs with these endings**, present tense forms are identified as "present" tense, "middle/passive" voice (abbreviated "M/P"). The future tense forms in this chapter are to be identified as "future" tense, "middle" voice. [This is enough information for now. Further information about voice will be given in Chapters 15, 17, and 18.]

One use for these endings involves a category of verbs called **deponents**. Deponent verbs appear with the new endings, but **still have an active translation**. [The term "deponent" comes from the Latin verb *deponere*, which means "to put aside." One way to understand this term is to say that a deponent verb has put aside its original force (either middle or passive) and replaced it with an active meaning (Wallace, p. 428).] Here is an example of a deponent verb:

```
* * * * * * * * * * * * * * * * * * * * * * * * * * * * *
*                     πορεύομαι – go                      *
*                                                         *
* Present Middle/Passive (M/P) Indicative   Future Middle Indicative   *
*                                                         *
*        Singular      Plural        Singular      Plural  *
*                                                         *
*  1ˢᵗ  πορεύομαι   πορευόμεθα    πορεύσομαι   πορευσόμεθα  *
*  2ⁿᵈ  πορεύῃ      πορεύεσθε     πορεύσῃ      πορεύσεσθε   *
*  3ʳᵈ  πορεύεται   πορεύονται    πορεύσεται   πορεύσονται  *
*                                                         *
* * * * * * * * * * * * * * * * * * * * * * * * * * * * *
```

IMPORTANT INFORMATION:

(1) These endings should be learned every bit as thoroughly as the active ones. They appear frequently!

(2) Deponent verbs appear in vocabulary listings in the present M/P form. *They have no present active form.* The present M/P is the first principal part of a deponent verb; the future middle is the second principal part.

(3) As with the active forms, present and future share a set of endings.

(4) The future stem is determined as in Chapter 6:

> Add sigma: πορεύομαι / πορεύσομαι
> Change the consonant: προσεύχομαι ("pray") / προσεύξομαι
> Learn a different stem: ἔρχομαι ("come") / ἐλεύσομαι

ADDITIONAL INFORMATION:

(1) Especially when it has the meaning "become," the verb γίνομαι functions as a "linking verb" (like εἰμί). For this reason it is followed grammatically *not* by a direct object, but by a *predicate nominative.*

> ὁ υἱός μου γίνεται διδάσκαλος.   My son is becoming a teacher.
> φίλοι γενήσονται οἱ διάκονοι.   The servants will become friends.

(2) A number of verbs which have active forms in most tenses have a *deponent form in the future (future middle).* The following list gives the verbs studied thus

far which have a deponent future. You may now return to the verb list in Chapter 9 and remove the brackets on these future forms. You should also mark these on your master verb list. [Do not, however, mark any future form with a circumflex over the vowel or diphthong of the personal ending.]

Present Active	*Future Middle*	*Aorist Active*
ἀκούω	ἀκούσομαι (sometimes)	ἤκουσα
ἐσθίω	φάγομαι	ἔφαγον
πίνω	πίομαι	ἔπιον
γινώσκω	γνώσομαι	[ἔγνων]
λαμβάνω	λήμψομαι	ἔλαβον
παραλαμβάνω	παραλήμψομαι	παρέλαβον
φεύγω	φεύξομαι	ἔφυγον

(3) The verb εἰμί also has a deponent (future middle) future, with a slightly irregular third person singular (no *epsilon* between the *sigma* and the *tau*):

```
* * * * * * * * * * * * * * * * * * * * * * * * * * *
*            Singular                    Plural              *
*                                                            *
* 1st  ἔσομαι  I will be          ἐσόμεθα  we will be        *
* 2nd  ἔσῃ  you (s.) will be       ἔσεσθε  you (pl.) will be  *
* 3rd  ἔσται  he/she/it will be    ἔσονται  they will be      *
*            there will be              there will be        *
*                                                            *
* * * * * * * * * * * * * * * * * * * * * * * * * * *
```

(4) The verb ἔρχομαι is deponent in the *present* (present M/P) and *future* (future middle), but has *active* forms in the aorist. (This is an exception. Usually if a verb starts out as a deponent it remains so in all its principal parts.) This verb has many compounds; see the vocabulary list below.

VOCABULARY

γίνομαι, γενήσομαι – The Danker lexicon describes this word as: "A verb with
   numerous nuances relating to being and manner of being" (p. 196).
   Among the many possible translations are: be made, be created; come
   about, happen; become [genesis]
πορεύομαι, πορεύσομαι – go; travel

ἐκπορεύομαι, ἐκπορεύσομαι – go / come out, proceed
δέχομαι, --- – receive, accept; welcome
εὔχομαι, --- – pray
προσεύχομαι, προσεύξομαι – pray
ἔρχομαι, ἐλεύσομαι, ἦλθον   come
ἀπέρχομαι, ἀπελεύσομαι, ἀπῆλθον – go away, depart
διέρχομαι, διελεύσομαι, διῆλθον – go through, cross
εἰσέρχομαι, εἰσελεύσομαι, εἰσῆλθον – go in(to), enter
ἐξέρχομαι, ἐξελεύσομαι, ἐξῆλθον – go out, proceed
παρέρχομαι, παρελεύσομαι, παρῆλθον – pass away, go by
προσέρχομαι, προσελεύσομαι, προσῆλθον – go to, approach
συνέρχομαι, συνελεύσομαι, συνῆλθον – go with, accompany; come together
        (with)
νῦν – now
πάλιν – again
οὐδέ – and not, nor (neither…nor)
οὐδείς – no one (nominative singular masculine)
οὐδέν – nothing (nominative / accusative singular neuter)
ὑπέρ (preposition with genitive) – for, for the sake of, on behalf of
        [preposition with accusative – over and above, beyond (hyperphagia)]

VOCABULARY NOTES:

(1) For εὔχομαι and προσεύχομαι note the following:

    a) The *person prayed to* goes in the dative case or appears in a
        prepositional phrase with πρός.
    b) The *thing prayed for* goes in the accusative case.
    c) The *person on behalf of whom or for whom* prayer is offered appears in
        a prepositional phrase with ὑπέρ ("for," "for the sake of," "on
        behalf of") and the **genitive** case. [ὑπέρ with the accusative case
        means "over and above" or "beyond," as in the English prefix
        "hyper–." You may learn this now, but it will not appear in the
        exercises The use with the genitive case will appear.]

(2) It is common in Greek to use a compound verb *and* then use the prepositional
prefix in a separate prepositional phrase.

Example: σὺν τῷ κυρίῳ ἐν τῷ πλοίῳ συνήλθομεν. – We went with the master in his (the) boat. [In this sentence τῷ κυρίῳ would be identified as "dative singular masculine / object of the preposition." If the separate preposition did *not* appear, τῷ κυρίῳ would be considered a "dative of association." This use is quite common following verbs compounded with σύν.]

(3) Expect to see the compounds of ἔρχομαι as follows:

ἀπέρχομαι – alone or with a prepositional phrase giving direction

διέρχομαι – accusative direct object or διά + genitive

εἰσέρχομαι – usually εἰς + accusative

ἐξέρχομαι – alone or with prepositional phrase giving direction

παρέρχομαι – alone, with accusative direct object, or with παρά + accusative

προσέρχομαι – usually with a ***dative of destination*** [This is a dative use which is lexically restricted to *intransitive* verbs incorporating a "to" idea. It is used primarily with ἔρχομαι and προσέρχομαι.]

συνέρχομαι – with a ***dative of association*** or σύν + dative

(4) The basic form of ἔρχομαι is usually translated "come" (though on occasion it may need to be translated "go"). The compounds, however, are usually translated using "go." The most common verbs meaning "go" are πορεύομαι and ὑπάγω, which can also mean "go away."

PREPARING FOR THE QUIZ:

(1) You should know what is meant by the term ***deponent verb***.

(2) You should be familiar with the ***new set of personal endings*** for present and future and the ***correct identification of forms with these endings***.

(3) Learn the ***deponent futures*** of verbs which are not otherwise deponent. Take this opportunity to review principal parts and update your verb lists.

(4) Add the ***dative of association*** and ***dative of destination*** to your ***uses for the dative case*** list. [Note carefully that both of these uses are "lexically limited." This means that they usually occur in very restricted circumstances with *certain types of verbs*.]

Chapter 14

ADJECTIVES: In Greek, as in English, adjectives modify or limit nouns, i.e., they give some special information about nouns. Examples: good friends, fine wine, the wise teacher, a righteous servant, the happy people.

AGREEMENT: In Greek an adjective must *agree* with the noun it modifies. This means that it must be the same case, number, and gender as the noun.

> οἱ φίλοι εἰσὶ σοφοί. The friends are wise. (Both "friends" and "wise" are nominative plural masculine.)

Adjectives, therefore, need to have endings to correspond to each case, number, and gender. Good news; there are no new endings in the paradigms below!

* *

σοφός, -ή, -όν – wise

	Singular			*Plural*		
	M.	F.	N.	M.	F.	N.
N.	σοφός	σοφή	σοφόν	σοφοί	σοφαί	σοφά
G.	σοφοῦ	σοφῆς	σοφοῦ	σοφῶν	σοφῶν	σοφῶν
D.	σοφῷ	σοφῇ	σοφῷ	σοφοῖς	σοφαῖς	οφοῖς
A.	σοφόν	σοφήν	σοφόν	σοφούς	σοφάς	σοφά

* *

Some first declension feminine adjectives, like some nouns (e.g., καρδία) have *alpha* (a long *alpha*) instead of *eta* in the singular forms. This will be noted in the lexicon entry.

ἄξιος, -α, -ον – worthy

N. ἀξία
G. ἀξίας
D. ἀξίᾳ
A. ἀξίαν

Adjective accents follow the same patterns as noun accents, the only difference being that the genitive plural feminine is *not* always accented on the ultima.

POSITION OF ADJECTIVES: The actual translating of Greek adjectives presents little problem once the issue of word order is clarified. There are two terms used to describe the position of the adjective in relation to the noun it modifies: *attributive* and *predicate.*

(1) The *attributive position* is used in phrases: "the good book," "the wise teacher," "the righteous commandment," etc. Phrases of this kind may be written *two ways* in Greek, with the adjective between the article and the noun or in the order: article-noun-article-adjective. Note that this always places an article *in front of* the adjective.

> τὸ ἀγαθὸν βιβλίον / τὸ βιβλίον τὸ ἀγαθόν
> ὁ σοφὸς διδάσκαλος / ὁ διδάσκαλος ὁ σοφός
> ἡ δικαία ἐντολή / ἡ ἐντολὴ ἡ δικαία

These are essentially the same in meaning, although in the first pattern the adjective receives a bit more emphasis. Note that in the last example, although the words all agree (nominative singular feminine), they are not identical. Each word follows its own pattern.

(2) The *predicate position* represents what we would call a predicate adjective. It is used in a whole clause rather than a phrase. It may be placed either before or after the verb.

> οἱ λόγοι τοῦ κυρίου εἰσὶ σοφοί. / σοφοί εἰσιν οἱ λόγοι τοῦ
> κυρίου. The words of the master are wise.

It is quite common in Greek, however, for the verb εἰμί to be omitted. When that happens, the appropriate form must be supplied by the translator based on the context. The predicate position of the adjective will serve as an indicator that this is, in fact, a complete clause and not just a noun-adjective phrase. Note that in the predicate position the article does *not* precede the adjective. Word order is either article-noun-adjective or adjective-article-noun.

> οἱ λόγοι τοῦ κυρίου σοφοί. / σοφοὶ οἱ λόγοι τοῦ κυρίου.

Note: It is, of course, possible to have a noun-adjective phrase with no article: μακάριος ἄνθρωπος: "a happy man." This could possibly mean "Happy is a man...," but you would have to figure this out from the context.

SUBSTANTIVES: As we saw in Chapter 12, the definite article can be used to create a substantive from certain kinds of words and phrases. This can also be done with adjectives. The article and noun ending will indicate the gender and number of the substantive and the case will provide information about the function in the sentence. Here are some examples:

> ὁ σοφός   the wise man / person / one (nominative singular masculine)
> τοῦ δικαίου   the just / righteous man / person / one (genitive singular masculine)
> οἱ ἅγιοι   the holy, the holy men, the holy people, the saints* (nominative plural masculine)
> τοῖς σοφοῖς   the wise, the wise men, the wise people (dative plural masculine)
> τὴν ἀγαθήν   the good woman (accusative singular feminine)
> τὰ ἀγαθά   the good things, the things which are good (nominative / accusative plural neuter)
> τὸ πονηρόν   the evil thing, that which is evil, what is evil, evil (nominative / accusative singular neuter)

*Sometimes a substantive adjective will acquire a noun definition of its own. Such noun definitions will be listed in a lexicon.

PREPOSITION: Like κατά and μετά, the preposition διά has different meanings depending on whether the object is in the genitive or accusative case.

> διὰ τῆς ἀγορᾶς   through the market-place
> διὰ τὸν λόγον   on account of the word

VOCABULARY

ἀγαθός, -ή, -όν – good [Agatha]
καλός, -ή, -όν – good; honorable; fine, beautiful (See the vocabulary note on synonyms.) [kaleidoscope]
σοφός, -ή, -όν – wise [sophomore]
κακός, -ή, -όν – bad, evil, wrong [cacophony]
πονηρός, -ά, -όν – evil, wicked
νεκρός, -ά, -όν – dead (*substantive*: dead body, corpse) [necropolis]
νέος, -α, -ον – new; young [prefix neo–]
δίκαιος, -α, -ον – righteous; just, right

ἄξιος, -α, -ον – worthy [axiom]

ἅγιος, -α, -ον – holy, sacred (*plural substantive*: holy ones, saints)
    [hagiography]

μακάριος, -α, -ον – blessed, happy, fortunate

αἰώνιος, -ον – eternal, everlasting (See the note regarding the endings of this
    adjective.) [aeonian]

διά (preposition with genitive) – through, by means of
  (preposition with accusative) – on account of, because of

NOTES:

(1) As your Greek vocabulary increases, you will continue to find a number of
words with either the same or very similar translations. At times some of these
words appear to be essentially synonymous, while at other times there are
noticeable distinctions. Sometimes they share one meaning or set of meanings
but diverge on others (as was the case with λύω and ἀπολύω). The Danker
lexicon is your best source for further information. As an example, we have in
this chapter two sets of such words.

First we have ἀγαθός and καλός. While both of these words can mean "good" in
a moral sense, there is a slight underlying difference. ἀγαθός, when applied to
things, has the sense of "meeting a relatively high standard of quality" or is
concerned with "social significance and worth" (Danker, pp. 3-4). When applied
to humans and deities, its "primary focus is on usefulness to humans and society
in general" (Danker, p. 3). καλός describes something or someone as "being in
accordance at a high level with the purpose of something or someone" (Danker, p.
504). George Berry in *A Dictionary of New Testament Greek Synonyms* says of
καλός, "It means *beautiful*, physically or morally. It is, however, distinctly the
beauty which comes from harmony, the beauty which arises from a symmetrical
adjustment in right proportion, in other words, from the harmonious completeness
of the object concerned" (p. 19).

Then we have κακός and πονηρός. Danker says that κακός has to do with being
"socially or morally reprehensible" or with being "harmful or injurious" (p. 501).
πονηρός he says "pertains to being morally or socially worthless" (p. 851). Berry
says that sometimes the two words appear to have little difference in meaning, but
may often have the following distinction: "κακός frequently means *evil* rather
negatively, referring to the absence of the qualities which constitute a person or
thing what it should be or what it claims to be. It is also used meaning *evil* in a
moral sense. It is a general antithesis to ἀγαθός. πονηρός is a word at once
stronger and more active, it means *mischief-making*, delighting in injury, doing

evil to others, dangerous, destructive. κακός describes the quality according to its nature, πονηρός, according to its effects" (p. 22).

(2) Adjectives such as αἰώνιος lack a separate feminine form. They are referred to as adjectives with two forms or two terminations. When such an adjective is used to modify a feminine noun, the *masculine* ending of the adjective will be used, e.g., ζωὴ αἰώνιος.

PREPARING FOR THE QUIZ:

(1) Take this opportunity to review all of the ***noun / adjective endings***.

(2) You should know what the terms ***"attributive position"*** and ***"predicate position"*** mean in regard to nouns and adjectives and the ***two possible word orders*** for each position.

(3) You should know how to recognize and translate adjectives being used as nouns (***substantives***).

(4) You should add the new preposition to the appropriate lists. There are a number of prepositional phrases on the quiz. Use this opportunity to review ***all the prepositions***.

Chapter 15

Deponent Verbs: Imperfect M/P and Aorist Middle Indicative /
Subordinate Causal Clauses

DEPONENT VERBS: In this chapter we will look at two more sets of new verb endings, one used for imperfect M/P *and* second aorist middle and the other used for first aorist middle. The correct identification of imperfect forms is "imperfect" tense, "M/P" voice. The correct identification of aorist forms is "aorist" tense, "middle" voice. These endings will be used for deponent verbs, though that is not their only function.

DEFINITION OF A DEPONENT VERB: When we combine the information in this chapter with that in Chapter 13, the following general observation may be made. In the present and imperfect tenses middle and passive forms are identical, hence the designation "M/P." In the future and aorist tenses middle and passive forms are *not* identical, hence the designation "middle." [The aorist passive is the sixth principal part of the verb (Chapter 30). The future passive is created from the aorist passive stem. For this reason, you will not see any aorist passives for quite some time. You will meet some future passives in Chapter 18; they have the same endings as future middle but a different stem.] Based on this information, the following definition of a deponent verb can be given: ***a verb with a middle and/or passive form, but an active translation***.

Here are the new forms. Remember that all translation information remains as you have learned it.

```
* * * * * * * * * * * * * * * * * * * * * *
*                                            *
*        Imperfect M/P of προσεύχομαι        *
*                                            *
*         Singular            Plural         *
*                                            *
*   1st   προσηυχόμην      προσηυχόμεθα       *
*   2nd   προσηύχου        προσηύχεσθε        *
*   3rd   προσηύχετο       προσηύχοντο        *
*                                            *
* * * * * * * * * * * * * * * * * * * * * *
```

<table>
<tr><td colspan="2" align="center">First Aorist Middle</td><td colspan="2" align="center">Second Aorist Middle</td></tr>
<tr><td colspan="2" align="center">Indicative of προσεύχομαι</td><td colspan="2" align="center">Indicative of γίνομαι</td></tr>
</table>

	Singular	Plural	Singular	Plural
1st	προσηυξάμην	προσηυξάμεθα	ἐγενόμην	ἐγενόμεθα
2nd	προσηύξω	προσηύξασθε	ἐγένου	ἐγένεσθε
3rd	προσηύξατο	προσηύξαντο	ἐγένετο	ἐγένοντο

NOTE: You may have noticed that the second person singular M/P and middle forms don't quite fit with the rest. They should, but this is what happened. In each form the ending originally included a sigma. This sigma has dropped out and the two vowels (a vowel and a diphthong in the present M/P and future middle) on either side of it have combined as follows:

$$\epsilon\sigma\alpha\iota - \epsilon(\sigma)\alpha\iota > \eta \qquad \epsilon\sigma o - \epsilon(\sigma)o > ov \qquad a\sigma o - a(\sigma)o > \omega$$

OBSERVATIONS: The parallels between the new M/P and middle forms and the active forms continue.

(1) Imperfect and second aorist share a set of endings.

(2) The first aorist endings (except the second person singular) include the letter *alpha*.

(3) The first person plural and second person plural imperfect (and therefore also the second aorist) have the same endings as the present and future tenses.

(4) Many first aorists have a regularly formed stem. Second aorists have an irregular stem which must be memorized. While there are certainly others, the only *second* aorist middle you will see with any regularity is that of γίνομαι.

CAUSAL CLAUSES: In Chapter 11 we saw our first example of a **subordinate clause**: the "if" clause of a conditional sentence. Another kind of subordinate clause is introduced by the subordinating conjunction ὅτι ("because," "since"). A causal clause gives the cause or reason for the main clause.

οὐκ ἀκούετε, ὅτι οὐκ ἐστε σοφοί.   You do not listen, because
you are not wise.

VOCABULARY

There is only one completely new verb in this chapter. The rest of the new forms are the imperfects (in parentheses) and some aorists of the verbs introduced in Chapter 13.

γίνομαι (ἐγινόμην), γενήσομαι, ἐγενόμην
ἔρχομαι (ἠρχόμην), ἐλεύσομαι, ἦλθον
δέχομαι (ἐδεχόμην), ---, ἐδεξάμην
εὔχομαι (εὐχόμην or ηὐχόμην), ---, εὐξάμην
προσεύχομαι (προσηυχόμην), προσεύξομαι, προσηυξάμην
πορεύομαι (ἐπορευόμην) πορεύσομαι, ---
ἐκπορεύομαι (ἐξεπορευόμην), ἐκπορεύσομαι, ---
ἐργάζομαι (ἠργαζόμην), ---, ἠργασάμην – work; do [energy]
ὅτι – because, since

PREPARING FOR THE QUIZ:

(1) Make sure you know all the ***deponent verb forms*** which we have covered so far. You should be able to recognize and correctly identify these forms.

(2) You should know the ***definition of a deponent verb*** as given in this chapter.

(3) You should know how to identify and translate a ***causal clause***.

REVIEW: The nouns we have studied so far may be summarized as follows:

(1) First declension feminine: nominative singular ends in –η or –α.
(2) Second declension masculine: nominative singular ends in –ος
(3) Second declension neuter: nominative singular ends in –ον.

FIRST DECLENSION MASCULINE NOUNS: There are also, however, some nouns of the *first declension* which are grammatically *masculine*. These generally refer to some category of people: tax-collectors, zealots, etc. They are recognizable in a lexicon by the following:

(1) The nominative singular ends in –ης (occasionally –ας).
(2) The genitive singular ends in –ου.
(3) The gender is indicated by the letter "m." or by the masculine definite article.

Examples: ἐργάτης, -ου, m. – worker
         τελώνης, -ου, m. – tax-collector
         ὀφειλέτης, -ου, m. – debtor; sinner

```
* * * * * * * * * * * * * * * * * * *
*          μαθητής – disciple        *
*                                    *
*        Singular        Plural      *
*                                    *
* N.  ὁ μαθητής      οἱ μαθηταί      *
* G.  τοῦ μαθητοῦ    τῶν μαθητῶν     *
* D.  τῷ μαθητῇ      τοῖς μαθηταῖς   *
* A.  τὸν μαθητήν    τοὺς μαθητάς    *
*                                    *
* * * * * * * * * * * * * * * * * * *
```

NOTES:

(1) Except for the nominative and genitive singular, all noun endings match first declension feminine.

(2) These nouns follow the same accent rules as first declension feminine nouns.

(3) Since these nouns are, in fact, grammatically *masculine*, the definite article and any adjectives used with them must also be masculine. [Lord's Prayer (Matthew 6:12): τοῖς ὀφειλέταις]

> ὁ σοφὸς μαθητής   the wise disciple (nominative singular masculine)
> τοὺς ἀξίους προφήτας   the worthy prophets (accusative plural masculine)

SECOND DECLENSION FEMININE NOUNS: There are also a few *feminine* nouns in the *second declension*. These are declined exactly like second declension masculine nouns. In context they will be noticeable by the feminine definite article. In a lexicon they will be indicated by the letter f. or the feminine definite article. They will be modified by *feminine* adjectives. Only two appear to any extent in the GNT: ὁδός ("road," "way") and ἔρημος ("desert," "deserted place").

```
* * * * * * * * * * * * * * * * * * *
*                                   *
*            ὁδός – way, road       *
*                                   *
*        Singular        Plural     *
*                                   *
*     N.  ἡ ὁδός        αἱ ὁδοί     *
*     G.  τῆς ὁδοῦ      τῶν ὁδῶν    *
*     D.  τῇ ὁδῷ        ταῖς ὁδοῖς  *
*     A.  τὴν ὁδόν      τὰς ὁδούς   *
*                                   *
* * * * * * * * * * * * * * * * * * *
```

τὴν ἀγαθὴν ὁδόν   the good way (accusative singular feminine)

NOUNS WITH CONTRACTED ENDINGS: There are a few nouns with what are called *contracted endings* (two vowels have combined to create a long vowel or diphthong). The contraction is marked with a circumflex accent.

```
* * * * * * * * * | | | * * * * * * * *
*
*    γῆ – earth              Ἰησοῦς – Jesus    |
*                                              *
*    N.  ἡ  γῆ               ὁ  Ἰησοῦς         *
†    G.  τῆς  γῆς            τοῦ  Ἰησοῦ        *
†    D.  τῆ  γῆ              τῷ  Ἰησοῦ         *
*    A.  τὴν  γῆν            τὸν  Ἰησοῦν       *
*                                              *
* * * * * * * * * * * * * * * * * * *
```

NOTES:

(1) There is no plural for γῆ. γῆ is a first declension feminine noun.

(2) Although the genitive and dative of Ἰησοῦς are identical, the frequent use of the definite article will help you out. Ἰησοῦς is a second declension masculine noun.

SECOND CLASS CONDITIONS: In Chapter 11 we looked at first class conditions. These conditions assume, for the sake of argument, that the "if" clause is true. Second class conditions assume, for the sake of argument, that the "if" clause is *not* true. For this reason, these conditions are sometimes called "contrary to fact." Second class conditions follow set patterns in Greek and require the use of specific translation formulas. In Greek these conditions use εἰ and either the imperfect or aorist (very occasionally other tenses) in the protasis (the "if" clause) and the same tenses in the apodosis (the "then" clause). The apodosis typically includes the untranslatable particle ἄν. Rather than translating the verb tenses as you normally would, you need to observe and practice the translation formulas.

present contrary to fact condition (Greek verbs are *imperfect*):

> εἰ ἐγινώσκετε τὸν πατέρα, τὸν υἱὸν ἄν ἐγινώσκετε. If you **knew** the Father [but we assume that you do not], you **would know** the Son.

past contrary to fact condition (Greek verbs are *aorist*):

> εἰ τὴν ἀλήθειαν εἶπεν, αὐτῷ ἐπίστευσεν ἄν ὁ διδάσκαλος. If he **had spoken** the truth [but we assume that he did not], the teacher **would have believed** him.

When working with second class conditions, you need to do the following: (1) spot the condition based on the εἰ and the ἄν, (2) determine whether the condition is in present or past time based on the tense of the verbs, and (3) apply the appropriate translation formula.

PREPOSITION: The preposition ἐπί may be used with an object in the genitive, dative, or accusative case. The meanings of this preposition are many and varied and even appear at times to overlap. At this point only a few meanings will be given for each case.

genitive: on, upon	ἐπὶ τῆς θαλάσσης	upon the sea
dative: on, at; near	ἐπὶ τῷ ἱερῷ	at the temple
accusative: on, upon; against; to	ἐπὶ τοὺς προφήτας	against the prophets

VOCABULARY

μαθητής, -οῦ, m. – disciple
στρατιώτης, -ου, m. – soldier
προφήτης, -ου, m. – prophet [prophet]
ὁδός, -οῦ, f. – way, road; way, way of life [odometer]
ἔρημος, -ου, f. – deserted place, uninhabited region, desert [hermit]
γῆ, γῆς, f. – earth [geography]
ἐπί (preposition with genitive) – on, upon [before, in the presence of; in the time of] [epidermis]
     (preposition with dative) – on, at; near
     (preposition with accusative) – on, upon; against; to

PREPARING FOR THE EXAM:

(1) Make sure you are clear on the two new categories of nouns: *first declension masculine* and *second declension feminine*. (This completes the picture of the first and second declensions.)

(2) Make sure you understand the basic concept of the *second class conditions*.

(3) Make sure you know how to spot second class conditions and how to distinguish second class conditions in present time from second class conditions in past time. *Be very sure that you know the correct translation formula for both.*

(4) Learn the meanings for the new preposition and add it to *all **three*** of your preposition lists

(5) ***Review*** the recent chapters; be sure to look at the "Preparing for the Quiz" sections.

Chapter 17

The Passive Voice: Both a Form and a Concept

VOICE: Chapters 17 and 18 are companion chapters continuing the topic of *voice* in Greek. Keep in mind that this concept is more complex than in English for reasons which will become clear as these chapters progress. The best way to understand this is to remember that in dealing with the voice of a Greek verb we are asking **two separate questions**. The first question asks, "What is the form of this verb?" This is the information given on a parsing chart. The second question asks, "How is this verb form to be translated **in this specific situation**?" Information about the form of the verb is given by the verb stem, the presence or absence of an augment, [the presence or absence of reduplication (a characteristic of the perfect and pluperfect tenses – Chapters 28 and 29)], and the personal ending. For verbs with an active form, the translation, with very few exceptions, will also be active in concept. For information about the translation of verbs with a middle and/or passive form, however, we must look at what we know, or can find out, about the specific verb.

REVIEW: In Chapters 13 and 15 we looked at deponent verbs. Most of the ones we looked at use *forms* called "middle/passive" in the present and imperfect tenses and *forms* called "middle" in the future and aorist, yet the *translation* of these verbs is active. (Remember the definition of a deponent: **a verb with a middle and/or passive form and an active translation**.)

CONCEPT OF PASSIVE: In this chapter we will discuss the *concept* of passive as it applies to verb translation. English also has a passive concept, so this should be fairly easy to grasp.

If the verb in a sentence is "active" (in concept), the subject does something. Examples:

> The soldiers are persecuting the disciples.
> Jesus was teaching the word of God.

If the verb is "passive" (in both form *and* concept), *something is done to the subject*. Examples:

> The disciples <u>are being persecuted</u> by the soldiers.
> The word of God <u>was being taught</u> by Jesus.

The issue of voice in Greek is complicated by two factors: (1) the existence of a third voice, the middle, and (2) deponent verbs. Remember the two points made previously:

(1) The middle and passive *forms* are identical in the present and imperfect tenses, but not in the future and aorist.

(2) Deponent verbs, though active in concept, use the middle and/or passive forms.

In the present and imperfect tenses the concept of passive (something done to the subject) is expressed in Greek by adding the **present and Imperfect M/P endings** to the first principal part of verbs which are **not** deponent.

The two passive sentences given above would be written like this in Greek:

oἱ μαθηταὶ <u>διώκονται</u> ὑπὸ τῶν στρατιωτῶν. (present M/P 3 pl.)

ὁ λόγος τοῦ θεοῦ <u>ἐδιδάσκετο</u> ὑπὸ τοῦ Ἰησοῦ. (imperfect M/P 3 s.)

PREPOSITION: The preposition ὑπό followed by the *genitive* case means "by" and is primarily used with the passive voice. [When followed by the *accusative* case, ὑπό means "under," "below"; thus the English prefix "hypo–."]

CONJUGATON AND TRANSLATION: The following is a conjugation of the verb διώκω in the present M/P and in the imperfect M/P. The appropriate *passive translation* for the present tense is usually "I am being persecuted," "you are being persecuted," etc. It is also possible to translate "I am persecuted," "you are persecuted," etc. if a *general* rather than a *particular* statement is being made. For the imperfect tense various translations are possible: "I was being persecuted," "you used to be persecuted," "they continued to be persecuted," but **not** "I was persecuted," "we were persecuted," etc. These translations must be reserved for the **aorist passive**. [**Note:** The concept of passive in the future and aorist tenses requires the use of the sixth principal part and will be learned later.]

* *

	Present M/P Indicative of διώκω		Imperfect M/P Indicative of διώκω	
	Singular	*Plural*	*Singular*	*Plural*
1st	διώκομαι	διωκόμεθα	ἐδιωκόμην	ἐδιωκόμεθα
2nd	διώκῃ	διώκεσθε	ἐδιώκου	ἐδιώκεσθε
3rd	διώκεται	διώκονται	ἐδιώκετο	ἐδιώκοντο

* *

As is evident from the paradigm above, the exact same *parsing information* is used for deponents and verbs which are not deponent but are instead being used to express the passive concept. (Remember that the parsing process just identifies the *form.*) Therefore **more than one step** is required to work with verbs which have middle and/or passive endings.

(1) Identify the form: ἔρχεται – present M/P indicative 3 s.

   βαπτίζεται – present M/P indicative 3 s.

(2) Translate the verb based on what you know about it. ἔρχομαι is a deponent, therefore the form given above will have an active translation ("he/she/it is coming"). βαπτίζω is not a deponent, therefore the form given above will have a passive translation ("he/she is being baptized").

OBSERVATIONS:

(1) Once again it becomes clear why it is important to know principal parts. You need to know which verbs are deponent (including deponent futures) and which are not in order to determine whether to use an active or passive translation for any middle and/or passive verb forms.

(2) Since deponents are already using a middle and/or passive form, they cannot somehow be made "more passive." For example, δέχομαι cannot be altered in some way to say something like "Guests were being welcomed." Another word or mode of expression would have to be used.

PREPARING FOR THE QUIZ:

(1) You should be able to articulate the **two step process** involved in dealing with Greek verbs.

(2) Make sure you remember the **definition of a deponent verb**.

(3) You should know the different possible ways to **translate the passive concept** in the present and imperfect tenses.

(3) You should know which of the verbs you have learned are **deponents** (including deponent futures). These will have an active translation. When M/P endings appear on *other* verbs in the present and imperfect tenses, these verbs may be expressing the *passive concept* and must be translated accordingly. (This will be true for all the exercises in this chapter.)

NOTE: The material in Chapter 18 builds on this chapter and further develops the process of learning more about the specific verb you are working with.

Chapter 18
The Middle Voice: Both a Form and a Concept

REVIEW: Before going on to discuss the middle voice, let's review what we have so far.

(1) The middle and passive *forms* are identical in the present and imperfect, but different in the future and aorist.

(2) We now have two possible uses for verbs with a middle and/or passive form. Such verbs may be deponents or, if the form is middle/passive or passive (but not middle), they may actually be expressing the passive concept of something done to the subject.

(3) So far we can only do the passive concept for present M/P and imperfect M/P forms. In these two tenses, parsing information will be the same for deponents and verbs expressing the passive concept; one must know more about the specific verb involved. Both πορεύονται and πέμπονται have the same parsing information: present M/P indicative third person plural. But πορεύονται is a deponent and so has an active translation: "they are going." Whereas πέμπονται is not a deponent and so must be expressing the passive concept: "they are being sent."

(4) Future and aorist forms, however, will be parsed as middle *or* passive. All of the deponent future and aorist forms which you have seen so far are middle:

ἐλεύσομαι – future middle 1 s.	προσευξόμεθα – future middle 1 pl.
λήμψονται – future middle 3 pl.	ἔσεσθε – future middle 2 pl.
ἐδέξαντο – 1st aorist middle 3 pl.	ἐγένετο – 2nd aorist middle 3 s.

(5) As has been stated already, the passive concept for the aorist and future tenses (something "was done" or "will be done") requires the use of the sixth principal part. For this reason we will not be able to express the passive concept in the aorist and future until that principal part is introduced (Chapter 30). The *form* of the future passive, however, will at times be used with an active translation. The future passive form is usually characterized by the letters θησ at the end of the stem, immediately before the personal ending (e.g., συναχθήσονται – future passive indicative 3 pl. of συνάγω· "they will gather," "come together"). **Note:** The future passive form uses the same endings as the future middle form, it is the *stem* that distinguishes them.

THE MIDDLE VOICE:

I. The function of the Greek middle voice is difficult for English speakers to comprehend, since we have nothing in our own language which corresponds to it. Furthermore, even in Greek, it is highly nuanced and subtle. If we look at some of the definitions which have been offered, however, we can begin to get a general sense of what the middle is about.

> "The basic notion is that the subject intimately participates in the results of the action. It is the voice of personal involvement." (Young, p. 134)

> "[I]n the middle voice the subject *performs* or *experiences the action* expressed by the verb in such a way that *emphasizes the subject's participation.*" (Wallace, p. 414)

> "The middle voice shows that the action is performed with special reference to the subject." (Smyth, p. 390)

> "The middle calls special attention to the subject...the subject acting in relation to himself somehow." (Robertson, p. 804)

> "In the middle voice the subject of the verb is involved in the action....In some way the action is in the interest of the subject." (Hewett, p. 82)

Wallace (p. 415) offers the further helpful comment, "The difference between the active and middle is one of emphasis. The active voice emphasizes the *action* of the verb; the middle voice emphasizes the *actor* [subject] of the verb."

II. So how is this expressed in English? Two major divisions are made in the broad category of middle: ***the direct middle*** and ***the indirect middle***. (There are some other classifications of the middle, based on specific nuances, but these need not concern beginning students.)

(1) In the direct middle the subject acts upon himself, herself, etc. The direct middle is generally translated using the English reflexive pronoun.

> In John 18:18 we read that "the servants and attendants, after they had made a charcoal fire, because it was cold, were standing there and <u>warming themselves</u>." The verb in question is ἐθερμαίνοντο [imperfect M/P 3 pl. θερμαίνω]. Clearly the subjects are involved in the action. The *active* voice would be used of someone warming someone else or something warming someone.

In Luke 12:37 we read that when the master comes and finds his slaves awake "he <u>will gird himself</u> and have them sit / recline at table and come by and serve them." The verb is περιζώσεται [future middle 3 s. περιζώννυμι / περιζωννύω]. The *active* voice would mean to gird someone else; the *passive* voice would mean to be girded [Among the most frequent uses of the direct middle in the GNT are those which refer to clothing oneself or putting on something.]

The direct middle is quite infrequent in the GNT. Increasingly an active verb form is used with a form of the reflexive pronoun. Occasionally one finds both the middle voice *and* a reflexive pronoun, a usage of the middle that may be termed "redundant." This use is also fairly rare in the GNT. It occurs with verbs which are deponent in the sense of not having active forms, but which still retain a middle nuance.

Matthew 16:24 ἀπαρνησάσθω ἑαυτὸν – "let him deny himself" [1st aorist middle imperative 3 s. ἀπαρνέομαι]

(2) In the indirect middle the subject acts for (sometimes by) himself, herself, etc., or in his, her, or their own interest. This is often not expressed in translations. If it is expressed, it is usually by adding "for himself," "for herself," etc. Even if this is not directly expressed in the translation, however, one needs to be aware of it when looking at the Greek.

In Luke 10:42 we read that "Mary <u>chose</u> the good part." The verb is ἐξελέξατο [1st aorist middle 3 s. ἐκλέγω]. The implication is that Mary chose the good part *for herself.*

In John 14:23 Jesus says, "If anyone loves me, he will keep my word, and my father will love him, and we will come to him and <u>make our abode</u> with him." The verb is ποιησόμεθα [future middle 1 pl. ποιέω]. The implication is that they will *make an abode for themselves (and then live in it).*

III. The good news is that you do not have to figure this out for yourself. The lexicon will let you know when verbs with middle forms are functioning in one of these two ways. (This is definitely true of the Danker lexicon, but is not always true of the one in the back of the UBS edition. The latter, for example, does not list the middle in the John 14:23 passage.) Often such verbs do not have active forms in use in the GNT, or even in other Koine Greek literature, and thus are listed as deponents. This is true for some of the verbs in the examples above, e.g., ἐκλέγομαι. In other instances, the lexicon will list the active form, but then give the notation "only middle in our (i.e., Koine) literature." It is useful, however, for you to have a general sense of the middle voice concept, since you will certainly encounter it at some point and it is helpful to see the logic behind some verbs which appear in the GNT as deponents but once had active forms. Even some deponent verbs which seem to have always been without any active forms have some sort of middle nuance. Among the deponents verbs which suggest the involvement of the subject in the results of the action are δέχομαι and εὔχομαι / προσεύχομαι. (For this reason, grammarians are divided as to whether they should properly be classified as deponents. For our purposes, however, we will continue to call verbs deponent if there is no active form in the GNT for the principal part involved.)

NOTE: You will not be asked to make decisions about the middle voice in your exercises, except for verbs which are listed as deponents and those which fall in the category discussed in the next section. You should keep it in the back of your mind, however, in preparation for reading in the GNT.

IV. This brings us, at last, to the *third* possible use for verbs with a middle and/or passive form and the one which will be the focus of the new vocabulary in this chapter. There are quite a number of verbs which have ***one definition for their active forms and another definition for either their middle forms or their passive forms***. These verbs will be listed in a lexicon under the active form with reference made to the middle or passive definition. Usually there is a noticeable relationship between the active meaning and the middle or passive meaning, although in a few verbs the definitions are, or appear to be, unrelated. (***Note:*** If a separate definition is given for middle forms it will also apply to forms that are middle/passive; it will *not*, however, apply to forms that are only passive. Likewise a separate definition for passive forms will apply to middle/passive forms, but *not* to those that are only middle.) Here is a typical lexicon entry:

> φυλάσσω guard, keep under guard; keep, obey, follow; keep safe, protect, defend; *midd.* be on one's guard against, look out for, avoid, beware of; abstain from (food offered in sacrifice to idols); keep, obey (Mark 10:20)

First the meanings for active forms are listed. Then, following the abbreviation "*midd.*," come the definitions for the middle forms. At the end of the entry are definitions which only apply in specific circumstances or only in specific passages, which will be cited.

VOCABULARY

Of the verbs we have seen so far, the following have separate middle or passive definitions in regular use. I will list the middle and/or passive forms in this vocabulary section. You need to be aware, however, that ***the first principal part***

is the present active form. That is where you will find the word in a lexicon; this is what you would list on a parsing chart. Only deponents which have no active forms in the present tense will be listed in a lexicon with a first principal part ending in -ομαι

NOTE. If active forms exist but do not appear in the GNT, a lexicon of only the New Testament will list the verb as a deponent. A more comprehensive lexicon, however, will list the active form.

1) ἄρχω – (active: rule); ***middle:*** begin [frequently used in the GNT with an infinitive]
   Present M/P ἄρχομαι
   Future middle ἄρξομαι
   Aorist middle ἠρξάμην

2) φυλάσσω – (active: guard; protect; keep); ***middle:*** be on one's guard (against), avoid, look out for, beware of
   Present M/P φυλάσσομαι
   No future middle or aorist middle

3) πείθω – (active: persuade, convince); ***passive*** [except for the perfect and pluperfect]: obey, follow, pay attention (to) (***dative direct object***); be persuaded, believe [(1) absolute, i.e. with nothing following, (2) with the ***dative*** of the thing by which one is persuaded, or (3) with an ***indirect statement*** (see Chapter 20) following]
   Present M/P πείθομαι
   Future passive πεισθήσομαι [The future passive form is not actually the second principal part. It is, however, the future form used for the passive meanings. This is also true for several of the following verbs.]
   No aorist middle

4) σκανδαλίζω – (active: cause to fall/sin, offend); ***passive:*** fall away, give up one's faith, fall into sin
   Present M/P σκανδαλίζομαι
   Future passive σκανδαλισθήσομαι
   No aorist middle

5) στρέφω – (active: turn, *transitive*); ***passive:*** turn, turn around (*intransitive*)
   Present M/P στρέφομαι

Future passive στραφήσομαι [The future form given here is a future *passive*, even though it lacks the *theta* which characterizes the majority of future passive forms. This will become more understandable when we look at the sixth principal part and learn how aorist and future passives are actually formed.]
No aorist middle

6) συνάγω – (active: gather, bring together, *transitive*); **passive:** come together, gather, assemble (*intransitive*)
Present M/P συνάγομαι
Future passive συναχθήσομαι
No aorist middle

7) ὑποτάσσω – (active: put in subjection, subordinate); **passive:** be subject to, submit to, obey (**dative direct object**)
Present M/P ὑποτάσσομαι
Future passive ὑποταγήσομαι [See the note on the future passive of στρέφω.]
No aorist middle

[*Occasionally* the passive of καταλείπω can mean "remain behind" and once the middle of ἀπολύω means "leave."]

The following two vocabulary entries involve new verb stems.

8) ἅπτω, ---, ἧψα – active: light, kindle / **middle:** touch, take hold of (**genitive direct object**)
Present M/P ἅπτομαι
No future middle
Aorist middle ἡψάμην

9) [μιμνήσκω, μνήσω, ἔμνησα – remind] **passive:** remember (**genitive direct object**) [mnemonic]
Present M/P μιμνήσκομαι
Future passive μνησθήσομαι
No aorist middle

NOTE: The active forms of ἅπτω do appear in the GNT, but the middle forms are much more common. The active forms of μιμνήσκω, however, do not appear at all (though they are used in compounds), so μιμνήσκομαι may be considered the first principal part (though μιμνήσκω would be technically correct).

SUMMARY OF BASIC INFORMATION ABOUT VOICE:

I. The first step in working with a verb is to parse it. When you parse a verb you use information about various features of the verb (augment, reduplication, stem, endings) to identify its *form*. With experience this can usually be done whether or not you know the specific word in question. When the parsing reveals an *active* verb form, you know that the verb will have an active translation

> λέγει – he is speaking (present active 3 s.)
>
> ἐδιδάσκομεν – we were teaching (imperfect active 1 pl.)
>
> εὑρήσω – I will find (future active 1 s.)
>
> εἴδετε – you saw (2nd aorist active 2 pl.)

II. When, however, the parsing reveals a *middle and/or passive* form, you need **more information about the specific verb** before you can determine how to translate it. If you know the verb, you should have this information available to you in the principal parts and the definitions you have learned. If you do not know the verb, a lexicon will provide what you need to know. There are three possibilities that you need to consider.

(1) Begin by asking if the verb is a deponent. If so, it will have an active translation (though there may be some passive sounding options). This includes verbs which are entirely or mostly deponent (i.e., they have no, or only a few, active forms) and deponent futures for some verbs which are not otherwise deponent. Deponent verbs will be listed in a lexicon with middle and/or passive endings.

> ἔρχονται – they are coming (present M/P 3 pl.)
>
> λήμψεται – he/she will take (future middle 3 s.)
>
> ἠργάζεσθε – you were working (imperfect M/P 2 pl.)
>
> ἐδεξάμην – I received (1st aorist middle 1 s.)

(2) If the verb is not a deponent, ask whether there are any special meanings for middle or passive forms. If so, one of those meanings will be used if the form permits (i.e., a middle meaning for middle or M/P forms, a passive meaning for passive or M/P forms).

> σκανδαλίζεσθε – you are falling into sin (present M/P 2 pl.
>   σκανδαλίζω)
>
> συνηγόμεθα – we were gathering [*intransitive*] (imperfect M/P 1 pl.
>   συνάγω)
>
> πεισθήσονται – they will obey (future passive 3 pl. πείθω)

ἤρξατο – he/she began (1ˢᵗ aorist middle 3 s. ἄρχω)

(3) If neither (1) nor (2) applies, then you are looking at a verb expressing the passive concept (something done to the subject) and that will have to be reflected in your translation. Remember that at this time you are only able to do this for verbs in the present and imperfect tenses.

πειράζονται – they are being tested (present M/P 3 pl.)

ἐδιωκόμεθα – we were being persecuted (imperfect M/P 1 pl.)

PREPARING FOR THE QUIZ:

(1) You should have a basic understanding of the primary nuance of the *middle voice* and how this is often expressed.

(2) You should know the *three possibilities* for dealing with verbs which have middle and/or passive forms, how to determine which one is operative in a given verb, and how to translate each.

(3) There are several verbs in the vocabulary which need to be added to your lists of verbs with a *direct object in the genitive case* and verbs with a *direct object in the dative case*.

Chapter 19
Personal Pronouns / Intensive Pronoun /
Reflexive Pronouns / Dative of Means / Punctuation

PERSONAL PRONOUNS: Pronouns take the place of nouns in a sentence. Since they have essentially the same function as nouns, pronouns are identified in the same way: case, number, gender (if possible), and use in the sentence. The first pronouns we will consider in this chapter are called *personal pronouns*. The following examples illustrate some of the most common uses of the personal pronouns:

> ὁ κύριος ἡμῖν εἶπεν. The master spoke to <u>us</u>. [dative plural / indirect object]
>
> σὲ εἶδον ἐν τῇ ἀγορᾷ. I saw <u>you</u> (s.) in the market place. [accusative singular / direct object]
>
> συνῆλθον σὺν ἐμοί. They came with <u>me</u>. [dative singular / object of preposition]
>
> μιμνησκόμεθα <u>αὐτῶν</u>. We remember <u>them</u>. [genitive plural masculine, feminine, or neuter / genitive direct object]
>
> τοὺς λόγους <u>αὐτοῦ</u> ἠκούσαμεν. We listened to <u>his</u> words. [genitive singular masculine / possession]

EMPHATIC SUBJECT: Notice that one very common use is missing: subject. Since the subject of the sentence is expressed by the verb ending, it is not necessary to use the nominative of the personal pronouns for this purpose. The nominative personal pronouns are, however, used quite frequently. While at times the nominative personal pronoun appears to be just a subject (in which case it is technically redundant), it is far more common for it to be giving some sort of emphasis to the subject. The emphasis may convey various connotations, such as importance, surprise, anger, contrast, comparison, or identity. For example, after Jesus' disciples have told him what others are saying about his identity, he asks them pointedly, Ὑμεῖς δὲ τίνα με λέγετε εἶναι; "But who do <u>you</u> say that I am?" (Matthew 16:15). In speaking, the emphasis can be expressed by the tone of voice; in writing it is best expressed by italics or underlining. [With the exception discussed in the next section, you should assume for now that any nominative personal pronoun is emphatic and indicate this by underlining it.]

The translation of the personal pronoun depends on how it is functioning in the sentence.

Nominative pronouns are used as subjects (generally emphatic): "I," "you" (s.), "we," "you" (pl.), ["he," "she," "it," " they"].

If the *genitive case* of the pronoun is being used to show *possession*, the English possessive is used: "my," "your," "our," "your" (pl.), "his," "her," "its," "their."

If the pronoun is used in any other way (direct object, indirect object, object of a preposition, objective genitive, etc.), the English translation will be "me," "you," "us," "you" (pl.), "him," "her," "it," "them."

FORMS OF PERSONAL PRONOUNS:

	First Singular (I, me, my)	*First Plural* (we, us, our)	*Second Singular*	*Second Plural* (you, your)
N.	ἐγώ	ἡμεῖς	σύ	ὑμεῖς
G.	ἐμοῦ, μου	ἡμῶν	σοῦ, σου	ὑμῶν
D.	ἐμοί, μοι	ἡμῖν	σοί, σοι	ὑμῖν
A.	ἐμέ, με	ἡμᾶς	σέ, σε	ὑμᾶς

	Third Singular			*Third Plural*		
	M. (he, him, his)	F. (she, her)	N. (it, its)	M.	F. (they, them, their)	N.
N.	αὐτός	αὐτή	αὐτό	αὐτοί	αὐταί	αὐτά
G.	αὐτοῦ	αὐτῆς	αὐτοῦ	αὐτῶν	αὐτῶν	αὐτῶν
D.	αὐτῷ	αὐτῇ	αὐτῷ	αὐτοῖς	αὐταῖς	αὐτοῖς
A.	αὐτόν	αὐτήν	αὐτό	αὐτούς	αὐτάς	αὐτά

NOTES ON PERSONAL PRONOUNS:

(1) When the possessive genitive is used, the noun it is modifying generally has an article (unlike English). The possessive genitive usually follows the noun, though it occasionally precedes the article. Only *very rarely* is it found between the article and the noun.

τὰ βιβλία μου   my books   ὁ υἱὸς αὐτοῦ   his son

(2) Except for the nominative case, there are two forms for the "I," "me," "my" (first person singular) and the "you," "your" (second person singular) pronouns. The unaccented forms are enclitic (closely associated and accented together with the *preceding word*). [See Chapter 10 for the accent rules governing enclitics.] The accented forms were considered somewhat more emphatic and are often used with prepositions.

(3) There is no gender distinction made for first and second person pronouns, but there is for third.

(4) The nominative / accusative neuter singular form of the third singular reflects the *article* ending rather than that of the noun. (We will see this with other pronouns as well.)

(5) Although the translations above are correct for most situations, in the case of the third person singular ("he", "she", "it") pronouns there is sometimes a discrepancy arising from the gender of certain nouns which are masculine or feminine in Greek but would be neuter in English, or occasionally neuter in Greek but personal in English (e.g., "child," "spirit"). In such instances, Greek will accurately reproduce the gender of the noun to which the pronoun refers, but the translation should reflect our English usage. Example: "House" is masculine in Greek, so if a pronoun is referring to a house, the Greek masculine form will be used. But in English "house" is neuter, so we would translate the pronoun with "it." ("We looked for your house and finally found it.")

TWO ADDITIONAL USES FOR αὐτός: There are two additional uses for the pronoun αὐτός, apart from its use as a personal pronoun.

I. When used *as a modifier in the attributive position* αὐτός functions as an adjective meaning "same." (Remember that the modifier must agree with the noun in case, number, and gender. / See Chapter 14 for a review of what is meant by "attributive" and "predicate" position.)

> ἐν τῷ αὐτῷ οἴκῳ / ἐν τῷ οἴκῳ τῷ αὐτῷ   in the same house
> τὰ αὐτὰ τέκνα / τὰ τέκνα τὰ αὐτά   the same children

II. αὐτός also functions as the *intensive pronoun*. The purpose of the intensive pronoun is to strengthen or intensify the word it modifies. Although this seems very much like the emphatic pronoun subject, there is a difference in the way they are translated. The emphatic subject is, of course, nominative and is stressed by voice or italics / underlining; the intensive pronoun may modify a word in any case and adds a word to the translation: "myself," "yourself," "himself," etc. [English prefix aut– / auto–]

There are two distinct situations in which you will encounter the intensive pronoun.

(1) The intensive pronoun may appear as a ***modifier in the predicate position*** (or with a proper noun which does not have an article):

> ὁ κύριος αὐτὸς / αὐτὸς ὁ κύριος ἐλεύσεται. The Lord himself will
> come.
> εἶπον τοῖς στρατιώταις αὐτοῖς / αὐτοῖς τοῖς στρατιώταις. I
> spoke to the soldiers themselves.

(2) The intensive pronoun can also modify the ***unwritten pronoun subject***. This use is especially troublesome, due to the tendency to associate αὐτός with the third person pronouns. One must keep in mind that this is a *separate use* and may be associated with ***any person and number***: "I myself," "you yourself," etc. When a nominative form of αὐτός appears alone (i.e., not modifying a noun which you can see) in the sentence, it is modifying the pronoun subject. The key is to watch the verb ending!

> αὐτὸς / αὐτὴ ἐλεύσεται.   He himself / She herself will come.
> αὐτοὶ / αὐταὶ ἐλευσόμεθα.   We ourselves will come. [The use of
> the feminine form would indicate that the speakers are females.]

When the nominative singular or plural of αὐτός modifies the "he," "she," "it," or "they" subject of a third person singular or plural verb, a somewhat ambiguous situation occurs. Should one assume that it is the intensive pronoun and translate "he himself, "she herself," etc.? Or should one consider it an emphatic subject and translate "<u>he</u>," "<u>she</u>," etc.? Or what about the possibility that it is only a redundant subject and should just be translated "he," she," etc.? Since all of these options are possible, one needs to carefully consider the context. ***For now, however, you should assume that when such forms appear in the exercises or quizzes they are intended to be the intensive pronoun and you should translate them accordingly.***

REFLEXIVE PRONOUNS: By combining the forms of αὐτός with the prefixes ἐμ–, σε–, and ἑ– we get the ***reflexive pronouns*** (myself, yourself, himself, etc.).

Here are the forms of the reflexive pronoun. It is the nature of the reflexive pronoun to "bend back" and refer to the same person(s) as the subject. The reflexive pronoun, therefore, cannot *be* the subject and so there are no nominative forms. All plural forms are the same except for gender. This should not create a problem, since the translation of the reflexive pronoun depends on the subject.

```
* * * * * * * * * * * * * * * * * * * * * * * * * * *
*         Singular (myself)          Plural (ourselves)       *
*                                                             *
*         M.           F.            M.          F.           *
*                                                             *
*  G    ἐμαυτοῦ     ἐμαυτῆς       ἑαυτῶν      ἑαυτῶν        *
*  D    ἐμαυτῷ      ἐμαυτῇ        ἑαυτοῖς     ἑαυταῖς       *
*  A    ἐμαυτόν     ἐμαυτήν       ἑαυτοῖς     ἑαυτάς        *
*                                                             *
* * * * * * * * * * * * * * * * * * * * * * * * * * *
```

```
* * * * * * * * * * * * * * * * * * * * * * * * * * *
*         Singular (yourself)         Plural (yourselves)       *
*                                                               *
*         M.           F.            M.          F.             *
*                                                               *
*  G.   σεαυτοῦ     σεαυτῆς       ἑαυτῶν      ἑαυτῶν          *
*  D.   σεαυτῷ      σεαυτῇ        ἑαυτοῖς     ἑαυταῖς         *
*  A.   σεαυτόν     σεαυτήν       ἑαυτούς     ἑαυτάς          *
*                                                               *
* * * * * * * * * * * * * * * * * * * * * * * * * * *
```

```
* * * * * * * * * * * * * * * * * * * * * * * * * * * * *
*              Singular                     Plural               *
*                                                                *
*     M.        F.        N.          M.        F.        N.      *
*  (himself) (herself)  (itself)           (themselves)          *
*                                                                *
* G. ἑαυτοῦ   ἑαυτῆς   ἑαυτοῦ     ἑαυτῶν    ἑαυτῶν    ἑαυτῶν   *
* D. ἑαυτῷ    ἑαυτῇ    ἑαυτῷ      ἑαυτοῖς   ἑαυταῖς   ἑαυτοῖς  *
* A. ἑαυτόν   ἑαυτήν   ἑαυτό      ἑαυτούς   ἑαυτάς    ἑαυτά    *
*                                                                *
* * * * * * * * * * * * * * * * * * * * * * * * * * * * *
```

EXAMPLES:

γινώσκω ἐμαυτόν / ἐμαυτήν.   I know myself.

γινώσκεις σεαυτόν / σεαυτήν.   You (s.) know yourself.

γινώσκει ἑαυτόν / ἑαυτήν.   He / She knows himself / herself.

γινώσκομεν ἑαυτούς / ἑαυτάς.   We know ourselves.

γινώσκετε ἑαυτούς / ἑαυτάς.   You (pl.) know yourselves.

γινώσκουσιν ἑαυτούς / ἑαυτάς / ἑαυτά.   They know themselves.

NOTES ON THE REFLEXIVE PRONOUNS:

(1) The possessive genitive of the reflexive pronoun may be used to emphasize that something belongs to the subject. The translation is "my own," "your own," etc. It is usually, but not always, placed between the article and the noun. In the GNT the possessive use of the reflexive possessive is not always clearly distinguished from that of the personal possessive.

> αὐτὸν ἤνεγκα πρὸς τὸν ἐμαυτοῦ οἶκον.   I brought him to <u>my own</u> house.

(2) It is a quirk of *English* that both the intensive and reflexive ideas are expressed with English words ending in –self / –selves. They do not look the same in Greek. Be sure to observe the distinction between the two. The intensive pronoun is **always a modifier** for another word, even if this is the unwritten pronoun subject. The reflexive pronoun, on the other hand, **has its own grammatical function** in the sentence (direct object, indirect object, etc.).

DATIVE OF MEANS: One of the most common uses of the dative case is called the "dative of means" or the "dative of instrument." As the name implies, it is used to indicate the means or instrument which is used to accomplish the action of the verb. In order to express this idea in English, the **translator must add "by," "with," or even "by means of" to the word(s) in the dative case**. (When checking for a dative of means, you can ask the question "By using what?" in regard to the action of the verb.)

> ἡμᾶς τῇ σοφίᾳ αὐτοῦ ἔπεισεν.   He persuaded us <u>by / with / by means of</u> his <u>wisdom</u>. [Persuaded us "By using what"? Answer: "Wisdom."]

> ἐγὼ ἐβάπτισα ὑμᾶς ὕδατι.   <u>I</u> baptized you <u>with water</u>. (Mark 1:8) [ὕδατι is a third declension noun form which is why the ending is not familiar to you.]

PUNCTUATION: Two new punctuation marks are officially added at this point. The mark used to indicate a question mark in Greek is ;. There is no change to the word order as there is when asking a question in English; you must depend on noticing the punctuation mark. A strong break between clauses is indicated by a raised dot (·). This is usually the equivalent of our semicolon. Try to represent these punctuation marks accurately in your translations.

VOCABULARY

The majority of the new vocabulary consists of the pronouns which are introduced in this chapter

ἄλλος, -η, -ο – other, another (Note that the neuter nominative / accusative singular ending matches the article rather than the noun ending. Note also that the neuter plural nominative / accusative form ἄλλα appears on the *Accents and Breathing Marks That Matter* list because it is spelled the same as ἀλλά meaning "but.") [allosaurus]

ἕτερος, -α, -ον – the other (of two); other, another (To a certain extent, ἕτερος and ἄλλος are used interchangeably, though only ἕτερος is used to mean the other of two. Both words can also be used to refer to something as "different" or even "strange," though this is more common with ἕτερος.) [heterodox]

ἕκαστος, -η, -ον – each

PREPARING FOR THE QUIZ:

(1) Learn all the **new pronoun forms**. Pay special attention to those personal pronoun forms with endings which are different from those you have seen before.

(2) Be sure you understand the **three** possible uses for forms of αὐτός. The intensive pronoun is fairly common and yet it is frequently missed.

(3) Make sure you understand the difference in translation between the **emphatic personal pronoun** subject and the **intensive pronoun** modifying a pronoun subject in the verb ending.

(4) Be sure you can identify and translate the **reflexive pronouns**, including the reflexive possessive.

(5) Remember that the intensive pronoun is **always a modifier** (though sometimes it modifies the pronoun subject in the verb ending), whereas the reflexive pronoun has **its own function in the sentence**

(6) Add the **dative of means** to your list of dative case uses. Remember that you must add "by," or "with" to your translation. The **correct identification**, however, is dative of means, not object of the preposition (no Greek preposition).

(7) Note the two **punctuation marks** introduced in this chapter. Let your English translation reflect the Greek punctuation as much as possible.

Chapter 20
Epsilon Contract Verbs / Indirect Statement (Indirect Discourse)

CONTRACT VERBS: When a verb stem ends in a *short* vowel (ε, α, or o), this vowel **contracts** with the personal verb endings in the **present** and **imperfect** *tenses*, producing a different, though similar, set of endings.

RULES FOR EPSILON CONTRACT VERBS: It is often helpful to realize what the rules of formation are, although your main responsibility is to recognize the contracted forms in context.

(1) The vowels contract as follows (example: ζητέω – "seek," "search / look for"):

      ε drops out before long vowels or diphthongs *(ζητέ ει > ζητεῖ)*

      ε plus *o* becomes *ου (ζητέ ομεν > ζητοῦμεν)*

      ε plus ε becomes ει *(ζητέ ετε > ζητεῖτε)*

(2) The accent stays on the syllable where it would have fallen if the contraction had not occurred. If the accent would have fallen on the *first* of the two contracted vowels, the accent is a circumflex. If the accent would have fallen on the *second* of the two vowels, the acute accent remains.

      ζητέ ουσι > ζητοῦσι   ζητε όμεθα > ζητούμεθα

```
* * * * * * * * * * * * * * * * * * * * * * * * * * * * * *
*                  ζητέω, ζητήσω, ἐζήτησα                  *
*                                                          *
*      Present Active Indicative        Present M/P Indicative   *
*                                                          *
*      Singular      Plural        Singular       Plural   *
*                                                          *
*  1st  ζητῶ         ζητοῦμεν       ζητοῦμαι       ζητούμεθα *
*  2nd  ζητεῖς       ζητεῖτε        ζητῇ           ζητεῖσθε  *
*  3rd  ζητεῖ        ζητοῦσι(ν)     ζητεῖται       ζητοῦνται *
*                                                          *
* * * * * * * * * * * * * * * * * * * * * * * * * * * * * *
```

	Imperfect Active Indicative		Imperfect M/P Indicative	
	Singular	Plural	Singular	Plural
1st	ἐζήτουν	ἐζητοῦμεν	ἐζητούμην	ἐζητούμεθα
2nd	ἐζήτεις	ἐζητεῖτε	ἐζητοῦ	ἐζητεῖσθε
3rd	ἐζήτει	ἐζήτουν	ἐζητεῖτο	ἐζητοῦντο

NOTES:

(1) ζητέω is not a deponent and there are no special meanings for middle or passive, so the English passive translation applies: "I am being sought," "he was being sought," etc. You need to consider this information each time you encounter a new verb.

(2) Epsilon contract verbs are *extremely* common. Apart from the vowel contractions in the present and imperfect tenses, they are generally regular with first aorists. Learn to watch for them in your reading.

(3) The second person singular and third person singular imperfect active forms are probably the most difficult to recognize in context, because the vowel contractions create what appear to be *present* active endings. Watching carefully for the augment and knowing your vocabulary are the keys to identification. In four out of the six imperfect active forms, the word accent is on the syllable *before* the short vowel and thus is not involved at all in the contractions.

(4) All contract verbs are listed in lexicons **with the short vowel**. You should learn this as the first principal part, even though it will never actually appear in a text. The rationale for this is that, after the vowel contractions occur, the present active first person singular forms look alike for all three types of contract verbs. Therefore you need, at some point, to see which of the three vowels is part of the stem.

FUTURE AND AORIST: These are usually formed by lengthening the *epsilon* to *eta* and adding a *sigma* to the stem. Regular future and first aorist endings are then used.

> ποιέω, ποιήσω, ἐποίησα ("make," "do")
> αἰτέομαι, αἰτήσομαι, ἠτησάμην ("ask," "ask for")

A few verbs keep the *epsilon* and just add *sigma*.

καλέω, καλέ<u>σω</u>, ἐκάλ<u>εσα</u> ("call," "name"; "invite")

INDIRECT STATEMENT (INDIRECT DISCOURSE): In Greek, as in English, a person's words (or thoughts, feelings, sense perceptions, etc.) can be reported or quoted directly or indirectly.

Direct statement: λέγει, Ἔρχομαι. He says, "I am coming."

Indirect statement: λέγει ὅτι ἔρχεται. He says that he is coming.

The introductory word for an indirect statement ("that") is ὅτι (occasionally ὡς). Note that ὅτι also means "because." In most instances the context will enable you to decide which translation to use.

IMPORTANT TRANSLATION INFORMATION:

(1) In translating Greek indirect statements, there is an important point to keep in mind about tense. ***The verb in the indirect statement is relative in time to the introductory verb.*** A present tense indicates simultaneous time, an aorist tense indicates prior time, and a future tense indicates future time. This presents no problem when the introductory verb is present or future; you simply translate each verb as what it looks like. When the introductory verb is aorist (or, less often, imperfect), however, a **shift in tense** needs to be made in order to convey the thought correctly in English. The present tense will *sound like* an imperfect, the aorist tense will *sound like* the English pluperfect tense (helping verb "had"), and the future tense will add the helping verb "would." [The need to make this kind of relative time shift will occur again in several other situations, so, even though it feels odd at first, it would be a good idea to master it now.]

εἶπεν ὅτι ἔρχεται. He said that he <u>was coming</u>. (at the same time)
εἶπεν ὅτι ἦλθεν. He said that he <u>had come</u>. (previously)
εἶπεν ὅτι ἐλεύσεται. He said that he <u>would come</u>. (in the future)

(2) Sometimes ὅτι will be used to introduce a ***direct statement / quotation***. When this happens, the ὅτι is serving the same function as a comma and beginning quotation mark in English; it lets you know that a quotation is coming. Do ***not*** translate it. The editors of the some editions of the GNT (e.g., the United Bible Societies edition) begin *all* direct quotations with a capital letter, so you should

have no trouble distinguishing direct quotations from indirect ones. If you see ὅτι followed by a word (other than a proper noun) beginning with a capital letter, you are looking at a direct quotation. [The other way that you will see the start of a direct quotation punctuated is a comma at the end of the introductory clause followed by a word beginning with a capital letter. Unfortunately there is no punctuation mark to signal the *end* of a direct quotation, so there are times (though not very many) when it is not entirely clear where the end is.]

εἶπεν ὅτι Συνελεύσομαι σὺν ὑμῖν. He said, "I will go with you."

VOCABULARY

φιλέω, ---, ἐφίλησα – love [philanthopist]

ποιέω, ποιήσω, ἐποίησα – do, make (Plus many other meanings based on the context. Sometimes used with a **double accusative**: to make [in the sense of "appoint"] someone something, to make something [into] something else, to make someone or something an attribute, e.g. "to make him well.") [poetry]

λαλέω, λαλήσω, ἐλάλησα – talk, speak [glossolalia]

ἀκολουθέω, ἀκολουθήσω, ἠκολούθησα – follow (both literally and in the sense of "be a disciple" – **dative direct object**) [acolyte]

ζητέω, ζητήσω, ἐζήτησα – seek, search / look for; strive for, try to obtain; investigate

τηρέω, τηρήσω, ἐτήρησα – keep; observe, obey, keep (laws, commandments)

μισέω, μισήσω, ἐμίσησα – hate [misanthrope]

μαρτυρέω, μαρτυρήσω, ἐμαρτύρησα – bear witness, testify [martyr]

περιπατέω (imperfect: περιεπάτουν), περιπατήσω, περιεπάτησα – go about, walk; live, conduct oneself (Note that the *iota* does not drop out before the augment.) [peripatetic]

καλέω, καλέσω, ἐκάλεσα – call, name; invite (Sometimes with a **double accusative**: to call or name someone something.)

τελέω, τελέσω, ἐτέλεσα – finish, complete, end [teleology]

αἰτέω, αἰτήσω, ᾔτησα – ask, ask for (Sometimes with a **double accusative**: the person[s] asked and the thing[s] asked for.) – The **middle** is translated the *same way as the active* (present M/P: αἰτοῦμαι, future middle αἰτήσομαι, 1st aorist middle: ᾐτησάμην).

λυπέω, ---, ἐλύπησα – grieve (*transitive*: cause grief or pain), vex; offend, insult; **passive**: "grieve" (*intransitive*), "be sad / sorrowful," "be distressed" (present M/P: λυποῦμαι, future passive: λυπηθήσομαι, no aorist middle)

φοβέομαι, φοβηθήσομαι (future passive), no aorist middle – fear, be afraid
(of); fear, reverence (God) (***Note:*** As was the case with μιμνῄσκομαι,
this is being taught as a deponent, since there are no active forms in the
GNT. Active forms did exist, however, in an earlier stage of the language,
having the meaning "put to flight" or "terrify." So technically "fear," etc.
would be special meanings for the passive. Therefore either φοβέω [as
listed in the Danker lexicon] or φοβέομαι [as listed in the UBS lexicon in
the back of the GNT text] is acceptable as the first principal part.)
[phobia]

ὅτι (ὡς) – that (introducing indirect statement)

PREPARING FOR THE QUIZ:

(1) You should know what is meant by the term *"**contract verb**."*

(2) Make sure that you can identify the ***present and imperfect forms*** of the
epsilon contract verbs.

(3) You should know how the ***regular future and aorist*** of the majority of
contract verbs are formed (lengthen the *epsilon* to *eta* and add *sigma* to the stem).
Be sure you can identify these in context. This will help you identify these forms
even if the vocabulary is unfamiliar.

(4) Note ***deponent forms*** and ***special meanings*** for middle or passive which
appear in the vocabulary list.

(5) Be sure you know how to spell the ***first principal part*** of these verbs so you
give this information when parsing them.

(6) You should know how to recognize and translate ***indirect statements***,
including the information about ***tense relationships***.

(7) You should know how to distinguish a ***direct statement*** introduced by ὅτι
from an indirect statement.

Chapter 21

Demonstrative Pronouns / Possessive Pronouns /
Reciprocal Pronoun / Dative of Time

DEMONSTRATIVE PRONOUNS: The term "demonstrative" comes from the Latin verb *demonstrare* ("to point out") and that is the function of the demonstrative pronouns. Here are the forms of the demonstrative pronouns:

```
* * * * * * * * * * * * * * * * * * * * *
*                Singular: "this"                 *
*                                                 *
*        M.          F.           N.              *
*                                                 *
*   N.  οὗτος      αὕτη        τοῦτο              *
*   G.  τούτου     ταύτης      τούτου             *
*   D.  τούτῳ      ταύτῃ       τούτῳ              *
*   A.  τοῦτον     ταύτην      τοῦτο              *
*                                                 *
*                Plural: "these"                  *
*                                                 *
*   N.  οὗτοι      αὗται       ταῦτα              *
*   G.  τούτων     τούτων      τούτων             *
*   D.  τούτοις    ταύταις     τούτοις            *
*   A.  τούτους    ταύτας      ταῦτα              *
*                                                 *
* * * * * * * * * * * * * * * * * * * * *


* * * * * * * * * * * * * * * * * * * * *
*                Singular: "that"                 *
*                                                 *
*        M.          F.           N.              *
*                                                 *
*   N.  ἐκεῖνος    ἐκείνη      ἐκεῖνο             *
*   G.  ἐκείνου    ἐκείνης     ἐκείνου            *
*   D.  ἐκείνῳ     ἐκείνῃ      ἐκείνῳ             *
*   A.  ἐκεῖνον    ἐκείνην     ἐκεῖνο             *
*                                                 *
* * * * * * * * * * * * * * * * * * * * *
```

```
* * * * * * * * * * * * * * * * * * * * * *
*                                          *
*            Plural: "those"               *
*                                          *
*        M.          F.          N.        *
*                                          *
*  N.  ἐκεῖνοι     ἐκεῖναι     ἐκεῖνα      *
*  G.  ἐκείνων     ἐκείνων     ἐκείνων     *
*  D.  ἐκείνοις    ἐκείναις    ἐκείνοις    *
*  A.  ἐκείνους    ἐκείνας     ἐκεῖνα      *
*                                          *
* * * * * * * * * * * * * * * * * * * * * *
```

(1) The demonstrative pronoun can be used either alone or as a modifier for another word. When it is used as a modifier, it agrees with the noun it modifies in case, number, and gender. It goes in the ***predicate position*** and the definite article is used with the noun.

> ἐν τούτῳ τῷ οἴκῳ / ἐν τῷ οἴκῳ τούτῳ   in this house
>
> εἰς τὸ ἱερὸν ἐκεῖνο / εἰς ἐκεῖνο τὸ ἱερόν   into that temple
>
> ἐκεῖνοι οἱ προφῆται / οἱ προφῆται ἐκεῖνοι   those prophets
>
> ἡ θάλασσα αὕτη / αὕτη ἡ θάλασσα   this sea

(2) When the demonstrative pronoun is used alone, it is serving as a substantive. The translator often, but not always, needs to add "man," "people," "women," "things," etc., based on the gender and number of the pronoun.

> ἐκεῖνος   that man / person / one (nominative singular masculine)
>
> ἐκείναις   those women (dative plural feminine)
>
> οὗτοι   these men / people (nominative plural masculine)
>
> ταύτην   this woman (accusative singular feminine)
>
> τοῦτο   this [thing] (nominative / accusative singular neuter)
>
> ταῦτα   these things (nominative / accusative plural neuter.)

(3) Notice that the nominative singular and plural feminine forms of οὗτος (αὕτη and αὗται) are on the *Accents and Breathing Marks That Matter* list. They are spelled exactly like the corresponding forms of αὐτός.

(4) Sometimes, depending on the *context*, a demonstrative pronoun may be translated as a third person personal pronoun: "he," "she," "it," "they." ***For the time being, stay away from this and concentrate on learning the meanings given above.***

POSSESSIVE PRONOUNS: Although technically classified as pronouns, these words look and function *exactly like adjectives*. They agree with the word they modify in case, number, and gender and are placed in the *attributive position*.

> ἐμός, -ή, -όν   my   ἡμέτερος, -α, -ον   our
> σός, ή, -όν   your (s.)   ὑμέτερος, -α, -ον   your (pl.)

> ὁ ἐμὸς ἀδελφός = ὁ ἀδελφός μου   my brother
> τὸν σὸν φίλον = τὸν φίλον σου   your friend
> τοῖς υἱοῖς τοῖς ἡμετέροις = τοῖς υἱοῖς ἡμῶν   our sons
> αἱ ψυχαὶ αἱ ὑμέτεραι = αἱ ψυχαὶ ὑμῶν   your souls

There is no corresponding possessive pronoun for "his," "her," "its," and "their." The genitive of the personal pronoun must be used.

RECIPROCAL PRONOUN: The reciprocal pronoun has no nominative and is translated "each other" or "one another." Only masculine forms appear in the GNT.

> G. ἀλλήλων
> D. ἀλλήλοις
> A. ἀλλήλους

DATIVE OF TIME: The dative case is used with or without the preposition ἐν (translated "in," "on," or "at") to indicate a definite time. If there is no preposition, the translator must add the "in," "on," or "at."

> ἐν ἐκείναις ταῖς ἡμέραις   in those days
> ταύτῃ τῇ ὥρᾳ   at this hour

VOCABULARY

The demonstrative, possessive, and reciprocal pronouns which are introduced in the chapter.

τοσοῦτος, τοσαύτη, τοσοῦτον/ο – so large, so great, so much (*plural*: so many)

τοιοῦτος, τοιαύτη, τοιοῦτον/ο – such, of such a kind

ὧδε – here (in this place *or* to this place)

ἐκεῖ – there (in that place *or* to that place)

χρόνος, -ου, m. – time (period of time) [chronology]

καιρός, -οῦ, m. – time (viewed as an occasion), appointed time, proper time

NOTE: Two extra bits of information regarding the use of Greek appear in the exercises. These should be added to your working vocabulary:

(1) διὰ τοῦτο, which literally means "on account of this [thing]," is often translated as "for this reason" or "therefore."

(2) κἀγώ is a combination (called "crasis") of καί and ἐγώ. Other combinations occur (such as κἀμοί = καί + ἐμοί and κἀκεῖνος = καί + ἐκεῖνος), but this is the most common one. You can tell that there is something unusual about κἀγώ because of the breathing mark. Normally breathing marks only appear on words which begin with a vowel or diphthong.

PREPARING FOR THE QUIZ:

(1) Be sure that you have thoroughly learned *all the new pronoun forms*. Be careful to distinguish the forms of οὗτος which have ου in the stem from those which have αυ. Most of the ones with αυ are feminine; the big exception is ταῦτα (the nominative / accusative plural *neuter*).

(2) Be sure you know how to *translate the demonstrative pronouns* when they are used alone and when they are modifying another word.

(3) You should know how to recognize and translate a *dative of time*. Identify this as "dative of time," even if the preposition ἐν is used. (It became much more common in Koine Greek to use prepositions for ideas which could also be expressed by the case use alone.)

Chapter 22
Alpha Contract Verbs / Omicron Contract Verbs /
Regular Formation of Adverbs

ALPHA CONTRACT VERBS: As with the *epsilon* contract verbs (Chapter 20), when the verb stem ends in *alpha*, this is contracted with the connecting vowel of the personal endings. The basic principle is the same, the combinations, of course, are different. Accent rules are the same as for epsilon contract verbs. Example: τιμάω – honor

α drops out before long vowels (τιμά ω > τιμῶ)
α plus ε becomes α (τιμά ετε > τιμᾶτε)
α plus ει or η becomes ᾳ (τιμά εις > τιμᾷς)
α plus ο becomes ω (τιμά ομεν > τιμῶμεν)
α plus ου becomes ω (τιμά ουσι > τιμῶσι)


```
* * * * * * * * * * * * * * * * * * * * * * * * * * * * * * *
*                    τιμάω, τιμήσω, ἐτίμησα                    *
*                                                             *
*       Present Active Indicative         Present M/P Indicative    *
*                                                             *
*       Singular      Plural          Singular        Plural  *
*                                                             *
*  1st   τιμῶ      τιμῶμεν          τιμῶμαι       τιμώμεθα    *
*  2nd   τιμᾷς     τιμᾶτε           τιμᾷ          τιμᾶσθε     *
*  3rd   τιμᾷ      τιμῶσι(ν)        τιμᾶται       τιμῶνται    *
*                                                             *
*                                                             *
*      Imperfect Active Indicative       Imperfect M/P Indicative   *
*                                                             *
*       Singular      Plural          Singular        Plural  *
*                                                             *
*  1st   ἐτίμων     ἐτιμῶμεν        ἐτιμώμην      ἐτιμώμεθα   *
*  2nd   ἐτίμας     ἐτιμᾶτε         ἐτιμῶ         ἐτιμᾶσθε    *
*  3rd   ἐτίμα      ἐτίμων          ἐτιμᾶτο       ἐτιμῶντο    *
*                                                             *
* * * * * * * * * * * * * * * * * * * * * * * * * * * * * * *
```


NOTES:

(1) As a result of the vowel contractions, the present active third person singular and the present M/P second person singular look alike. You will need to use in-

formation about the specific verb or the context to help you determine which form is being used.

(2) As with the *epsilon* contract verbs, the imperfect active singular forms are the most troublesome. The second person singular and third person singular are often mistaken for first aorists. This is also true for the other forms with *alpha* in the endings, but those with a circumflex are more easily identified as contract verbs. The key to identification is knowing your vocabulary.

FUTURE AND AORIST: The future and regular first aorist are usually formed by lengthening the *alpha* to *eta* and adding *sigma* plus regular endings.

ἀγαπάω, ἀγαπήσω, ἠγάπησα – love

Note the *irregular future and second aorist* of ὁράω:

ὁράω, ὄψομαι, εἶδον – see

THE VERB ζάω: The verb ζάω ("live") uses η or ῃ where most alpha contract verbs use α or ᾳ. [*Note*: ζάω has no present or imperfect M/P forms.]

Present Active Indicative		Imperfect Active Indicative	
Singular	*Plural*	*Singular*	*Plural*
1st ζῶ	ζῶμεν	ἔζων	ἐζῶμεν
2nd ζῇς	ζῆτε	ἔζης	ἐζῆτε
3rd ζῇ	ζῶσι(ν)	ἔζη	ἔζων

OMICRON CONTRACT VERBS: When the verb stem ends in *omicron*, these are the vowel combinations. Example: πληρόω – fill, fulfill

o drops out before long vowels and ου (πληρό ω > πληρῶ)
o plus ε becomes ου (πληρό ετε > πληροῦτε)
o plus ει or η becomes οι (πληρό εις > πληροῖς)
o plus ο becomes ου (πληρό ομεν > πληροῦμεν)

NOTE: As with the *alpha* contract verbs, the present active third person singular and the present M/P second person singular are identical.

* *

$$\pi\lambda\eta\rho\acute{o}\omega, \ \pi\lambda\eta\rho\acute{\omega}\sigma\omega, \ \acute{\epsilon}\pi\lambda\acute{\eta}\rho\omega\sigma\alpha$$

	Present Active Indicative		Present M/P Indicative	
	Singular	*Plural*	*Singular*	*Plural*
1st	$\pi\lambda\eta\rho\hat{\omega}$	$\pi\lambda\eta\rho o\hat{\upsilon}\mu\epsilon\nu$	$\pi\lambda\eta\rho o\hat{\upsilon}\mu\alpha\iota$	$\pi\lambda\eta\rho o\acute{\upsilon}\mu\epsilon\theta\alpha$
2nd	$\pi\lambda\eta\rho o\hat{\iota}s$	$\pi\lambda\eta\rho o\hat{\upsilon}\tau\epsilon$	$\pi\lambda\eta\rho o\hat{\iota}$	$\pi\lambda\eta\rho o\hat{\upsilon}\sigma\theta\epsilon$
3rd	$\pi\lambda\eta\rho o\hat{\iota}$	$\pi\lambda\eta\rho o\hat{\upsilon}\sigma\iota(\nu)$	$\pi\lambda\eta\rho o\hat{\upsilon}\tau\alpha\iota$	$\pi\lambda\eta\rho o\hat{\upsilon}\nu\tau\alpha\iota$

	Imperfect Active Indicative		Imperfect M/P Indicative	
	Singular	*Plural*	*Singular*	*Plural*
1st	$\acute{\epsilon}\pi\lambda\acute{\eta}\rho o\upsilon\nu$	$\acute{\epsilon}\pi\lambda\eta\rho o\hat{\upsilon}\mu\epsilon\nu$	$\acute{\epsilon}\pi\lambda\eta\rho o\acute{\upsilon}\mu\eta\nu$	$\epsilon\pi\lambda\eta\rho o\acute{\upsilon}\mu\epsilon\theta\alpha$
2nd	$\acute{\epsilon}\pi\lambda\acute{\eta}\rho o\upsilon s$	$\acute{\epsilon}\pi\lambda\eta\rho o\hat{\upsilon}\tau\epsilon$	$\acute{\epsilon}\pi\lambda\eta\rho o\hat{\upsilon}$	$\acute{\epsilon}\pi\lambda\eta\rho o\hat{\upsilon}\sigma\theta\epsilon$
3rd	$\acute{\epsilon}\pi\lambda\acute{\eta}\rho o\upsilon$	$\acute{\epsilon}\pi\lambda\acute{\eta}\rho o\upsilon\nu$	$\acute{\epsilon}\pi\lambda\eta\rho o\hat{\upsilon}\tau o$	$\acute{\epsilon}\pi\lambda\eta\rho o\hat{\upsilon}\nu\tau o$

* *

FUTURE AND AORIST: The future and first aorist are usually formed by lengthening the *omicron* to *omega* and adding *sigma* plus regular endings.

$\psi\alpha\nu\epsilon\rho\acute{o}\omega, \ \phi\alpha\nu\epsilon\rho\acute{\omega}\underline{\sigma}\omega, \ \acute{\epsilon}\phi\alpha\nu\acute{\epsilon}\rho\omega\sigma\alpha$ – make known, reveal

ADVERBS: Often, but not always, a Greek adverb is formed regularly from the adjective stem. The characteristic ending is $-\omega s$. The accent is as it would be on the genitive plural of the adjective. There is also an adverbial form of the demonstrative pronoun $o\mathring{\upsilon}\tau os$: $o\mathring{\upsilon}\tau\omega s$ ("thus," "in this way").

$\kappa\alpha\kappa\acute{o}s$ – bad	$\kappa\alpha\kappa\hat{\omega}s$ – badly
$\mathring{\alpha}\delta\iota\kappa os$ – unjust	$\mathring{\alpha}\delta\acute{\iota}\kappa\omega s$ – unjustly
$\mathring{o}\rho\theta\acute{o}s$ – right, straight	$\mathring{o}\rho\theta\hat{\omega}s$ – rightly, correctly

VOCABULARY

τιμάω, τιμήσω, ἐτίμησα – honor   [Timothy]

ἐπιτιμάω, ---, ἐπετίμησα – rebuke; warn (***dative direct object***)

ἐρωτάω, ἐρωτήσω, ἠρώτησα – ask (either question or request)

ἀγαπάω, ἀγαπήσω, ἠγάπησα – love

νικάω, νικήσω, ἐνίκησα – conquer, overcome   [Nike]

γεννάω, γεννήσω, ἐγέννησα – beget, be / become the father of; bear, give birth
     to; ***passive***: be born (present M/P: γεννῶμαι, future passive:
     γεννηθήσομαι, no aorist middle)

πλανάω, πλανήσω, ἐπλάνησα – lead astray, mislead, deceive; ***passive***: go
     astray, wander; be mistaken; be misled / deceived (present M/P:
     πλανῶμαι, future passive: πλανηθήσομαι, no aorist middle) [planet]

ὁράω (imperfect: ἑώρων), ὄψομαι, εἶδον – see; ***passive***: appear (present M/P:
     ὁρῶμαι, future passive: ὀφθήσομαι, no aorist middle) ***Note***: ὄψομαι is
     a future *middle* (a deponent future). The meaning is "will see." The
     future *passive* form means "will appear."

ζάω, ζήσω (ζήσομαι), ἔζησα – live ***Note***: The future of ζάω is sometimes
     active and sometimes middle (deponent). Both are translated "will live."

πληρόω, πληρώσω, ἐπλήρωσα – fulfill; fill; bring to completion

δικαιόω, δικαιώσω, ἐδικαίωσα – justify, vindicate, treat as righteous

φανερόω, φανερώσω, ἐφανέρωσα – show, reveal, make known; ***passive***: be
     revealed, become known (present M/P: φανεροῦμαι, future passive:
     φανερωθήσομαι, no aorist middle)

σταυρόω, σταυρώσω, ἐσταύρωσα – crucify

οὕτως – thus, in this way

τότε – then, at that time

PREPARING FOR THE QUIZ:

(1) You should learn to recognize the ***present and imperfect*** of *alpha* and
omicron contract verbs and know the ***regular formation*** for the future and aorist.

(2) Know the peculiarity regarding the ***conjugation of ζάω*** and the ***irregular
principal parts*** of ὁράω.

(3) Learn to recognize the ***ending for adverbs*** which are formed in a regular way
from adjectives.

Chapter 23
Interrogative Pronouns and Adverbs / Indefinite Pronoun and Adverbs / Partitive Genitive (Genitive of the Whole) / Historical Present

INTERROGATIVE PRONOUN τίς, τί: The most common interrogative pronoun is τίς, τί. Its primary function is to ask an *identifying question*. Here are the forms of τίς and τί

```
* * * * * * * * * * * * * * * * * * * * * * * * * *
*        Singular                    Plural          *
*                                                     *
*     M. / F.        N.           M. / F.       N.    *
*                                                     *
*  N. τίς          τί            τίνες        τίνα     *
*  G. τίνος        τίνος         τίνων        τίνων    *
*  D. τίνι         τίνι          τίσι(ν)      τίσι(ν)  *
*  A. τίνα         τί            τίνας        τίνα     *
*                                                     *
* * * * * * * * * * * * * * * * * * * * * * * * * *
```

NOTES ON τίς AND τί:

(1) These endings, although not familiar to you now, will be seen again. They are the **basic endings for the third declension** (Chapters 24 and 27).

(2) The stem of the pronoun is τιν. This is modified in front of the *sigma* ending in the nominative singular masculine / feminine form and the dative plural forms.

(3) There is only one form for masculine and feminine and *all three genders* are the same in the genitive and dative.

(4) The accusative singular masculine / feminine is identical to the nominative / accusative plural neuter (a three way overlap).

(5) The acute accent on the interrogative τίς and τί is never altered to a grave.

(6) Since English does not distinguish between singular and plural interrogatives, your translation will sound the same for both.

EXAMPLES: The following examples will illustrate the most common substantival (pronoun used alone) uses of τίς and τί and the appropriate English translations.

Nominative case:

>   τίς ἐποίησε ταῦτα;   Who / Which one (person) did these things?
>   (personal subject)
>   τί ἐγένετο;   What happened? (impersonal subject)

Genitive case:

>   τίνος (τίνων) υἱός ἐστιν;   Whose son is he? (possession)
>   ὑπὸ τίνος (τίνων) ταῦτα ποιεῖται;   By whom are these things being
>   done? (object of preposition)
>   τίνος (τίνων) ἥψατο ὁ ᾽Ιησοῦς;   Whom did Jesus touch? (genitive
>   direct object)

Dative case:

>   τίνι (τίσιν) ἐλέγετε;   To whom were you speaking? (indirect object)
>   σὺν τίνι (τίσιν) συνήλθετε;   With whom did you come? (object of
>   preposition)
>   τίνι (τίσιν) ἀκολουθεῖς;   Whom do you follow? (dative direct object)

Accusative case:

>   τίνα (τίνας) πέμψομεν;   Whom shall we send? (personal direct
>   object)
>   τί (τίνα) ποιοῦσιν;   What (What things) are they doing? (impersonal
>   direct object)
>   πρὸς τίνα (τίνας) τὰ δῶρα πέμψομεν;   To whom shall we send the
>   gifts? (object of preposition)

NOTES:

(1) If the neuter is used in the genitive or dative case, the translation would be "what?" The neuter, however, is used primarily as a subject or direct object or as the object of a preposition.

(2) Occasionally both τίς and τί encroach on the territory of ποῖος (see below) and ask "What sort of?"

INTERROGATIVE PRONOUN AS A MODIFIER: In addition to its use as a substantive (illustrated above), the interrogative pronoun can also be used as an *interrogative modifier for a noun.* When this is done, it will agree with the noun in case, number, and gender. Remember, however, that there is only one form to be used with masculine *and* feminine nouns. The translation is "which?" or "what?"

> τίνες μαθηταὶ συνῆλθον σοί;   Which disciples accompanied you?

> ἐν τίνι οἴκῳ ταῦτα εἴδετε;   In which / what house did you see these things?

> τί δῶρον / τίνα δῶρα προσοίσετε τῷ τέκνῳ;   What gift(s) will you offer to the child?

τί AS AN INTERROGATIVE ADVERB: The *accusative singular neuter* form τί also serves as the interrogative adverb "why?" (It is quite common in Greek for the accusative singular neuter form of an adjective to be used as an adverb.) Obviously you will have to distinguish carefully between the two uses of τί.

> τί διώκουσιν ἡμᾶς;   Why are they persecuting us?

ADDITIONAL INTERROGATIVE PRONOUNS πόσος AND ποῖος: Like the possessive pronouns (Chapter 21), these two interrogative pronouns look and function just like adjectives.

πόσος, -η, -ον asks questions about quantity or degree (how great? how much? how many?).

ποῖος, -η, -ον asks questions about category or quality (what kind / sort of?). *Very occasionally* ποῖος functions like τίς, τί and asks an identity question (which? what?).

INTERROGATIVE ADVERBS: These words seek various kinds of adverbial information.

πῶς – how?	ποῦ – where?
πότε – when?	πόθεν – from where?

INDEFINITE PRONOUN: The indefinite pronoun is *identical to the interrogative pronoun in spelling.* It is accented, however, as an enclitic. In practical terms this means:

(1) Under normal circumstances, the singular forms τις and τι will have **no accent**.

(2) All other forms will have either **no accent** or *an accent on the **second** syllable.* (Remember that all two syllable interrogatives arc accented on the **first** syllable.)

```
* * * * * * * * * * * * * * * * * * * * * * * *
*        Singular                  Plural         *
*                                                 *
*    M. / F.      N.          M. / F.      N.      *
*                                                 *
*  N. τις        τι           τινές       τινά     *
*  G. τινός      τινός        τινῶν       τινῶν    *
*  D. τινί       τινί         τισί(ν)     τισί(ν)  *
*  A. τινά       τι           τινάς       τινά     *
*                                                 *
* * * * * * * * * * * * * * * * * * * * * * * *
```

The indefinite pronoun, like the interrogative, may be used either substantivally (alone as a noun substitute) or as a modifier for a noun. When used alone it is translated: "anyone," "anything"; "someone," "something"; plural: "some" (men / people).

> εὕρετέ τινα ἐκεῖ; Did you find anyone (or possibly "any things") there?

> τοῖς τοῦ κυρίου λόγοις τινὲς οὐ πιστεύουσιν. Some (people) do not believe the words of the Lord.

When used as a modifier it is translated: "certain," "some."

> τις οἶκος   a certain house
> ἄνθρωποί τινες   certain / some people

INDEFINITE ADVERBS: Like the pronouns, these are enclitics. They are **spelled** like the interrogatives, but **accented** differently.

πως – somehow, anyhow

που – somewhere, anywhere

ποτε *(ποτέ)* – sometime, anytime, once, ever

NOTE ON ACCENTS: Sometimes in a sentence two words (occasionally more) which would not normally have an accent appear in sequence. When this happens, the last one remains unaccented, but the preceding ones each acquire an *acute accent*. This can create real difficulty, because it is possible that the acquisition of an accent will cause a word to look like something which it is not. You will need to be alert to this possibility and figure out logically what must be meant. [*Examples*: "For someone said somewhere…" εἶπε γάρ πού τις… Note that the accent on γάρ does not change to a grave and the indefinite που picks up an acute accent. This does not present a translation problem because the interrogative would have a circumflex. But in John 6:18 the words ἥ τε θάλασσα ("and the sea") appear. The ἥ is just the feminine definite article, but because of the accent it has acquired it looks like the nominative singular feminine of the relative pronoun (Chapter 26). Context should help you, but you do need to be careful.]

PARTITIVE GENITIVE: The genitive case can be used to denote the *whole* of which something is a part. The head noun or pronoun represents the part. (This use of the genitive case is sometimes called **genitive of the whole**.) It is very common with the indefinite pronoun and can also be used with the interrogative (as well as other words, e.g., numbers, "few," "many"). Sometimes the partitive genitive idea is expressed by ἐκ *(ἐξ)* with the genitive case. ***In such situations the preposition is translated "of" rather than "from" or "out of."***

> ἐν τῇ ἀγορᾷ τινας τῶν στρατιωτῶν εἴδομεν.   We saw <u>some of the soldiers</u> in the market place.

> ταῦτα ἔλεγόν τινες ἐκ τῶν μαθητῶν αὐτοῦ.   <u>Some of his disciples</u> were saying these things.

> τίς ἐξ ὑμῶν συνελεύσεται σὺν ἐμοί;   <u>Who / which one of you</u> will go with me?

HISTORICAL PRESENT: Fairly often, in narrative literature, we find the present tense used where we would expect an aorist to describe a past event. The usual reason given for this is that it portrays an event "*vividly*, as though the reader were in the midst of the scene as it unfolds" (Wallace, p. 526). In the case of λέγει or other verbs introducing direct or indirect discourse, however, this use has essentially become idiomatic and has lost the original sense of vividness. When you see the historical present, translate it as if it were aorist.

VOCABULARY

All the pronouns and adverbs in the chapter. (Note that, for obvious reasons, the interrogatives and indefinites all appear on the list of *Accents and Breathing Marks That Matter.*)

ἔτι – still, yet
οὐκέτι – no longer
οὔπω – not yet
οὐδέποτε – never

NOTE: διὰ τί, which literally means "on account of what?" can also be translated as "why?"

PREPARING FOR THE QUIZ:

(1) Learn the **new pronoun forms** thoroughly. Remember that in doing so you are also learning the basic third declension noun endings.

(2) Learn how to make the **distinction** between the interrogative τίς, τί and the indefinite τις, τι.

(3) Make sure you know how to **translate** the interrogative and indefinite pronouns, both as substantives and adjectival modifiers, as they are used in sentences.

(4) Add the new **interrogative and indefinite adverbs** to your vocabulary. They are easily confused; make sure you have them straight.

(5) Add **partitive genitive** to your list of genitive case uses. Note that it may appear with or without the preposition ἐκ (ἐξ).

(6) Make a note of the **historical present**. It appears in one of the translation sentences in the exercises, and will appear regularly from now on in GNT quotations.

Chapter 24

THIRD DECLENSION NOUNS: The third declension category is a large and diverse one, including many theologically significant words and providing a pattern which will be repeated later by certain participles. In this chapter we will look at *third declension masculine and feminine nouns.* The important facts about these nouns will be illustrated by a detailed examination of four words. χάρις ("grace"), γυνή ("woman"), ἄρχων ("ruler"), and πατήρ ("father").

1) The **endings** for third declension masculine and feminine nouns are identical. One must learn the gender along with the noun, since there is no way to discern it just by looking at the word. Of the nouns listed above, two are masculine (ἄρχων and πατήρ) and two are feminine (χάρις and γυνή). Logic, of course, tells you that "father" is masculine and "woman" is feminine, but what about "city," "foot," "night," etc.? (**Reminder**: Gender is indicated in lexicons by the letter "m.," "f.," or "n." or by the definite article.) The basic endings are as follows:

```
* * * * * * * * * * * * * * * * * * * * * *
*            M. / F. Singular         M. / F. Plural  *
*                                                     *
*    N.    –ς or no distinct ending      –ες         *
*    G.    –ος                           –ων         *
*    D.    –ι                            –σι(ν)      *
*    A.    –α or –ν                      –ας         *
*                                                     *
* * * * * * * * * * * * * * * * * * * * * *
```

Reminder: These are also the endings of the masculine / feminine interrogative and indefinite pronouns (Chapter 23)

2) The **stem** of the noun is found in the **genitive singular**. This, not the nominative singular, is the stem to which the other endings are added. This too *must be memorized.*

Nom.	χάρις	γυνή	ἄρχων	πατήρ
Gen.	χάριτος	γυναικός	ἄρχοντος	πατρός

3) The **nominative singular** is the "odd man out" of the third declension. It does not contain the basic noun stem nor is it consistent in any way from one word to another (although there are some patterns). It must simply *be memorized.* Of our four paradigm words, only χάρις has the *sigma* ending.

4) This gives a total of *three* pieces of information to be learned for each noun: **nominative singular, genitive singular**, and **gender.** If this is done carefully, the third declension nouns are generally not too difficult to work with.

5) Once the stem is established, the other case endings are added to it. For most forms this presents no problem. In the **dative plural** (and sometimes **nominative singular**), however, a consonant at the end of the stem must make some accommodation with the *sigma* of the ending. For the most part, this follows the same patterns as the changes made in forming the future tense (see Chapter 6). Study the following four paradigms for some of the options.

```
* * * * * * * * * * * * * * * * * * * * * * * * * * * * * *
*                                                          *
*      Singular      Plural           Singular      Plural *
*                                                          *
* N.   γυνή          γυναῖκες         χάρις         χάριτες *
* G.   γυναικός      γυναικῶν         χάριτος       χαρίτων  *
* D.   γυναικί       γυναιξί(ν)       χάριτι        χάρισι(ν)*
* A.   γυναῖκα       γυναῖκας         χάριν         χάριτας  *
*                                                          *
* * * * * * * * * * * * * * * * * * * * * * * * * * * * * *


* * * * * * * * * * * * * * * * * * * * * * * * * * * * * *
*                                                          *
*      Singular      Plural           Singular      Plural *
*                                                          *
* N.   ἄρχων         ἄρχοντες         πατήρ         πατέρες  *
* G.   ἄρχοντος      ἀρχόντων         πατρός        πατέρων  *
* D.   ἄρχοντι       ἄρχουσι(ν)       πατρί         πατράσι(ν)*
* A.   ἄρχοντα       ἄρχοντας         πατέρα        πατέρας  *
*                                                          *
* * * * * * * * * * * * * * * * * * * * * * * * * * * * * *
```

NOTES ON PARADIGMS:

(1) In the dative plural of γυνή the *kappa* of the stem combines with the *sigma* of the case ending to produce *xi*.

(2) The accusative singular of χάρις uses the alternate ending *nu* (though there are a few instances in the GNT of χάριτα).

(3) In the dative plural of ἄρχων both stem consonants have dropped out and the *omicron* has been lengthened to *ou*. We will see this happening again with certain dative plural participles. In fact, ἄρχων *is* actually the present active nominative

singular masculine participle of the verb ἄρχων. Note that this produces a form
which looks exactly like the present active indicative third person plural.

(4) With πατήρ there is a stem fluctuation between πατρ– and πατερ–. Such
internal stem changes do not need to be memorized, as long as you can recognize
the case and number of the noun.

(5) Although these nouns have different endings from the ones learned previously,
the *definite article* will remain as you have learned it. Furthermore, all the
adjectives you have learned so far are first / second declension and will *not* take
on third declension endings. This means that noun-adjective phrases, while
agreeing in case, number, and gender, will often not "match."

> τὴν ἀγαθὴν γυναῖκα   the good woman (accusative singular feminine)
> οἱ ἄρχοντες οἱ σοφοί   the wise rulers (nominative plural masculine)

(6) Accents – It is difficult, if not impossible, to establish consistent rules for third
declension noun accents. The paradigms above illustrate some of the possible
patterns. Other accents may be learned by observation in texts or by consulting a
lexicon.

VOCABULARY

The vocabulary is in four groups, based on gender and whether the stem ends in a
consonant or a vowel.

1) *Masculine* nouns with a stem ending in a consonant:

αἰών, αἰῶνος, m. – age; eternity (εἰς τὸν αἰῶνα, εἰς τοὺς αἰῶνας:
       "forever" / εἰς τοὺς αἰῶνας τῶν αἰώνων: "forever and ever" / *dative
       plural*: αἰῶσι) [aeon/eon]
ἀνήρ, ἀνδρός, m. – man (in contrast with woman); husband (*dative plural*:
       ἀνδράσι) [androgen]
ἄρχων, ἄρχοντος, m. – ruler [monarchy]
μάρτυς, μάρτυρος, m. – witness; martyr (*dative plural*: μάρτυσι) [martyr]
πατήρ, πατρός, m. – father [patriarch]
πούς, ποδός, m. – foot (*dative plural*: ποσί) [podiatrist]
σωτήρ, σωτῆρος, m. – savior (*dative plural*: σωτῆρσι) [soteriology]

2) **Feminine** nouns with a stem ending in a consonant:

ἐλπίς, ἐλπίδος, f. – hope (*dative plural*: ἐλπίσι)
γυνή, γυναικός, f. – woman; wife [gynecology]
μήτηρ, μητρός, f. – mother (*dative plural*: μητράσι) [matriarch]
νύξ, νυκτός, f. – night (dative plural: νυξί)
σάρξ, σαρκός, f. – flesh (both literal "flesh" or "body" and to represent our
        humanness – *dative plural*: σαρξί This word is often used in a
        prepositional phrase with κατά: κατὰ σάρκα. This phrase may have
        several different implications. It can mean "by earthly descent,"
        "under the control of one's sinful nature," or "by human standards," "as
        far as external standards are concerned.") [sarcophagus]
χάρις, χάριτος, f. – grace
χείρ, χειρός, f. – hand (*dative plural*: χερσί) [chirography, chiropractic]

3) **Masculine** nouns with a stem ending in a vowel. The stem of most forms ends
in *epsilon* (ευ appears in the nominative singular and dative plural). The genitive
singular ends in –ως instead of –ος. All the nouns in this group have the same
declension pattern. *Learn one model for the pattern.* [**Note:** The nominative and
accusative plural are identical.] The βασιλεύς ("king") pattern:

```
* * * * * * * * * * * * * * * *
*                             *
*     Singular      Plural    *
*                             *
*  N. βασιλεύς     βασιλεῖς    *
*  G. βασιλέως     βασιλέων    *
*  D. βασιλεῖ      βασιλεῦσι(ν)*
*  A. βασιλέα      βασιλεῖς    *
*                             *
* * * * * * * * * * * * * * * *
```

Other nouns in the βασιλεύς pattern:

ἀρχιερεύς, ἀρχιερέως, m. – high priest
γραμματεύς, γραμματέως, m. – scribe
ἱερεύς, ἱερέως, m. – priest [hieroglyphic]

4) **Feminine** nouns with a stem ending in a vowel. The stem of most forms ends in epsilon (iota appears in the nominative / accusative singular). All the nouns in this group have the same declension pattern. *Again learn one model for the pattern.* [Again, the genitive singular ends in –ως instead of –ος and the nominative and accusative plural are identical.] The πόλις ("city") pattern:

```
* * * * * * * * * * * * * * * * *
*                                *
*      Singular      Plural      *
*                                *
*  N.   πόλις       πόλεις       *
*  G.   πόλεως      πόλεων       *
*  D.   πόλει       πόλεσι(ν)    *
*  A.   πόλιν       πόλεις       *
*                                *
* * * * * * * * * * * * * * * * *
```

Other nouns in the πόλις pattern:

ἀνάστασις, ἀναστάσεως, f. – resurrection
δύναμις, δυνάμεως, f. – power, might; work of power, mighty work, miracle
      [dynamic]
θλίψις, θλίψεως, f. – tribulation
κρίσις, κρίσεως, f. – judgment   [crisis]
πίστις, πίστεως, f. – faith, belief, trust

Note: Nouns in the πόλις pattern are usually feminine, but you will occasionally come across a masculine one (e.g., ὄφις – "serpent," "snake")

VOCATIVE CASE: A separate case exists for the purpose of addressing someone. It is called the vocative case from the Latin *vocare* ("to call"). In many instances (including *all plurals*) its form is identical to that of the nominative, for which reason it is not generally listed with the other cases. The exceptions to this are:

(1) First declension masculine nouns endings in –ης (or –ας): the vocative singular ends in –α.
      μαθητά   προφῆτα

(2) Second declension masculine nouns: the vocative singular ends in –ε.
      ἀδελφέ   φίλε   κύριε

(3) Third declension nouns: the vocative singular is *sometimes* the stem alone or an abbreviated version of the stem, other times it is identical to the nominative.

γύναι   πάτερ

The vocative case is generally set off by commas and is grammatically independent of the rest of the sentence. Its proper identification is: **vocative s. or pl. (plus gender) / direct address**.

> εἶπέν τις τῶν μαθητῶν αὐτοῦ πρὸς αὐτόν, <u>Κύριε</u>, δίδαξον ἡμᾶς προσεύχεσθαι.

> A certain one of his disciples said to him, "<u>Lord</u>, teach us to pray." (Luke 11:1)

GENITIVE OF TIME: The genitive case is used to express an indefinite time *within which* something happens. Sometimes this is explained as the *type of time* within which an activity takes place.

> νυκτός   by night, in the night, at night, during the night

> καὶ οἱ πυλῶνες αὐτῆς οὐ μὴ κλεισθῶσιν <u>ἡμέρας</u>, νὺξ γὰρ οὐκ ἔσται ἐκεῖ.

> And its gates shall never be shut <u>by day</u>, for there shall not be night there. (Revelation 21:25)

THE PREPOSITION εἰς TO EXPRESS PURPOSE: Frequently the use of a preposition is expanded beyond its literal meaning. One example of this is the use of εἰς to convey the idea of **purpose**. When this happens, the preposition can be translated "for" or, if the noun involved represents a verbal action, the entire phrase can be re-written using either an English infinitive or a clause introduced by "may" or "might."

> εἰς ἄφεσιν ἁμαρτιῶν – for the forgiveness of sins; to forgive sins; that sins may / might be forgiven [Note that ἁμαρτιῶν is an objective genitive following the verbal head noun "forgiveness."]
> εἰς τοῦτο – for this reason; for this purpose
> εἰς σωτηρίαν – for salvation; that (someone) may / might be saved

εἰς μαρτύριον — An testimony; to testify, that (someone) may / might testify

καὶ ἰδοὺ πᾶσα ἡ πόλις ἐξῆλθεν <u>εἰς</u> ἀπάντησιν τῷ <u>Ἰησοῦ</u>.

And behold, the whole city went out to meet Jesus. (Matthew 8:34) [The
    verb to which the noun ὑπάντησις is related has a dative direct
    object, so, since the prepositional phrase is serving the verbal
    function of expressing purpose, the dative continues to be used.]

PREPARING FOR THE QUIZ:

(1) Since this is primarily a form and vocabulary chapter, your main responsibility
is to learn the **new endings** for third declension masculine and feminine nouns
and to recognize and be able to identify such nouns when you see them in context.

(2) Try writing out the declension for a few of the nouns just to get the endings set
in your mind.

(3) You should know how to spot, translate, and identify a noun in the **vocative
case**.

(4) You should know what is meant by the term **genitive of time** and how to
identify and translate a noun expressing this concept.

(5) You should have an understanding of the use of the preposition **εἰς *to express
a purpose idea*** and know how to translate such phrases when they appear.

Chapter 25
Contract Futures / Liquid Stem Verbs / Aorist
Active Indicative of γινώσκω / Indirect Questions

CONTRACT FUTURES: Some verbs have a future tense (second principal part active or middle) which uses the same endings as the ***present active*** or ***present M/P*** of an *epsilon* contract verb. If the second principal part is listed with a circumflex accent on the personal ending, this indicates that it will use epsilon contract endings.

λέγω, ἐρῶ ("will say"), εἶπον
ἀποθνῄσκω, ἀποθανοῦμαι (deponent future: "will die"), ἀπέθανον

* *

	Future Active Indicative of λέγω		Future Middle Indicative of ἀποθνῄσκω	
	Singular	*Plural*	*Singular*	*Plural*
1st	ἐρῶ	ἐροῦμεν	ἀποθανοῦμαι	ἀποθανούμεθα
2nd	ἐρεῖς	ἐρεῖτε	ἀποθανῇ	ἀποθανεῖσθε
3rd	ἐρεῖ	ἐροῦσι(ν)	ἀποθανεῖται	ἀποθανοῦνται

* *

NOTES:

(1) Occasionally, as with ἀποθνῄσκω, the future will *also* be deponent.

(2) If you did not know the vocabulary and principal parts, you would initially parse these contract futures as present. The lexicon would correct this for you.

LIQUID STEM VERBS: There are some verbs whose present tense stem ends in what are called "liquid consonants": λ, λλ, ν, or ρ. These verbs often display certain irregularities in forming the future and aorist. One such irregularity is that many of the future tense forms have contract verb (always the present of an *epsilon* contract verb) endings, e.g., βάλλω, βαλῶ, ἔβαλον. Usually there is also some change to the stem. There are two verbs, however, which require special attention, because the ***present and future stems are identical***.

κρίνω, κρινῶ, ἔκρινα – judge
μένω, μενῶ, ἔμεινα – remain

Most liquid stem verbs have a *first aorist* (βάλλω is an exception) and the stem frequently has an *internal vowel change*, e.g., ἔμεινα

AORIST OF γινώσκω: The verb γινώσκω has a *second* aorist active indicative conjugated using the letter *omega*.

	Singular	Plural
1st	ἔγνων	ἔγνωμεν
2nd	ἔγνως	ἔγνωτε
3rd	ἔγνω	ἔγνωσαν

INDIRECT QUESTION: Questions as well as statements, thoughts, etc. may be quoted both directly and indirectly. (This is another aspect of indirect discourse.) An indirect question may be part of a sentence which is a statement ("He asked me <u>where I was going</u>.") or a question ("Does anyone know <u>where our friends are</u>?").

Study the following patterns for *agreement of tenses*:

γινώσκω τί γίνεται.　I know what is happening.
γινώσκω τί ἐγένετο.　I know what happened.
γινώσκω τί γενήσεται.　I know what will happen.

ἠρώτησέ με τί ποιῶ.　He asked me what I <u>was doing</u>.
ἠρώτησέ με τί ἐποίησα.　He asked me what I <u>had done</u>.
ἠρώτησέ με τί ποιήσω.　He asked me what I <u>would do</u>.

Many indirect questions are easily identified by the presence of one of the interrogatory words. If there is no such word, an indirect question is introduced by εἰ ("if" or "whether").

ἠρώτησέ με εἰ μενῶ ἐκεῖ.　He asked me whether / if I would stay there.

A double indirect question is introduced by πότερον...ἤ ("whether.....or").

ἠρώτησέ με πότερον μενῶ ἢ πορεύσομαι.   He asked me whether I
would stay or go.

PREPOSITION: The preposition παρά can have its object in the genitive,
dative, or accusative case. See the vocabulary list for some of the meanings of
παρά. [***Reminder regarding prepositions***: These definitions do not exhaust the
possibilities, but simply give a representative sampling.]

παρὰ ἀνθρώπου   from a man / person / human being
παρὰ τοῦ πατρός μου   from my Father
παρὰ τῷ θεῷ   with God / in the sight of God
παρ᾽ ἑαυτοῖς   among (literally "with") themselves
παρὰ τὴν θάλασσαν   by the sea
παρὰ τοὺς πόδας   at (literally "by") the feet [of someone]

VOCABULARY

[For all but two of the verbs, you already know the vocabulary meaning and two
of the first three principal parts.]

βάλλω, βαλῶ, ἔβαλον
ἐκβάλλω, ἐκβαλῶ, ἐξέβαλον
ἐλπίζω, ἐλπιῶ, ἤλπισα
λέγω, ἐρῶ, εἶπον
ἀποθνῄσκω, ἀποθανοῦμαι, ἀπέθανον
πίπτω, πεσοῦμαι, ἔπεσον
μένω, μενῶ, ἔμεινα – stay, remain, abide
κρίνω, κρινῶ, ἔκρινα – judge, pass judgment; condemn (if the context requires
     this translation)
γινώσκω, γνώσομαι, ἔγνων
εἰ – whether (in indirect questions)
πότερον...ἤ – whether.....or
παρά (with genitive) – from (*the side of*) (usually with a person as object)
       (with dative) – with, near, at the side of, in the presence of; in the sight of,
           in the judgment of (with a person as object)
       (with accusative) – by, beside; along (The additional definitions for παρά
           with the accusative – "than," "more than," "rather than" – do not
           appear in the exercises.) [paramedic]

PREPARING FOR THE EXAM:

(1) Make a note about the fact that some verbs use *present tense epsilon* contract verb endings in the future tense. Learn the verbs from this chapter which have this characteristic. Update your master verb list with these future tense forms.

(2) Note that κρίνω and μένω appear on the *Accents and Breathing Marks That Matter* list. Check them off or highlight them.

(3) Be sure you know what is meant by the term "*liquid stem verb*."

(4) Add the *second aorist of γινώσκω* to your master verb list.

(5) You should know how to recognize and translate *indirect questions*, including the tense shift after a past tense introductory verb.

(6) Add the *preposition παρά* to the appropriate lists.

(7) Do whatever *review* of the previous chapters is necessary and look over the supplementary materials accompanying this chapter

Chapter 26
Relative Pronoun / Indefinite Relative Pronoun /
Relative Adjectives / Conjunctions

RELATIVE PRONOUN: In Greek, as in English, a noun (or pronoun) may be modified by a ***relative clause***. In the English sentence "Where is the slave whom you sent?" the relative clause is "whom you sent." The first word of the clause, "whom," is a ***relative pronoun***. The purpose of the relative clause is to give information about the slave. Note that, as a clause, "whom you sent" has its own subject ("you") and verb ("sent"). The word "whom" functions as the direct object of the clause. A relative clause is a subordinate (dependent) clause; it cannot stand alone as a separate sentence.

In the sentence above, the word "slave" is called the ***antecedent*** of the relative pronoun. The antecedent is the word in the main clause which the relative pronoun modifies and by means of which the relative clause is connected to the rest of the sentence.

NOTES:

(1) It is very important to be certain of the grammatical function of the relative pronoun, since it generally appears *at the beginning* of the relative clause. It will generally be either the first word in the clause or, if it is the object of a preposition, the second.

(2) Since relative pronouns and interrogative pronouns sound the same *in English*, students need to be sure they understand the difference between the two.

(3) Relative pronouns are gradually disappearing from English, causing many people to forget about their existence. However, they are very much present in Greek and have to be dealt with!

(4) Appropriate translations for the relative pronoun are as follows:

> masculine and feminine [when referring to persons(s)]
>> subject: "who"
>> object: "whom"
>> possessive: "whose"
>
> neuter – "which" or "that" [unless referring to person(s)]

FORMS OF THE RELATIVE PRONOUN:

	M.	F.	N.	M.	F.	N.
	Singular			*Plural*		
N.	ὅς	ἥ	ὅ	οἵ	αἵ	ἅ
G.	οὗ	ἧς	οὗ	ὧν	ὧν	ὧν
D.	ᾧ	ᾗ	ᾧ	οἷς	αἷς	οἷς
A.	ὅν	ἥν	ὅ	οὕς	ἅς	ἅ

Warning! Many of the relative pronouns appear in the *Accents and Breathing Marks That Matter* list.

The rule for the use of the relative pronoun in Greek reflects its connection to both the antecedent and its own clause. *The relative pronoun will be the same* **gender** *and* **number** *as the antecedent, but its* **case** *will be determined by its use in the relative clause.* The English example given above would be written in Greek as:

> ποῦ ἐστιν ὁ δοῦλος <u>ὃν</u> ἔπεμψας;

Since δοῦλος is **masculine singular**, the masculine singular relative pronoun is used. Since "whom" is the **direct object** of the relative clause, the **accusative** case is used.

INDEFINITE RELATIVE PRONOUN: The *indefinite relative pronoun* is formed by combining the relative pronoun with the indefinite pronoun. *Both parts are fully declined and the relative part has the accent it would have if it were alone.* This makes a rather unusual looking word. The neuter nominative / accusative singular form is written as two words to avoid confusion with ὅτι.

```
* * * * * * * * * * * * * * * * * * * * *
*                    Singular                 *
*                                             *
*           M.          F.          N.        *
*                                             *
*   N.    ὅστις      ἥτις        ὅ τι         *
*   G.    οὗτινος    ἧστινος     οὗτινος      *
*   D.    ᾧτινι.     ᾗτινι       ᾧτινι        *
*   A.    ὅντινα     ἥντινα      ὅ τι         *
*                                             *
*                     Plural                  *
*                                             *
*   N.    οἵτινες    αἵτινες     ἅτινα        *
*   G.    ὧντινων    ὧντινων     ὧντινων      *
*   D.    οἷστισι(ν) αἷστισι(ν)  οἷστισι(ν)   *
*   A.    οὕστινας   ἅστινας     ἅτινα        *
*                                             *
* * * * * * * * * * * * * * * * * * * * *
```

In actual usage, this form appears most frequently in the *nominative case*. It may be used with or without an antecedent. Without an antecedent, the use is a generalizing one: "whoever," "whichever," "everyone who," "everything which," "all who." With an antecedent, it is sometimes used to emphasize the nature or a quality or characteristic of the antecedent. At other times it functions exactly the same way as the basic relative pronoun. (The latter two uses are not always easy to distinguish from one another.)

> ὅστις γὰρ ἔχει, δοθήσεται αὐτῷ καὶ περισσευθήσεται· ὅστις δὲ οὐκ ἔχει, καὶ ὃ* ἔχει ἀρθήσεται ἀπ' αὐτοῦ.

> For whoever has, to him shall it be given and increased; but whoever does not have, even that which he has shall be taken away from him. (Matthew 13:12) [*The use of the basic relative pronoun in this sentence will be discussed later in this chapter.]

RELATIVE ADJECTIVES: There are also two *relative adjectives*:

ὅσος, -η, -ον: "as much as," "as many as"; with or without the Greek adjective πάντες / πάντα (Chapter 27): "all...who," "all...which/that"; *used as a substantive*: "all those who," "all the things which," "everything which" (Compare πόσος and τοσοῦτος.)

καὶ ὅσοι ἦσαν ἐκ γένους ἀρχιερατικοῦ

and <u>all those who / as many as</u> were of high priestly descent (Acts 4:6)

οἷος, α, ον "such as," "as," "of what sort" (Compare πηλίκος and τοιοῦτος.)
[There are no examples of this word in the exercises.]

RELATIVE PARTICLES AND CONJUNCTIONS: Certain particles and conjunctions correspond to the interrogative or demonstrative particles and adverbs:

(1) ὡς – as, like; while (with present or imperfect), when (with aorist) (Compare πῶς and οὕτως.)

> Τότε οἱ δίκαιοι ἐκλάμψουσιν <u>ὡς</u> ὁ ἥλιος ἐν τῇ βασιλείᾳ τοῦ πατρὸς αὐτῶν.

> Then the righteous will shine <u>as / like</u> the sun in the kingdom of their Father. (Matthew 13:43a)

> Οὐχὶ ἡ καρδία ἡμῶν καιομένη ἦν ἐν ἡμῖν <u>ὡς</u> ἐλάλει ἡμῖν ἐν τῇ ὁδῷ, <u>ὡς</u> διήνοιγεν ἡμῖν τὰς γραφάς;

> Were not our hearts burning within us, <u>while</u> he was speaking to us on the road, <u>while</u> he was explaining to us the Scriptures?   (Luke 24:32)

> <u>ὡς</u> ἤκουσεν τὸν ἀσπασμὸν τῆς Μαρίας ἡ Ἐλισάβετ

> <u>when</u> Elizabeth heard Mary's greeting (Luke 1:41)

(2) καθώς, ὥσπερ – as, just as (often paired in the sentence with οὕτως)

> <u>ὥσπερ</u> γὰρ ὁ πατὴρ ἐγείρει τοὺς νεκροὺς καὶ ζῳοποιεῖ, οὕτως καὶ ὁ υἱὸς οὓς* θέλει ζῳοποιεῖ.

> For <u>just as</u> the Father raises the dead and makes them alive, thus / so also the Son makes alive those whom he wishes. (John 5:21) [*See the note on the preceding page.]

(3) ὅτε – when (Compare πότε and τότε.)

ἔρχεται νὺξ <u>ὅτε</u> οὐδεὶς δύναται ἐργάζεσθαι.

A night is coming <u>when</u> no one can work.   (John 9:4b)

(4) οὗ (also ὅπου) – where (Compare ποῦ.) Be careful; οὗ is also the genitive singular masculine and neuter of the basic relative pronoun! See the *Accents and Breathing Marks That Matter* list.

<u>οὗ</u> γάρ εἰσιν δύο ἢ τρεῖς συνηγμένοι εἰς τὸ ἐμὸν ὄνομα, ἐκεῖ
    εἰμι ἐν μέσῳ αὐτῶν.

For <u>where</u> two or three have gathered / are gathered together in my name,
    I am there in their midst / in the midst of them.   (Matthew 18:20)

<u>ὅπου</u> γάρ ἐστιν ὁ θησαυρός σου, ἐκεῖ ἔσται καὶ ἡ καρδία σου.

For <u>where</u> your treasure is, there will your heart be also.   (Matthew 6:21)

(5) ὅθεν – from where, from which, whence (Compare πόθεν.)

τότε λέγει, Εἰς τὸν οἶκόν μου ἐπιστρέψω <u>ὅθεν</u> ἐξῆλθον.

Then it [an unclean spirit] says, "I will return to my house <u>from which</u> I
    went out." (Matthew 12:44a)

TWO SPECIAL SITUATIONS INVOLVING RELATIVE PRONOUNS:
Two additional comments need to be made at this time concerning the use of the basic relative pronoun:

(1) Sometimes the antecedent, generally a pronoun, may be omitted and must be understood from the relative pronoun. This is especially common with the subject and direct object. See the previous sentences marked with an asterisk and the examples below. (***Hint:*** If the sentence starts with a relative pronoun, assume you will have to supply the antecedent. There cannot be one in the sentence, since no words precede the relative pronoun.) In the case of both the neuter singular and neuter plural, it has become common to condense "that which" and "the things which" to just "what." While this is not totally incorrect, it is also not the very best choice, since it blurs the distinction between the use of the relative pronoun and that of the interrogative pronoun.

ὃν γὰρ ἀπέστειλεν ὁ θεὸς τὰ ῥήματα τοῦ θεοῦ λαλεῖ.

For he whom / the one whom God sent speaks the words of God.   (John
3:34)

ὑμεῖς προσκυνεῖτε ὃ οὐκ οἴδατε· ἡμεῖς προσκυνοῦμεν ὃ
οἴδαμεν.

You worship that which / what you do not know; *we* worship that which /
what we know. (John 4:22)

Note: From now on emphatic pronoun subjects in examples and answer keys will
be italicized rather than underlined in order to avoid confusion with the new
material which is being underlined.

Πορευθέντες ἀπαγγείλατε Ἰωάννῃ ἃ ἀκούετε καὶ βλέπετε.

Go and tell John the things which you hear and see.   (Matthew 11:4)

(2) When the relative pronoun would naturally be in the accusative case as the
direct object of its clause, it is often ***assimilated*** (or ***attracted***) to the case of a
genitive or dative antecedent.

μνημονεύετε τοῦ λόγου οὗ ἐγὼ εἶπον ὑμῖν.

Remember the word which *I* spoke to you.   (John 15:20a)

We would expect the relative pronoun to be in the accusative case (ὅν) as the
direct object of "said"; but instead it is genitive, having been assimilated to the
case of the antecedent τοῦ λόγου.

καὶ νῦν δόξασόν με σύ, πάτερ, παρὰ σεαυτῷ τῇ δόξῃ ᾗ εἶχον
πρὸ τοῦ τὸν κόσμον εἶναι παρὰ σοί.

And now, Father, you glorify me together with yourself, with the glory
which I had in your presence before the world existed. (John 17:5)

VOCABULARY: All the vocabulary words are included in the chapter.   There is
no additional new vocabulary.

PREPARING FOR THE QUIZ:

(1) Learn the ***forms of the basic relative pronoun***. Note that these are the basic first and second declension noun / adjective endings, with the usual exception for pronouns that the neuter nominative / accusative singular reflects the article ending rather than that of the noun.

(2) Be sure you know how to ***recognize and translate*** a relative clause in relation to the sentence in which it appears.

(3) Know the meaning of the term ***"antecedent"*** and how to identify the antecedent of a relative pronoun.

(4) You should know how to ***recognize and translate*** the indefinite relative pronoun. Remember that this may appear with or without an antecedent. You are only responsible at this time for the *nominative case forms.*

(5) Know how to translate the relative adjective ὅσος. Note especially the ***substantive uses*** "all those who" and "all the things which."

(6) Learn the various relative particles and conjunctions and be sure you can recognize and translate each in context. Note especially the ***two distinct categories of meaning*** for ὡς.

(7) Know how to recognize situations where the ***relative pronoun has been omitted*** and you must supply it from the context. Note the various possibilities for the word which you will have to supply.

(8) Know what it means to say that the relative pronoun has been ***assimilated*** or ***attracted*** to the case of its antecedent. Think about how you will recognize such situations. Be able to use these terms correctly in describing such situations.

Chapter 27

Third Declension Neuter Nouns / Adjectives and Numbers with Third Declension Forms / Comparative Adjectives / Genitive of Comparison

THIRD DECLENSION NEUTER NOUNS: Third declension neuter nouns do not have as much variety in the nominative singular as do third declension masculine and feminine nouns. There are two large groups and one considerably smaller one. All share the common third declension characteristic of showing the true stem in the genitive singular. They also have the usual neuter characteristic of having the same form for the nominative and accusative singular and for the nominative and accusative plural. The endings are as follows. (Note that these, like masculine and feminine third declension nouns, parallel the interrogative / indefinite pronoun endings.)

	Singular	Plural
N.	no distinct ending	–α
G.	–ος	–ων
D.	–ι	–σι(ν)
A.	same as N.	–α

The first of the two large groups exhibits what may be called the –μα / –ματος pattern (example: πνεῦμα – "spirit," "wind," "breath" [pneumatic]). Learn one paradigm well; all other nouns having this pattern will follow it exactly.

	Singular	Plural
N.	πνεῦμα	πνεύματα
G.	πνεύματος	πνευμάτων
D.	πνεύματι	πνεύμασι(ν)
A.	πνεῦμα	πνεύματα

Other third declension neuter nouns in the –μα / –ματος pattern:

αἷμα, αἵματος, n. – blood [hematology]
θέλημα, θελήματος, n. – will [monothelite – one who holds that Christ had only one will, the divine]

ὄνομα, ὀνόματος, n. – name [onomatopoeia]
ῥῆμα, ῥήματος, n. – word, saying; thing, matter
σπέρμα, σπέρματος, n. – seed; offspring, descendants [sperm]
στόμα, στόματος, n. – mouth [stomach, -ostomy]
σῶμα, σώματος, n. – body [psychosomatic]

The other large group, which may be called the –ος / –ους pattern, is more difficult because some of the endings have undergone certain changes. The true stem ends in a *sigma*. This *sigma*, however, drops out between the *epsilon* of the stem and any vowel in the case ending, whereupon the two vowels contract in similar fashion to those in the personal endings of contract verbs. This is true in the genitive and dative singular and the nominative, genitive, and accusative plural. In the dative plural, the sigma drops out, but there is no question of vowel contractions because the case ending begins with another *sigma*. Using as an example the noun ὄρος ("mountain"), we can observe how these changes take place. The forms in parentheses are the uncontracted ones.

```
* * * * * * * * * * * * * * * * * * * * * * * * * * * *
*                                                        *
*          Singular            Plural                    *
*                                                        *
*   N.    ὄρος              ὄρη (ὄρεσα)                  *
*   G.    ὄρους (ὄρεσος)    ὀρῶν (ὀρέσων)                *
*   D.    ὄρει (ὄρεσι)      ὄρεσι(ν) (ὄρεσσι)            *
*   A.    ὄρος              ὄρη                          *
*                                                        *
* * * * * * * * * * * * * * * * * * * * * * * * * * * *
```

Not only do these forms look different from the standard third declension patterns, several of the endings resemble either first declension feminine or second declension masculine noun forms. In order to avoid confusion, it is a good idea to make an extra effort to remember which nouns belong to this group.

Other third declension neuter nouns in the –ος / –ους pattern:

γένος, γένους, n. – race, nation; family; descendant
ἔθνος, ἔθνους, n. – nation; Gentile [ethnic]
ἔτος, ἔτους, n. – year [Etesian – winds which blow annually in the Mediterranean]
μέλος, μέλους, n. – member, part, limb (of the body, either literal or figurative)
μέρος, μέρους, n. – part

πλῆθος, πλήθους, n. – multitude [plethora]
σκότος, σκότους, n. – darkness
τέλος, τέλους, n – end, goal [teleology]

There are also some third declension neuter nouns with stems ending in a liquid consonant or *tau* (but not –ματ–). These do not belong to either of the preceding patterns; they do, however, use the basic endings given at the beginning of the chapter. Two of these, πῦρ ("fire") and φῶς ("light"), have no plural forms in use in the GNT. [***Note:*** The nominative / accusative singular of οὖς appears on the *Accents and Breathing Marks That Matter* list.]

```
* * * * * * * * * * * * * * * * * * * *
*
*      οὖς, ὠτός, n.            πῦρ, πυρός, n.        *
*      ear [otoscope]          fire [pyrotechnics]   *
*                                                    *
*      Singular  Plural        Singular              *
*                                                    *
*   N.  οὖς       ὦτα            πῦρ                  *
*   G.  ὠτός      ὦτων           πυρός                *
*   D.  ὠτί       ὠσί(ν)         πυρί                 *
*   A.  οὖς       ὦτα            πῦρ                  *
*                                                    *
*      ὕδωρ, ὕδατος, n.         φῶς, φωτός, n.        *
*      water [hydro–]           light [photography]  *
*                                                    *
*      Singular  Plural         Singular             *
*                                                    *
*   N   ὕδωρ      ὕδατα          φῶς                  *
*   G.  ὕδατος    ὑδάτων         φωτός                *
*   D.  ὕδατι     ὕδασι(ν)       φωτί                 *
*   A.  ὕδωρ      ὕδατα          φῶς                  *
*                                                    *
* * * * * * * * * * * * * * * * * * * *
```

ADJECTIVES: There are also adjectives which have third declension forms. The adjective ἀληθής ("true"; "real") follows a third declension pattern similar to nouns of the ὄρος pattern. The actual stem is ἀληθέσ–. Two other adjectives with this form are μονογενής, -ές ("only," "unique") and πλήρης, -ες ("full").

```
* * * * * * * * * * * * * * * * * * * * * * * * * * * * * *
*              Singular                        Plural                    *
*                                                                        *
*        M. / F.              N.            M. / F.              N.       *
*                                                                        *
*  N.  ἀληθής           ἀληθές        ἀληθεῖς           ἀληθῆ           *
*  G.  ἀληθοῦς          ἀληθοῦς       ἀληθῶν            ἀληθῶν          *
*  D.  ἀληθεῖ           ἀληθεῖ        ἀληθέσι(ν)        ἀληθέσι(ν)      *
*  A.  ἀληθῆ            ἀληθές        ἀληθεῖς           ἀληθῆ           *
*                                                                        *
* * * * * * * * * * * * * * * * * * * * * * * * * * * * * *
```

There are other adjectives which have a combination of first declension and third declension forms or even a combination of all three declensions. We will look at several of these in this chapter. The first one to be considered is πᾶς ("each," "every," "all," "whole"). It is extremely common in its own right and also illustrates the paradigm of the first aorist active participle. It has third declension forms for masculine and neuter and first declension forms for feminine. This may be called the "3-1-3 pattern." The feminine forms have both the endings and the genitive plural accent of the δόξα pattern (Chapter 8). This adjective gives us the common prefix "pan–" [Pandora, pandemonium]. The much less common adjective ἅπας has essentially the same meaning and follows the same pattern.

```
* * * * * * * * * * * * * * * * * * * * * * * * * * * * * *
*              Singular                            Plural                *
*                                                                        *
*     M.        F.        N.          M.         F.         N.           *
*                                                                        *
* N. πᾶς      πᾶσα      πᾶν        πάντες    πᾶσαι     πάντα          *
* G. παντός   πάσης     παντός     πάντων    πασῶν     πάντων         *
* D. παντί    πάσῃ      παντί      πᾶσι(ν)   πάσαις    πᾶσι(ν)        *
* A. πάντα    πᾶσαν     πᾶν        πάντας    πάσας     πάντα          *
*                                                                        *
* * * * * * * * * * * * * * * * * * * * * * * * * * * * * *
```

NOTES:

(1) In the singular *without the article* the most common translation is "every" or "each."

> πᾶν δένδρον – every tree / each tree
> πᾶσα πόλις – every city
> πᾶς ἄνθρωπος – every person

(2) The singular can also be translated "all" and "whole," depending on the context.

πᾶσα σάρξ – all flesh
πᾶσα Ἱεροσόλυμα – all Jerusalem
πᾶσα ἡ πίστις – all faith
πᾶσα ἡ κτίσις – the whole creation
ὁ πᾶς νόμος – the whole law

(3) The plural translation is generally "all."

πάντες οἱ μαθηταί – all the disciples
πάντα ταῦτα – all these things

(4) It is especially common to see the plural forms used as substantives. Masculine forms are translated as "all" or "all men / people" and neuter forms are "all things."

(5) Whenever the masculine or masculine / feminine forms of an adjective and the neuter forms use a third declension pattern, there will be a ***three way overlapping form*** in the *accusative singular masculine* or *masculine / feminine* and the *nominative and accusative plural neuter*.

Two other adjectives have third declension endings only in the *nominative and accusative singular masculine* and *nominative and accusative singular neuter*. (These four forms also have a *different stem*.) Elsewhere they are normal first / second declension adjectives. These are πολύς ("much", "many") and μέγας ("great", "large"). These adjectives provide common English prefixes: "poly–" [e.g., polyphonic, polytheism] and "mega–" / "megal–" [e.g., megaphone, megalopolis] The underlined forms have the different stem and the third declension endings.

```
* * * * * * * * * * * * * * * * * * * * * * *
*                                           *
*                  Singular                 *
*                                           *
*        M.           F.           N.       *
*                                           *
*  N.  πολύς       πολλή        πολύ        *
*  G.  πολλοῦ      πολλῆς       πολλοῦ      *
*  D.  πολλῷ       πολλῇ        πολλῷ       *
*  A.  πολύν       πολλήν       πολύ        *
*                                           *
* * * * * * * * * * * * * * * * * * * * * * *
```

```
* * * * * * * * * * * * * * * * * * * * * *
*                      Plural                 *
*                                             *
*          M.           F.           N.       *
*                                             *
*  N.   πολλοί       πολλαί       πολλά       *
*  G.   πολλῶν       πολλῶν       πολλῶν      *
*  N.   πολλοῖς      πολλαῖς      πολλοῖς     *
*  A.   πολλούς      πολλάς       πολλά       *
*                                             *
* * * * * * * * * * * * * * * * * * * * * *


* * * * * * * * * * * * * * * * * * * * * *
*                     Singular                *
*                                             *
*          M.           F.           N.       *
*                                             *
*  N.   μέγας        μεγάλη       μέγα        *
*  G.   μεγάλου      μεγάλης      μεγάλου     *
*  D.   μεγάλῳ       μεγάλῃ       μεγάλῳ      *
*  A.   μέγαν        μεγάλην      μέγα        *
*                                             *
*                      Plural                 *
*                                             *
*  N.   μεγάλοι      μεγάλαι      μεγάλα      *
*  G.   μεγάλων      μεγάλων      μεγάλων     *
*  D.   μεγάλοις     μεγάλαις     μεγάλοις    *
*  A.   μεγάλους     μεγάλας      μεγάλα      *
*                                             *
* * * * * * * * * * * * * * * * * * * * * *
```

NOTE: Beyond the basic translations of πολύς and μέγας, these two words often adapt their translations to specific situations. These will be listed in the lexicon. Here are a few examples. You do not need to try to do this with your translation unless you wish to, but you should be aware of it for New Testament work.

πολὺς ὄχλος – a great crowd   μέγα φῶς – a bright light
λόγος πολύς – a long speech   μεγάλη φωνή – a loud voice

NUMBERS: As indicated in Chapter 12, most Greek number words are not declined (i.e., they do not change endings for the different cases and genders). There are, however, a few which are declined. All, of course, are plural except "one." The number "one" follows a third declension pattern in the masculine and neuter forms and a first declension pattern in the feminine forms (the 3-1-3 pattern). The adjective οὐδείς, οὐδεμία, οὐδέν is a compound of the number and follows the same declension pattern. As an adjective οὐδείς means "no"; as a substantive it means "no one," "nothing." (The forms οὐθέν and οὐθενός also appear.)

```
* * * * * * * * * * * * * * * * * * * * * * * * * * * * * * * * * *
*      M.      F.      N.          M.          F.          N.        *
*                                                                    *
* N.  εἷς     μία     ἕν         οὐδείς      οὐδεμία     οὐδέν      *
* G.  ἑνός    μιᾶς    ἑνός       οὐδενός     οὐδεμιᾶς    οὐδενός    *
* D.  ἑνί     μιᾷ     ἑνί        οὐδενί      οὐδεμιᾷ     οὐδενί     *
* A.  ἕνα     μίαν    ἕν         οὐδένα      οὐδεμίαν    οὐδέν      *
*                                                                    *
* * * * * * * * * * * * * * * * * * * * * * * * * * * * * * * * * *
```

The numbers "three" (τρεῖς, τρία [triad]) and "four" (τέσσαρες, τέσσαρα [tessera]) have third declension patterns. The neuter τέσσαρα can also be spelled τέσσερα.

```
* * * * * * * * * * * * * * * * * * * * * * * * * * * * * * * * * *
*      M. / F.           N.              M. / F.            N.       *
*                                                                    *
* N.  τρεῖς           τρία            τέσσαρες         τέσσαρα       *
* G.  τριῶν           τριῶν           τεσσάρων         τεσσάρων      *
* D.  τρισί(ν)        τρισί(ν)        τέσσαρσι(ν)      τέσσαρσι(ν)   *
* A.  τρεῖς           τρία            τέσσαρας         τέσσαρα       *
*                                                                    *
* * * * * * * * * * * * * * * * * * * * * * * * * * * * * * * * * *
```

For the number "two" there are only two forms: δύο is nominative, genitive, and accusative, and δυσί(ν) is dative.

All numbers are adjectives and must agree in case, number, and gender with the word they modify, if possible.

COMPARATIVE ADJECTIVES: Many adjectives have a form which is used to make a comparison. Words or phrases like "wiser," "better," "slower," and "more interesting" are examples of English comparatives. In Greek, many comparative adjectives are formed by adding the first / second declension suffix $-\tau\epsilon\rho o\varsigma$, -α, -ον to the adjective stem. You should learn to ***recognize this suffix*** as a sign of a comparative adjective. ***Example***: μικρός ("small") / μικρότερος ("smaller")

The comparative adjective μείζων, -ον ("greater": the comparative of μέγας) has third declension endings.

```
* * * * * * * * * * * * * * * * * * * * * * * * * * * * * * * * *
*              Singular                         Plural              *
*                                                                   *
*       M. / F.          N.              M. / F.          N.        *
*                                                                   *
* N.  μείζων          μεῖζον          μείζονες        μείζονα        *
* G.  μείζονος        μείζονος        μειζόνων        μειζόνων       *
* D.  μείζονι         μείζονι         μειζόνοσι(ν)    μειζόνοσι(ν)   *
* A.  μείζονα         μεῖζον          μείζονας        μείζονα        *
*                                                                   *
* * * * * * * * * * * * * * * * * * * * * * * * * * * * * * * * *
```

The less common adjective πλείων, -ον ("more": the comparative of πολύς) is similarly declined.

NOTE: There are also ***superlative*** adjectives in Greek ("greatest," "best," "very wise," etc.). The superlative ***forms*** can be handled with the help of a lexicon. For questions regarding the ***use of positive, comparative, and superlative adjectives*** and the occasional substitution of one for another, see Wallace (pp. 296-305).

COMPARATIVE ADJECTIVES IN CONTEXT: There are two ways to indicate a comparison in Greek. The first involves using the word ἤ (translated in this context as "than") between the two words being compared. ***Note***: This word can also be used with comparative adverbs.

> μείζων ἐστὶν ὁ ἐν ὑμῖν ἢ ὁ ἐν τῷ κόσμῳ.

> The one who is in you is <u>greater than</u> the one who is in the world. (1 John 4:4)

GENITIVE OF COMPARISON: The other way to indicate a comparison is to use a *genitive of comparison* for the second of the two words being compared. (Note that this construction requires the translator to add the word "than.")

ἀμὴν ἀμὴν λέγω ὑμῖν, οὐκ ἔστιν δοῦλος <u>μείζων τοῦ κυρίου</u> αὐτοῦ.

Truly truly I say to you, a slave is not <u>greater than</u> his master. (John 13:16)

SUMMARY: This chapter brings to an end our study of noun, adjective, and pronoun forms. There are a few other pronoun and adjective forms, but these are not common and can be looked up if and when you encounter them. There are, however, a number of other case uses, especially for the genitive and dative cases. These can be handled by consulting Wallace (or another upper level Greek grammar). The basic course material will include ***one more genitive case use*** and ***two more accusative case uses***. At this point, however, it would be a good idea to do a quick review of the uses we have encountered thus far. You can use the review sheet accompanying Chapter 25, with the addition of the genitive of comparison.

VOCABULARY: All the new vocabulary is included in the chapter.

PREPARING FOR THE QUIZ:

(1) Since this is primarily a ***form and vocabulary*** chapter, that should be the focus of your attention. Third declension forms are exceedingly common and you need to be able to recognize them quickly. Work on the form and vocabulary exercise to help you learn this material.

(2) Make sure you know the ***regular endings*** and then look at the ***exceptions***.

(3) Learn the suffix which indicates a regularly formed ***comparative*** and learn the comparative adjective μείζων.

(4) Know how to recognize and translate the two possible contexts of a comparative adjective. Add ***genitive of comparison*** to your list of noun case uses.

Chapter 28

The Verb: Perfect Active Indicative / Pluperfect Active Indicative / Fourth Principal Part

GREEK PAST TENSES: We have already looked at two Greek verb tenses used to describe actions in the past. To review, the *imperfect* describes a past action as continuous, on-going, or repeated and the *aorist* describes an action as a whole (it summarizes the action). It is important to remember that the action could be the same one, it is a question of which aspect the writer chooses to emphasize. (For example, Mark 1:45 talks about Jesus out in the country with people coming to him from all directions. The verb used is ἤρχοντο (imperfect M/P 3 pl. ἔρχομαι), yet it is often just translated as "they came." This indeed tells what happened, but it loses the dramatic picture that is painted by the imperfect: "they kept coming.") In addition to the imperfect and aorist, Greek has two other tenses which describe past actions: the *perfect* and the *pluperfect*. We can describe the aspect of the perfect and pluperfect by saying that both speak of an event accomplished in the past, but ***rather than focusing primarily on the event itself they focus primarily on the continuing results of the action.***

FUNCTION OF THE PERFECT TENSE: The perfect tense describes an event which took place in the past and has continuing results existing in the present time (from the standpoint of the speaker or writer). As such, it combines elements of both the present (continuing results / effect) and the aorist (past action). Although the focus of the perfect tense is *always* on the present situation, the emphasis may shift slightly toward the past action or toward the resulting state. For this reason, there are ***two separate ways*** to translate the perfect.

(1) The so-called ***extensive perfect*** shifts the emphasis slightly toward the *completed action* from which a present state results. The usual translation is "I have…," "you have…," etc.

> αὕτη δέ ἐστιν ἡ κρίσις ὅτι τὸ φῶς <u>ἐλήλυθεν</u> εἰς τὸν κόσμον
> καὶ ἠγάπησαν οἱ ἄνθρωποι μᾶλλον τὸ σκότος ἢ τὸ φῶς.

> And this is the judgment, that the light <u>has come</u> into the world and the people loved the darkness rather / more than the light. (John 3:19a)

(2) The ***intensive perfect*** *shifts the emphasis slightly toward the results* produced by a past action. Often the best translation of an intensive perfect ***sounds like the English present tense***. This is especially common in the perfect M/P, as we shall see in Chapter 29. There are several words, however, which provide good examples in the intensive perfect active.

> γινώσκω – perfect: ἔγνωκα – I have come to know = I know

πιστεύω   perfect : πεπίστευκα   I have come to believe and still do
    I believe

ἐγγίζω (new in this chapter) – perfect: ἤγγικε (3 s.) – It has drawn
    near – It is at hand

λέγει αὐτῷ, Ναί κύριε, ἐγὼ <u>πεπίστευκα</u> ὅτι σὺ εἶ ὁ Χριστός.

She said to him, "Yes, Lord, *I* <u>believe</u> that *you* are the Christ / Messiah."
    (John 11:27)

<u>Πεπλήρωται</u> ὁ καιρὸς καὶ <u>ἤγγικεν</u> ἡ βασιλεία τοῦ θεοῦ.

The time <u>is fulfilled</u> (perfect M/P) and the kingdom of God <u>is at hand</u>.
    (Mark 1:15a)

PERFECT WITH A PRESENT FORCE: A small number of verbs have a perfect tense which is used as the equivalent of the present tense. These perfects (unlike the examples under intensive perfect) do not have the option of using "have / has" in the translation. For these verbs the result and the action are virtually the same and all focus on the action is lost. Among the most common are:

πέποιθα – perfect of πείθω: trust [in], depend on, rely on; be convinced / certain / sure
ἕστηκα – perfect of ἵστημι (Chapter 31): stand
οἶδα (new this chapter): know

VERY IMPORTANT NOTE: These different tenses tend to be confusing to beginning Greek students and often they either ignore them or mix them up randomly. This is a big mistake, because the Greek writers did not use the tenses haphazardly and a correct analysis of the tense is often helpful in exegetical work. One of the most common mistakes is to translate an aorist as if it were a perfect (i.e., with "have" or "has") because it "sounds better." This is understandable because the English perfect tense does not necessarily have the same focus as the Greek. (And there is *occasionally* a justification for doing this.) At this point, however, you need to practice making the distinctions among the imperfect, aorist, and perfect. For this reason, you should avoid using "have" or "has" as a helping verb when translating the aorist and reserve these for the extensive perfect.

FORMATION OF THE PERFECT ACTIVE:

(1) Reduplication – This goes on the beginning of the word; it is often a very easily observed characteristic of the perfect tense. Although there are some unusual exceptions, reduplication is generally done as follows:

> An initial consonant is repeated + *epsilon.* πεπιστευ– / τετηρε–
> An initial *phi* is reduplicated with *pi* + *epsilon.* πεφιλε–
> An initial *theta* is reduplicated with *tau* + *epsilon.* τεθεραπευ–
> An initial *chi* is reduplicated with *kappa* + *epsilon.*
> An initial *alpha* or *epsilon* lengthens to *eta.* ἠγαπα–
> An initial *omicron* lengthens to *omega.*
> An initial *zeta* and certain consonant clusters are reduplicated with just
>   *epsilon.* ἐγνω–

For compound verbs, reduplication (like an augment) goes between the prefix and the stem. περιπεπατε–.

(2) Regular verbs with a stem ending in a vowel or diphthong add *kappa* to the stem (most contract verbs first lengthen the stem vowel).

πεπιστευκ–	τετηρηκ–	ἠγαπηκ–
πεφιληκ–	περιπεπατηκ–	

Many other perfect active forms also have a stem ending in *kappa* (e.g., γινώσκω: ἐγνωκ–). Though not totally predictable, these are usually easily recognizable. There is a distinction made between the so-called *first perfect* and *second perfect*. It is, however, a distinction of *form only* and applies only to the *stem*, not the endings. First perfects are those which have a stem ending in *kappa*, second perfects have some other letter at the end of the stem. Since second perfects generally cannot be predicted and therefore must be memorized and even some first perfects have somewhat irregular formations, the perfect active is the ***fourth principal part*** of the verb.

(3) Add the personal endings:

† † † † † † † † † † † † ¥ ¥ ¥ ¥ * * * ж ж ж ж

	Singular	Plural	
	First Perfect Active Indicative of φιλέω		
1st	πεφίληκα	πεφιλήκαμεν	
2nd	πεφίληκας	πεφιλήκατε	
3rd	πεφίληκε(ν)	πεφιλήκασι(ν)	

Second Perfect Active Indicative of ἔρχομαι

1st	ἐλήλυθα	ἐληλύθαμεν
2nd	ἐλήλυθας	ἐληλύθατε
3rd	ἐλήλυθε(ν)	ἐληλύθασι(ν)

VOCABULARY: There are only five completely new words in this chapter. The rest of the vocabulary work consists of learning to recognize and work with the fourth principal part for the verbs from the preceding chapters. We will use the master verb list for this purpose. (This will also provide an opportunity to review the principal parts of the verbs which you have already learned.) As you go through this list, think about which fourth principal parts you can easily recognize based on recognizing a familiar root in them plus the typical perfect active features. You should not need, for example, to memorize πεποίηκα. You should be able to recognize the reduplication, the root ποιε– with the *epsilon* lengthened to *eta*, and the *kappa* of the first perfect. Simply note this and move on. Only when you encounter a perfect active stem which differs significantly from the previous stems do you need to stop and memorize it, e.g., εἴληφα (the fourth principal part of λαμβάνω). Even here you will find some good news, because the stem changes seen in the fourth principal part often carry over to the fifth and sixth. An example of this is the new word in this chapter: ἀποστέλλω. The fourth principal part is ἀπέσταλκα, but then the final two principal parts repeat the ἀπεσταλ (though you need to remember that the *upsilon* is reduplication in the perfect and augment in the aorist).

New words (first four principal parts need to be learned, except as noted):

ἀναβαίνω, ἀναβήσομαι, [ἀνέβην], ἀναβέβηκα – go up, come up, ascend
    (The stem verb βαίνω has many compounds and only the compounds

appear in the GNT. Note the deponent future. The aorist is in brackets until Chapter 30. This is a liquid stem verb [Chapter 25], but it does not have the typical characteristics of one.) [anabasis]

καταβαίνω, καταβήσομαι, [κατέβην], καταβέβηκα – go down, come down, descend [katabatic]

ἀποστέλλω, ἀποστελῶ, ἀπέστειλα, ἀπέσταλκα – send; send out, send away (This verb does have the characteristic features of a liquid stem verb: the single *lambda* and the *epsilon* contract endings in the future and the internal vowel change in the aorist.) [apostle]

ἐγγίζω, ἐγγιῶ, ἤγγισα, ἤγγικα – come near, draw near, approach; *perfect –* be at hand

οἶδα – There are no other principal parts for this verb. It is a second perfect and is translated "know" (***not*** "have known"). It is related to the stem εἰδ–, as will become evident as we look at other verbal forms. The general distinction between γινώσκω and οἶδα is that the former is nuanced toward experiential knowledge of a person or thing (Danker, p. 199), though this distinction is not always closely observed in use.

```
* * * * * * * * * * * * * *
*                            *
*          οἶδα – know        *
*                            *
*      Singular      Plural   *
*                            *
* 1st  οἶδα       οἴδαμεν     *
* 2nd  οἶδας      οἴδατε      *
* 3rd  οἶδε(ν)    οἴδασι(ν)   *
*                            *
* * * * * * * * * * * * * *
```

[There are a few forms of οἶδα which appear only one or two times: ἴσασιν (third person plural), ἴστε (second person plural), and εἰδήσουσιν (a third person plural *future* form). You do not need to learn these forms now.]

FUNCTION OF THE PLUPERFECT TENSE: The pluperfect describes an event which was completed in the past and had results existing *in the past as well*. (Nothing is implied about whether or not the results existed into the time of speaking or writing.) The pluperfect tense is not especially common.

(1) Most pluperfect actives are translated as ***extensive*** (*shifting the emphasis slightly toward the completed action*), using the helping verb "had."

εὗραν καθὼς εἰρήκει αὐτοῖς.

They found [everything] just as <u>he had told</u> them.   (Luke 22:13)

(2) In some instances, an ***intensive*** translation is possible, *shifting the emphasis slightly toward the results of an action.* In the following sentence, the first of the two pluperfects could be either extensive or intensive. In such situations, it is up to the translator to decide where to place the emphasis.

> καὶ σκοτία ἤδη <u>ἐγεγόνει</u> καὶ οὔπω <u>ἐληλύθει</u> πρὸς αὐτοὺς ὁ ᾿Ιησοῦς.

> And it <u>had</u> already <u>become</u> dark [extensive – NASB / literally: "darkness had already happened"] / And <u>it was</u> now dark [intensive – RSV], and Jesus <u>had</u> not yet <u>come</u> to them. (John 6:17b)

PLUPERFECT WITH A SIMPLE PAST FORCE: Finally, just as a few perfects have an entirely present tense force, a small number of pluperfects express a simple past tense idea. One of the most common of these is ἤδειν, the pluperfect of οἶδα. Since οἶδα is translated "know," the pluperfect is generally translated "knew." The other pluperfect commonly used this way is that of the verb ἵστημι which we will meet in Chapter 31. The perfect of this word is translated as "stand" and the pluperfect is translated as "stood" (also "was / were standing").

FORMATION OF THE PLUPERFECT ACTIVE: The perfect active (fourth principal part) stem is re-used for the pluperfect active. For this reason the pluperfect (like the imperfect which uses the present stem) is *not* considered a separate principal part. To the perfect active stem (including the reduplication) are added the endings: –ειν, –εις, –ει, –ειμεν, –ειτε, –εισαν. (***Note:*** Technically the ει is regarded as a "coupler" between the stem and the actual ending, but it is generally more convenient to regard the coupler + ending as a single unit.) Sometimes there is an augment on the beginning of the pluperfect, but often there is not. Again the distinction is made between a *first pluperfect* (stem ends in *kappa*) and a *second pluperfect* (stem ends in something other than *kappa*).

```
* * * * * * * * * * * * * * * * * * * * * * * * * *
*              Singular              Plural              *
*                                                         *
*        First Pluperfect Active Indicative of πιστεύω    *
*                                                         *
*   1ˢᵗ  (ἐ)πεπιστεύκειν      (ἐ)πεπιστεύκειμεν          *
*   2ⁿᵈ  (ἐ)πεπιστεύκεις      (ἐ)πεπιστεύκειτε           *
*   3ʳᵈ  (ἐ)πεπιστεύκει       (ἐ)πεπιστεύκεισαν          *
*                                                         *
*        Second Pluperfect Active Indicative of ἔρχομαι   *
*                                                         *
*   1ˢᵗ  ἐληλύθειν            ἐληλύθειμεν                *
*   2ⁿᵈ  ἐληλύθεις            ἐληλύθειτε                 *
*   3ʳᵈ  ἐληλύθει             ἐληλύθεισαν                *
*                                                         *
*        Second Pluperfect Active Indicative of οἶδα      *
*                                                         *
*   1ˢᵗ  ᾔδειν                ᾔδειμεν                    *
*   2ⁿᵈ  ᾔδεις                ᾔδειτε                     *
*   3ʳᵈ  ᾔδει                 ᾔδεισαν                    *
*                                                         *
* * * * * * * * * * * * * * * * * * * * * * * * * *
```

PREPARING FOR THE QUIZ:

(1) Make sure you understand the **aspect** of the perfect and pluperfect tenses, i.e. the way these two tenses look at the action of the verb.

(2) Be sure you understand what is meant by the terms **extensive** and **intensive** perfect and how the distinction can affect translation.

(3) Be sure you know what is meant by **perfect with a present force**. Know the two verbs which we have seen so far which fall into this category.

(4) Know how to **recognize the perfect and pluperfect active** when you see them (reduplication and personal endings).

(5) Learn **the first four principal parts** for the completely new verbs and the **perfect active** for verbs which we have already had. **Note:** This may mean actual memorization or it may mean just knowing enough about how the perfect is formed that you can recognize it when you see it. (This will be easier to do for verbs with regular principal parts.)

Chapter 29
The Verb: Perfect M/P Indicative / Pluperfect M/P Indicative / Fifth Principal Part / Perfect M/P Participle / Periphrastic Constructions

ASPECT: The aspect of these two tenses is the same in the middle / passive as it was in the active – *both describe a past action or event but with the focus on the continuing results*.

(1) The *extensive* perfect and pluperfect M/P shift the emphasis slightly toward the past action. The perfect is translated "have / has been…"

> ἡ ἀγάπη τοῦ θεοῦ ἐκκέχυται ἐν ταῖς καρδίαις ἡμῶν.

> The love of God <u>has been poured out</u> in our hearts.   (Romans 5:5)

The extensive pluperfect M/P is translated "had been…"

> καὶ γυναῖκές τινες αἳ <u>ἦσαν τεθεραπευμέναι</u> ἀπὸ πνευμάτων πονηρῶν καὶ ἀσθενειῶν

> and some women who <u>had been healed</u> from evil spirits and illnesses (Luke 8:2)

(2) The *intensive* perfect M/P is quite frequent. Like the perfect active, it will *sound* like the present tense, but must be carefully distinguished from it. The present M/P represents an action as on-going but not completed (e.g., νικᾶται – "he is being conquered"), whereas the intensive perfect M/P represents the action as completed with the focus on the continuing results (e.g., νενίκηται – "he is conquered"). Another way to express this is to say that the perfect M/P describes the *present state of the subject*. A frequently used perfect M/P is γέγραπται. This could be translated "it has been written," but, in fact, is generally translated "it is written" to emphasize the present significance of the written word. It should be pointed out that many perfects are open to interpretation and could be either extensive or intensive, depending on which emphasis of the perfect tense the translator thinks the writer had in mind. There is a good example in Luke 16:26.

> μεταξὺ ἡμῶν καὶ ὑμῶν χάσμα μέγα ἐστήρικται.

> Between us and you a great chasm <u>has been / is fixed</u>.

Did the writer want to emphasize the past action (putting the chasm in place) or the fact that it is now there? Which one do you prefer? Check a couple of English translations and see what they say.

The intensive pluperfect M/P is not common, but can be illustrated by the following passage describing Lazarus as he emerges from the tomb. The emphasis is not on the fact that his face "had been wrapped," but on the fact that, even as he walked from the grave, his face "was wrapped" with a cloth.

> καὶ ἡ ὄψις αὐτοῦ σουδαρίῳ <u>περιεδέδετο</u>.

And his face <u>was wrapped around</u> with a cloth.   (John 11:44a)

One needs to be very careful in using this translation for the pluperfect M/P to avoid confusion with the aorist passive which is translated to indicate that something "was done" to the subject. Remember that the perfect and pluperfect may be said to describe the *state of the subject*. This describes the state of Lazarus' face, not something which at that time was done to his face.

PERFECT WITH A PRESENT FORCE: There are also a few perfect M/P forms that are always translated with a present force (i.e., without "have / has"). Examples are:

> πέπεισμαι – perfect M/P of πείθω: be convinced, be certain (of
>   something / that…) [e.g., Romans 8:38]
> μέμνημαι – perfect M/P of μιμνήσκομαι: remember

DEPONENTS AND SPECIAL MEANINGS FOR MIDDLE OR PASSIVE: As is the case for other middle and/or passive verb forms, not only will the perfect and pluperfect M/P be used to express the passive concept (something done to the subject), but they will also be used for deponents and for any verb which has a special meaning for the middle or passive. This means that in such situations the translation will *sound like* the perfect active.

> δέδεγμαι (perfect M/P 1 s. δέχομαι) – I have received
> ἐσκανδάλισται (perfect M/P 3 s. σκανδαλίζω) – he has fallen away
> ὑποτετάγμεθα (perfect M/P 1 pl. ὑποτάσσω) – we have subjected
>   ourselves / submitted
> (ἐ)πεπόρευντο (pluperfect M/P 3 pl. πορεύομαι) – they had gone

FORMATION OF THE PERFECT M/P: The perfect M/P is the *fifth principal part*. The distinctive *reduplication* follows the same patterns as in the perfect active. The endings (–μαι, –σαι, –ται, –μεθα, –σθε, –νται) are attached *directly to the stem* without any connecting *o* / ε. (Along with the reduplication, this lack of a connecting vowel is an easily recognizable feature of the perfect M/P.) The endings are familiar except for the *second person singular*. Remember that the –η ending which serves as the second singular ending for the present M/P and the future middle is the result of a vowel contraction after a *sigma* has dropped out: –ε(σ)αι. Since the perfect M/P has no *epsilon* before the ending, the *sigma* remains.

```
* * * * * * * * * * * * * * * * * * * * * * * * *
*            Perfect M/P Indicative of θεραπεύω        *
*                                                      *
*          Singular                Plural              *
*                                                      *
*   1st    τεθεράπευμαι       τεθεραπεύμεθα             *
*   2nd    τεθεράπευσαι       τεθεράπευσθε              *
*   3rd    τεθεράπευται       τεθεράπευνται             *
*                                                      *
* * * * * * * * * * * * * * * * * * * * * * * * *
```

Contract verbs lengthen the stem vowel before adding the personal endings.

> τετήρηνται – they have been kept
> πεπλανήμεθα – we have gone astray / we have been deceived
> δεδικαίωσθε – you have been justified / are justified

The above formations work when the stem ends in a vowel. When the stem ends in a consonant, however, the lack of a connecting vowel causes some incompatible consonant combinations. This in turn leads to changes to the stem consonant. The following paradigms are provided to illustrate the possibilities, but these **do not have to be memorized**. If one observes (1) the reduplication, (2) the lack of a connecting vowel, and (3) the endings, there should be no problem identifying a perfect M/P.

```
* * * * * * * * * * * * * * * * * * * * * * *
*                                               *
*           Stem ending in κ, γ, χ              *
*          Perfect M/P Indicative of ἄγω        *
*                                               *
*           Singular              Plural         *
*                                               *
*  1ˢᵗ      ἦγμαι              ἤγμεθα            *
*  2ⁿᵈ      ἦξαι               ἦχθε              *
*  3ʳᵈ      ἦκται             ἠγμένοι εἰσί(ν)     *
*                                               *
*                                               *
*           Stem ending in π, β, φ              *
*          Perfect M/P Indicative of πέμπω      *
*                                               *
*  1ˢᵗ      πέπεμμαι          πεπέμμεθα          *
*  2ⁿᵈ      πέπεμψαι          πέπεμφθε           *
*  3ʳᵈ      πέπεμπται         πεπεμμένοι εἰσί(ν)  *
*                                               *
*                                               *
*           Stem ending in τ, δ, θ, ζ           *
*          Perfect M/P Indicative of βαπτίζω    *
*                                               *
*  1ˢᵗ   βεβάπτισμαι         βεβαπτίσμεθα        *
*  2ⁿᵈ   βεβάπτισαι          βεβάπτισθε          *
*  3ʳᵈ   βεβάπτισται         βεβαπτισμένοι εἰσί(ν)*
*                                               *
*                                               *
*           Stem ending in λ, μ, ν, ρ           *
*          Perfect M/P Indicative of αἴρω       *
*                                               *
*  1ˢᵗ      ἦρμαι              ἤρμεθα            *
*  2ⁿᵈ      ἦρσαι              ἦρσθε             *
*  3ʳᵈ      ἦρται             ἠρμένοι εἰσί(ν)     *
*                                               *
* * * * * * * * * * * * * * * * * * * * * * *
```

PERFECT M/P PARTICIPLE and PERIPHRASTIC CONSTRUCTIONS:
Although the various consonant changes are able to take care of five of the six
verb forms, a problem occurs with the third person plural.   Attempts to combine

the νι with other consonants generally result in unpronounceable consonant clusters. So a different solution is employed: the ***perfect M/P participle*** is combined with the third person plural of a verb meaning "to be." While other verbs meaning "to be" (e.g., γίνομαι or ὑπάρχω) may be used in periphrastic constructions, εἰμί is by far the most common. This construction is called the ***periphrastic*** use of the participle and will be discussed again in Chapter 33. The concept is not difficult, however, and the perfect and pluperfect M/P periphrastic constructions may as well be learned now.

The participle is formed by removing the –μαι of the first person singular and adding –μένος, -η, -ον. The endings are those of a first / second declension adjective. (A participle, by definition, is a ***verbal adjective***.)   The basic translation of the perfect M/P participle *alone* is as follows:

> γεγραμμένος, -η, -ον – (having been) written
> τεθεραπευμένος, -η, -ον – (having been) healed
> βεβλημένος, -η, -ον – thrown
> κεκλημένος, -η, -ον – called

When the perfect M/P participle is combined with a form of the present tense of εἰμί, the combined form is the ***equivalent of the perfect M/P indicative***. (Note that the nominative plural masculine ending is used because of the third person plural verb with an unspecified "they" subject.)

> βεβαπτισμένοι εἰσί(ν) – they have been / are baptized
> σεσωσμένοι εἰσί(ν) – they have been / are saved

Although the periphrastic construction is used of necessity for the third person plural, it can be used in other forms as well. A change in the gender or number of the subject would require the participle ending to be changed to agree with the subject.

> σεσωσμένοι ἐστέ – you have been / are saved
> ἡτοιμασμένη ἐστί(ν) – she has been / is prepared [Note the nominative singular feminine ending on the participle.]

Finally, note that the participle may precede or follow the form of εἰμί and may even be separated from it in the sentence.

> ἡ θύρα ἐστὶν ἀνεῳγμένη.   The door has been / is opened.

VOCABULARY: Again we will use the master verb list to learn the fifth principal part for verbs from the preceding chapters. There are also three new vocabulary verbs for which all the principal parts need to be learned.

αἴρω, ἀρῶ, ἦρα, ἦρκα, ἦρμαι – take up, lift up; take away, remove (Note that both this verb and the following one are liquid stem verbs.)

ἐγείρω, ἐγερῶ, ἤγειρα, ---, ἐγήγερμαι – raise, raise up; wake; *passive*: get up, rise; arise; awaken (This is one of the two verbs used in the GNT to talk about Jesus' resurrection. It is also used, however, for ordinary situations where someone gets up from a sitting or lying position. It is difficult, especially when talking of Jesus' resurrection, to make a hard and fast rule about whether to translate the third person singular passive or M/P forms using the passive concept ["he has been raised"] or with the special meaning "he has risen / is risen.")

καθαρίζω, καθαριῶ, ἐκαθάρισα, ---, κεκαθάρισμαι – cleanse, make clean, purify [catharsis]

FORMATION OF THE PLUPERFECT M/P: As was the case for the pluperfect active, the perfect M/P stem (including reduplication) is re-used. The endings are –μην, –σο, –το, –μεθα, –σθε, –ντο. (Remember that the –ου ending used for the second person singular of the imperfect M/P and the second aorist middle is the result of the contraction of an *epsilon* and an *omicron* after a *sigma* has dropped out: –ε(σ)ο > –ου.) In this form also there is no connecting vowel, so once again consonant changes occur if the stem ends in a consonant. For the periphrastic third person plural the *imperfect of εἰμί* is used. The augment is optional.

```
* * * * * * * * * * * * * * * * * * * * *
*        Pluperfect M/P Indicative of τιμάω      *
*                                                *
*          Singular              Plural          *
*                                                *
*   1st  (ἐ)τετιμήμην      (ἐ)τετιμήμεθα       *
*   2nd  (ἐ)τετίμησο       (ἐ)τετίμησθε        *
*   3rd  (ἐ)τετίμητο       (ἐ)τετίμηντο        *
*                                                *
* * * * * * * * * * * * * * * * * * * * *
```

```
Y  Y  *  *  *  *  *  *  *  *  *  *  *  *  *  *  *  *  *
*           Pluperfect M/P Indicative of ἐγείρω              ·ŀ·
*                                                            ·Ψ·
*            Singular              Plural                     *
Y                                                            ·ŀ·
*      1ˢᵗ   ἐγηγέρμην          ἐγηγέρμεθα                    *
*      2ⁿᵈ   ἐγήγερσο          ἐγήγερσθε                     *
*      3ʳᵈ   ἐγήγερτο          ἐγηγερμένοι ἦσαν              *
*                                                            ·ŀ·
*  *  *  *  *  *  *  *  *  *  *  *  *  *  *  *  *  *  *  *
```

NOTE: Since the pluperfect augment is optional and the first person plural and second person plural endings are the same for both perfect and pluperfect M/P, it is possible for these two forms to be identical. The translator would need to try to determine the tense from the context.

$$ἀπεστάλμεθα – \text{we have been sent out / we had been sent out}$$
$$λέλυσθε – \text{you have been freed / you had been freed}$$

PREPARING FOR THE QUIZ:

(1) Review the basic *aspect* of the perfect and pluperfect tenses.

(2) Know how to *translate* both the extensive and intensive perfect and the extensive and the (rare) intensive pluperfect.

(3) Know the *basic endings* for the perfect and pluperfect M/P. Remember that the reduplication will be the same as it was for the perfect and pluperfect active.

(4) Study the patterns which illustrate the *possible consonant combinations* which can occur when the stem of the perfect M/P ends in a consonant.

(5) Know what is meant by the term "*periphrastic*" construction and what the two elements of the perfect M/P periphrastic and the pluperfect M/P periphrastic are.

(6) Know how to form, recognize, and translate the *perfect M/P participle* alone and how to translate the two periphrastic constructions given in this chapter.

(7) Learn the *three new verbs* in this chapter (all of which have a fifth principal part) and review the master list for the *fifth principal parts* of the verbs you have already learned.

Chapter 30

The Verb: Aorist Passive Indicative / Future Passive Indicative /
Sixth Principal Part / Overview of the Indicative

AORIST AND FUTURE PASSIVE: This chapter completes our study of the tenses of the indicative mood. The **sixth principal part** of the Greek verb is the **aorist passive**. The **future passive** re-uses the stem of the aorist passive and, for that reason, is not itself a principal part.

FUNCTION OF THE AORIST PASSIVE: The aorist passive indicative, like the aorist active (see Chapter 9), talks about a past action as a whole (sometimes called "unitary action"). It is sometimes described as a snapshot of the action, as compared with the motion picture view of the imperfect. The aorist says that "something happened," without any indication of how long it took or how often it happened or what the continuing results are. The usual translation of the aorist passive indicates that something "was done" to the subject.

ἐδιδάχθημεν (1st aorist passive 1 pl. διδάσκω) – we were taught

ἐβαπτίσθησαν (1st aorist passive 3 pl. βαπτίζω) – they were baptized

ἐπειράσθη (1st aorist passive 3 s. πειράζω) – he/she was tempted

ἀπεστάλην (2nd aorist passive 1 s. ἀποστέλλω) – I was sent out

Remember that the translation of aorist passive forms for **deponents** and any verbs with a **special meaning for passive forms** will *sound like an aorist active.*

ἐπορεύθητε (1st aorist passive 2 pl. πορεύομαι) – you went

ἐφοβήθησαν (1st aorist passive 3 pl. φοβέομαι) – they were afraid / they became afraid

ἠγέρθη (1st aorist passive 3 s. ἐγείρω) – he/she arose / got up / was raised

ἐστράφην (2nd aorist passive 1 s. στρέφω) – I turned [*intransitive*]

FORMATION OF THE AORIST PASSIVE:

(1) Like the aorist active, the aorist passive starts with an **augment,** either an *epsilon* or a lengthened vowel.

(2) For a **first aorist passive** the letters θη are added at the end of the stem. (Second aorist passives lack the distinctive *theta*.) If the stem ends in a vowel or diphthong (contract verbs lengthen the stem vowel), these letters attach with no problem. If the stem ends in a consonant, certain changes take place. Nevertheless, the first aorist passive is generally a very easy form to recognize.

ἐδιδάχθη (διδάσκω)
ἐπεμφθη (πέμπω)
ἐκλήθη (καλέω)
ἐπειράσθη (πειράζω)
ἤχθη (ἄγω)

(3) The personal endings of the aorist passive (–ν, –ς, ---, –μεν, –τε, –σαν) are familiar to you, but until now you have only seen them on active forms. Learn to recognize these forms as *passive* and you should have no problem with person and number. As with the perfect and pluperfect, a distinction is made between first and second aorist passive, but *the distinction only involves the stem.* If the stem ends with θη, it is a first aorist passive.

```
* * * * * * * * * * * * * * * * * * * * * *
*                                               *
*    First Aorist Passive Indicative of βαπτίζω  *
*                                               *
*        Singular            Plural             *
*                                               *
*  1ˢᵗ  ἐβαπτίσθην        ἐβαπτίσθημεν         *
*  2ⁿᵈ  ἐβαπτίσθης        ἐβαπτίσθητε          *
*  3ʳᵈ  ἐβαπτίσθη         ἐβαπτίσθησαν         *
*                                               *
* * * * * * * * * * * * * * * * * * * * * *
```

The **second aorist passive** has exactly the same personal endings, but lacks the *theta* of the first aorist passive; some other consonant will precede the *eta*. Since most verbs have a first aorist passive, it is necessary that second aorist passives be noted carefully and remembered. They are nowhere near as easy to spot.

```
* * * * * * * * * * * * * * * * * * * * * *
*                                               *
*      Second Aorist Passive Indicative         *
*              of ἀποστέλλω                      *
*                                               *
*        Singular            Plural             *
*                                               *
*  1ˢᵗ  ἀπεστάλην        ἀπεστάλημεν           *
*  2ⁿᵈ  ἀπεστάλης        ἀπεστάλητε            *
*  3ʳᵈ  ἀπεστάλη         ἀπεστάλησαν           *
*                                               *
* * * * * * * * * * * * * * * * * * * * * *
```

FUNCTION OF THE FUTURE PASSIVE: The future tense says that something "will happen." Like the aorist, the action is generally seen as a whole ("unitary"). The translation of the future passive indicates that something "will be done" to the subject. Again, remember that *deponents and verbs with a special meaning for the passive* will have an active sounding translation.

> ἀχθήσεσθε (future passive 2 pl. ἄγω) – you will be led
> κριθήσονται (future passive 3 pl. κρίνω) – they will be judged
> σωθήσῃ (future passive 3 s. σῴζω) – you will be saved
> ἀποσταλήσεσθε (future passive 2 pl. ἀποστέλλω) – you will be sent out
> πεισθησόμεθα (future passive 1 pl. πείθω) – we will obey / pay attention to
> μνησθήσομαι (future passive 1 pl. μιμνήσκομαι) – I will remember

FORMATION OF THE FUTURE PASSIVE:

(1) Remove the personal ending (*nu*) and the augment from the sixth principal part. In most situations removing the augment is no problem: take off the *epsilon* or return a lengthened vowel to its original form.

> ἤχθην becomes ἀχθη–
> ἐδιδάχθην becomes διδαχθη–

Sometimes, however, the sixth principal part is an irregular formation and it is a bit tricky to recognize the unaugmented stem.

> ἐρρήθην (sixth principal part of λέγω) becomes ῥηθη–
> ἠνέχθην (sixth principal part of φέρω) becomes ἐνεχθη–

(2) Add σ and then ο / ε.

(3) Add the same personal endings as were used for the present M/P and the future middle. (The **stem** is the key to distinguishing future middle from future passive.)

NOTE: The future passive is likely to be quite a long verb form. Future passives are generally easy to recognize, though those which are formed from second aorist passives are a bit more difficult since they lack the distinctive *theta*.

```
* * * * * * * * * * * * * * * * * * * * * * *
*           Future Passive Indicative of βαπτίζω           *
*                                                          *
*              Singular                    Plural          *
*                                                          *
*  1st   βαπτισθήσομαι        βαπτισθησόμεθα                *
*  2nd   βαπτισθήση           βαπτισθήσεσθε                 *
*  3rd   βαπτισθήσεται        βαπτισθήσονται                *
*                                                          *
* * * * * * * * * * * * * * * * * * * * * * *
```

Other examples:

    ῥηθήσεται – it will be said (λέγω)

    ἐγερθησόμεθα – we will arise / be raised (ἐγείρω)

    σκανδαλισθήσεσθε – you will fall away (σκανδαλίζω)

    ὀφθήσονται – they will appear (ὁράω)

OVERVIEW OF THE INDICATIVE: With the exception of the –μι verbs in Chapter 31, this chapter brings to a conclusion our study of the indicative mood. As you take one more look at the master list, consider now what you need to know about each verb. Is it a perfectly regular verb with regular principal parts (e.g., λύω, δοξάζω, and most contract verbs)? Are there easily recognizable relationships among the different stems, even though you might not have been able to predict them all (e.g., εὑρίσκω, γράφω, ἀποστέλλω, and γινώσκω)? The great majority of the verbs fall into one of these two categories. Is there a deponent future and/or a second aorist or some other unusual stem feature involved (e.g., ἀποθνῄσκω, λαμβάνω, and πίπτω)? Here a bit more memory work will be required. Finally, is this one of the small number of verbs which have joined together in the principal parts unrelated verb stems (e.g., λέγω, φέρω, and ὁράω)? Obviously, these will need to be memorized.

VOCABULARY: This time we will be looking at the master vocabulary list for the sixth principal part of the verbs. There are also five new vocabulary words,

ἀπαγγέλλω, ἀπαγγελῶ, ἀπήγγειλα, ---, ---, ἀπηγγέλην – report, tell; announce, proclaim (Note the distinctive liquid stem characteristics: the double *lambda* in the present tense reduced to one *lambda* in the other principal parts, contract endings in future, and internal vowel change in the aorist active stem. Remember that this is a *first* aorist active.)

Table of Indicative Verb Endings

Here is a summary of the verb endings for the indicative (except for some $-\mu\iota$ verb forms). Note that the connecting vowels are missing in the perfect and pluperfect M/P. The *eta* of the aorist passive is properly part of the stem, but is included here in parentheses. (Remember that in the present and imperfect of contract verbs the endings will look different because of the vowel contractions.)

Present Active and Future Active

$-\omega$	$-o\mu\epsilon\nu$
$-\epsilon\iota\varsigma$	$-\epsilon\tau\epsilon$
$-\epsilon\iota$	$-ou\sigma\iota(\nu)$

Present M/P, Future Middle, and Future Passive

$-o\mu\alpha\iota$	$-\acuteo\mu\epsilon\theta\alpha$
$-\epsilon(\sigma)\alpha\iota = -\eta$	$-\epsilon\sigma\theta\epsilon$
$-\epsilon\tau\alpha\iota$	$-o\nu\tau\alpha\iota$

Imperfect and Second Aorist Active

$-o\nu$	$-o\mu\epsilon\nu$
$-\epsilon\varsigma$	$-\epsilon\tau\epsilon$
$-\epsilon(\nu)$	$-o\nu$

Imperfect M/P and Second Aorist Middle

$-\acuteo\mu\eta\nu$	$-\acuteo\mu\epsilon\theta\alpha$
$-\epsilon(\sigma)o = ou$	$-\epsilon\sigma\theta\epsilon$
$-\epsilon\tau o$	$-o\nu\tau o$

First Aorist Active

$-\alpha$	$-\alpha\mu\epsilon\nu$
$-\alpha\varsigma$	$-\alpha\tau\epsilon$
$-\epsilon(\nu)$	$-\alpha\nu$

First Aorist Middle

$-\acute\alpha\mu\eta\nu$	$-\acute\alpha\mu\epsilon\theta\alpha$
$-\alpha(\sigma)o = \omega$	$-\alpha\sigma\theta\epsilon$
$-\alpha\tau o$	$-\alpha\nu\tau o$

Perfect Active

$-\alpha$	$-\alpha\mu\epsilon\nu$
$-\alpha\varsigma$	$-\alpha\tau\epsilon$
$-\epsilon(\nu)$	$-\alpha\sigma\iota$

Perfect M/P

$-\mu\alpha\iota$	$-\mu\epsilon\theta\alpha$
$-\sigma\alpha\iota$	$-\sigma\theta\epsilon$
$-\tau\alpha\iota$	$-\nu\tau\alpha\iota$

Pluperfect Active

$-\epsilon\iota\nu$	$-\epsilon\iota\mu\epsilon\nu$
$-\epsilon\iota\varsigma$	$-\epsilon\iota\tau\epsilon$
$-\epsilon\iota$	$-\epsilon\iota\sigma\alpha\nu$

Pluperfect M/P

$-\mu\eta\nu$	$-\mu\epsilon\theta\alpha$
$-\sigma o$	$-\sigma\theta\epsilon$
$-\tau o$	$-\nu\tau o$

Aorist Passive

$-(\eta)\nu$	$-(\eta)\mu\epsilon\nu$
$-(\eta)s$	$-(\eta)\tau\epsilon$
$-(\eta)$	$-(\eta)\sigma\alpha\nu$

ἀποκρίνομαι, ---, ἀπεκρινάμην, ---, ---, ἀπεκρίθην   answer

ἀποκτείνω, ἀποκτενῶ, ἀπέκτεινα, ---, ---, ἀπεκτάνθην – kill (Again
    the liquid stem verb characteristics.)

φαίνω, φανοῦμαι, ἔφηνα,   ,   , ἐφάνην – shine, give light (The second
    principal part is a deponent future.); *passive:* appear, be or become visible
    [phenomenon]

χαίρω, χαρήσομαι, ---, ---, ---, ἐχάρην – rejoice (All forms have an
    active translation. The present imperative second singular and second
    plural forms function as a word of greeting, more or less formal depending
    on the circumstances: "hail," "greetings," "welcome," etc.)

Finally, note that the *second aorist* **active** forms of ἀναβαίνω and καταβαίνω
(Chapter 28) use the *same endings* as a second aorist passive: ἀνέβην /
κατέβην. They are still parsed, however, as aorist active.

PREPARING FOR THE QUIZ:

(1) Make sure you understand the **aspect** of the aorist and future tenses and how
to translate these two tenses (both the passive concept and deponent or special
meaning for passive verbs).

(2) You should know how to **recognize** an aorist passive form when you see it,
including recognizing the difference between a first aorist passive and a second
aorist passive.

(3) You should understand how the future passive is **formed regularly** from the
aorist passive.

(4) Learn the new vocabulary words (all principal parts), including the **aorist
active** of the compounds of βαίνω.

(5) Go through the master verb list for all of the **sixth principal parts**.

Chapter 31

–μι Verbs

–μι VERBS: In this chapter we will look at a small group of Greek verbs known as *–μι verbs*. The reason for the name is that the present active indicative first person singular form ends in these two letters. All the other verbs we have studied, with the exception of εἰμί, belong to the so-called –ω conjugation. There are not a lot of –μι verbs, but several of them are quite important and occur frequently. Generally, the second, fourth, fifth, and sixth principal parts present no problems in conjugation once the stems are learned. (For this reason, paradigms for these principal parts will not be written out in their entirety. If you need to check endings, you can refer to the paradigms in the chapters in which these principal parts are introduced.) The first and third principal parts, however, have some peculiarities which must be carefully noted. During the Koine period, the –μι verbs were gradually being phased out by attaching the regular –ω verb endings to –μι verb stems. You should not be surprised, therefore, to see a combination of the two sets of endings on any given –μι verb stem.

(1) δίδωμι: Since this is basically a form and vocabulary chapter, we will look at each verb individually and comment on whatever characteristics and translations need to be specially noted. We will begin with the verb δίδωμι ("give"; "grant"), since this verb most completely illustrates the various –μι verb characteristics. Two compounds of this verb should also be learned: ἀποδίδωμι ("pay"; "give back," "return") and παραδίδωμι ("hand over," "deliver"; "betray"; "hand down"). The principal parts are as follows:

> **δίδωμι, δώσω, ἔδωκα, δέδωκα, δέδομαι, ἐδόθην** [antidote, apodosis]

In looking at the conjugation of the present tense, four things need to be noted.

1) Some, but not all, of the active endings are different from the –ω conjugation endings.

–μι	–μεν
–ς	–τε
–σι(ν)	–ασι(ν)

2) The stem ends in a vowel, but this fluctuates between a long and short vowel (in the case of δίδωμι between *omega* and *omicron*).

3) There are no connecting vowels; the endings are added directly to the stem (as in the perfect M/P).

4) The first principal part (used for both present and imperfect) has a kind of reduplication using *iota*. This is a very useful characteristic to note, since *only these two tenses* have it.

```
* * * * * * * * * * * * * * * * * * * * * * * * * * * * * *
*      Present Active Indicative         Present M/P Indicative        *
*                                                                      *
*     Singular      Plural            Singular         Plural          *
*                                                                      *
* 1st  δίδωμι        δίδομεν           δίδομαι          διδόμεθα        *
* 2nd  δίδως         δίδοτε            δίδοσαι          δίδοσθε         *
* 3rd  δίδωσι(ν)     διδόασι(ν)        δίδοται          δίδονται        *
*                                                                      *
* * * * * * * * * * * * * * * * * * * * * * * * * * * * * *
```

In the imperfect, the δι– reduplication remains and an augment is added. Endings are regular, except that –σαν is used in the third person plural, so there is no first singular / third plural overlap. *In the **singular active** forms the stem vowel lengthens to –ου.*

```
* * * * * * * * * * * * * * * * * * * * * * * * * * * * * *
*      Imperfect Active Indicative        Imperfect M/P Indicative      *
*                                                                       *
*     Singular      Plural            Singular         Plural           *
*                                                                       *
* 1st  ἐδίδουν       ἐδίδομεν          ἐδιδόμην         ἐδιδόμεθα        *
* 2nd  ἐδίδους       ἐδίδοτε           ἐδίδοσο          ἐδίδοσθε         *
* 3rd  ἐδίδου        ἐδίδοσαν          ἐδίδοτο          ἐδίδοντο         *
*                                                                       *
* * * * * * * * * * * * * * * * * * * * * * * * * * * * * *
```

In the aorist active, the *omega* stem vowel is used and the endings are first aorist. The stem, however, ends in a ***kappa*** and must be carefully distinguished from the perfect active. (Note that some of the other μι verbs share this characteristic.) There is no aorist middle in use in the GNT.

```
* * * * * * * * * * * * * * * *
*     First Aorist Active Indicative     *
*                                        *
*       Singular        Plural           *
*                                        *
*  1ˢᵗ  ἔδωκα          ἐδώκαμεν          *
*  2ⁿᵈ  ἔδωκας         ἐδώκατε           *
*  3ʳᵈ  ἔδωκε(ν)       ἔδωκαν            *
*                                        *
* * * * * * * * * * * * * * * *
```

Remember that the other principal parts are regular. Just note *which stem vowel* is used: *omega* in the future and perfect (and pluperfect) active and *omicron* in the perfect (and pluperfect) M/P and aorist passive (and future passive).

(2) τίθημι: Our second –μι verb is τίθημι ("put," "place," "lay," "set"; "lay down"; "lay aside"). **Middle** forms have essentially the same translation as the active (as is also true, for example, of αἰτέω), but *sometimes* in a M/P situation the true passive sense will prevail. This also has a compound which should be learned: ἐπιτίθημι ("lay on / upon," "put on"). The stem vowel fluctuates between *eta* and *epsilon* (and in some forms ει). The principal parts are:

τίθημι, θήσω, ἔθηκα, τέθεικα, τέθειμαι, ἐτέθην [synthesis]

```
* * * * * * * * * * * * * * * * * * * * * * * * * * * * *
*    Present Active Indicative              Present M/P Indicative      *
*                                                                        *
*      Singular      Plural            Singular         Plural           *
*                                                                        *
*  1ˢᵗ  τίθημι       τίθεμεν           τίθεμαι          τιθέμεθα          *
*  2ⁿᵈ  τίθης        τίθετε            τίθεσαι          τίθεσθε           *
*  3ʳᵈ  τίθησι(ν)    τιθέασι(ν)        τίθεται          τίθενται          *
*                                                                        *
*    Imperfect Active Indicative            Imperfect M/P Indicative     *
*                                                                        *
*  1ˢᵗ  ἐτίθην       ἐτίθεμεν          ἐτιθέμην         ἐτιθέμεθα         *
*  2ⁿᵈ  ἐτίθεις      ἐτίθετε           ἐτίθεσο          ἐτίθεσθε          *
*  3ʳᵈ  ἐτίθει       ἐτίθεσαν          ἐτίθετο          ἐτίθεντο          *
*                                                                        *
* * * * * * * * * * * * * * * * * * * * * * * * * * * * *
```

The aorist active is a first aorist using the *eta* stem vowel and, like δίδωμι, having a stem ending in *kappa*. There is also a **second aorist middle** which uses the *epsilon* stem vowel (and has the typical vowel contraction in the second person singular).

```
* * * * * * * * * * * * * * * * * * * * * * * * * * * *
*    First Aorist Active Indicative    Second Aorist Middle Indicative  *
*                                                                       *
*       Singular      Plural           Singular        Plural           *
*                                                                       *
*   1ˢᵗ  ἔθηκα        ἐθήκαμεν          ἐθέμην          ἐθέμεθα          *
*   2ⁿᵈ  ἔθηκας       ἐθήκατε           ἔθου            ἔθεσθε           *
*   3ʳᵈ  ἔθηκε(ν)     ἔθηκαν            ἔθετο           ἔθεντο           *
*                                                                       *
* * * * * * * * * * * * * * * * * * * * * * * * * * * *
```

The other principal parts are regular: future using the *eta* stem vowel, perfect (and pluperfect) active and M/P using ει (the sound equivalent of *eta*), and aorist (and future) passive using *epsilon*.

(3) ἵστημι: The third of the "big three" (in terms of importance and frequency) is ἵστημι. It is more complicated in its use than the others and needs more detailed explanation. The stem vowel fluctuates between *eta* and *alpha*. The reduplication is just *iota* with a rough breathing. (It should have been σι, but the *sigma* slipped off leaving the rough breathing mark in its place.) The principal parts are:

> *ἵστημι (ἱστάνω), στήσω, ἔστησα / ἔστην, ἕστηκα, ---, ἐστάθην*
> [αποσταзу, hypostasis]

The problem with this verb is keeping the translation straight for the different forms. There are **both a transitive meaning and an intransitive one**. The transitive meaning (which is used in only four places) is "set," "place,"; "establish." The intransitive meaning is "stand" (also, if the context requires it, "stand still," "stop"; "stand firm"). In order to sort out all the translation information, we will look at each principal part separately. (Numbers refer to the principal parts.)

1) The present and imperfect forms of ἵστημι appear very rarely in the GNT in the basic verb alone, but they appear more often in some of its many compounds. For that reason, I have included the paradigms here, but not in the exercises. Concentrate your efforts on the other tenses which appear more frequently. When

you encounter the various compounds, be sure to check for whatever difference there may be between the transitive meaning and the intransitive one.

The ***present active*** is the first of the four forms which use the transitive meaning. The ἱστάνω form uses regular –ω conjugation endings. In the ἵστημι form, the stem vowel and ending contract in the third person plural. The ***present M/P*** has the intransitive meaning.

```
* * * * * * * * * * * * * * * * * * * * * * * * * * * *
*    Present Active Indicative         Present M/P Indicative      *
*                                                                  *
*    Singular      Plural         Singular      Plural             *
*                                                                  *
*  1ˢᵗ  ἵστημι      ἵσταμεν        ἵσταμαι       ἱστάμεθα           *
*  2ⁿᵈ  ἵστης       ἵστατε         ἵστασαι       ἵστασθε            *
*  3ʳᵈ  ἵστησι(ν)   ἱστᾶσι(ν)      ἵσταται       ἵστανται           *
*                                                                  *
* * * * * * * * * * * * * * * * * * * * * * * * * * * *
```

The ***imperfect active*** is the second of the forms to have the transitive meaning: "was / were setting." There is no further augment, so second person singular, first person plural, and second person plural are identical to present active. The imperfect M/P has the intransitive meaning: "was / were standing." First person plural and second person plural are identical to the present M/P.

```
* * * * * * * * * * * * * * * * * * * * * * * * * * * *
*    Imperfect Active Indicative        Imperfect M/P Indicative   *
*                                                                  *
*    Singular      Plural         Singular      Plural             *
*                                                                  *
*  1ˢᵗ  ἵστην       ἵσταμεν        ἱστάμην       ἱστάμεθα           *
*  2ⁿᵈ  ἵστης       ἵστατε         ἵστασαι       ἵστασθε            *
*  3ʳᵈ  ἵστη        ἵστασαν        ἵστατο        ἵσταντο            *
*                                                                  *
* * * * * * * * * * * * * * * * * * * * * * * * * * * *
```

2) The ***future active (στήσω)*** is transitive, translated "will set." The ***future middle (στήσομαι)*** is intransitive, translated "will stand."

3) The ***first aorist active (ἔστησα)*** is transitive (the fourth and last of the transitive forms), translated "set," "placed." A first aorist middle (ἐστησάμην) appears in a few compounds.

The **second aorist active** (ἔστην) is intransitive, translated "stood." (The endings are those of an aorist passive: compare ἀνέβην). In the third person plural only, the first and second aorist are the same.

```
* * * * * * * * * * | | | * * * * * * * †
*        Second Aorist Active Indicative      *
*                                             *
*        Singular              Plural         *
*                                             *
*   1st    ἔστην           ἔστημεν            *
*   2nd    ἔστης           ἔστητε             *
*   3rd    ἔστη            ἔστησαν            *
*                                             *
* * * * * * * * * * * * * * * * * * * *
```

4) The **perfect active** (ἔστηκα) is translated as a **present tense**: "stand," or "am / are / is standing" (compare οἶδα).

> εἶπεν δέ τις αὐτῷ, Ἰδοὺ ἡ μήτηρ σου καὶ οἱ ἀδελφοί σου ἔξω
> ἑστήκασιν ζητοῦντές σοι λαλῆσαι.

> And someone said to him, "Behold, your mother and your brothers <u>are standing</u> outside, seeking to talk to you." (Matthew 12:47)

The **pluperfect active** (εἱστήκειν) is intransitive, translated as an **imperfect / aorist**: "stood" or "was / were standing" (compare ᾔδειν).

> Ἔτι αὐτοῦ λαλοῦντος τοῖς ὄχλοις ἰδοὺ ἡ μήτηρ καὶ οἱ ἀδελφοὶ
> αὐτοῦ <u>εἱστήκεισαν</u> ἔξω ζητοῦντες αὐτῷ λαλῆσαι.

> And while he was still speaking to the crowds, behold his mother and brothers <u>were standing / stood</u> outside, seeking to talk to him. (Matthew 12:46)

6) The **aorist passive** (ἐστάθην) is intransitive, translated "stood."

> καὶ ἰδοὺ ὁ ἀστήρ, ὃν εἶδον ἐν τῇ ἀνατολῇ, προῆγεν αὐτούς,
> ἕως ἐλθὼν <u>ἐστάθη</u> ἐπάνω οὗ ἦν τὸ παιδίον.

> And behold the star, which they had seen in the east, kept going on ahead
> of them, until it came and <u>stood / stopped</u> over the place where the
> young child was. (Matthew 2:9)

The *future passive (σταθήσομαι)* is intransitive, translated "will stand."

***Summary*:**

(1) Remember the four places where the transitive translation is used (present active, imperfect active, future active, and *first* aorist active). All others are intransitive.

(2) Remember that first and second aorist have different translations and that the second aorist active has endings which look like aorist passive.

(3) Remember that the perfect and pluperfect will not use "have / has" and "had," but rather sound like present and imperfect / aorist. The perfect active form is quite common, since it is being used with a present translation.

There is also a compound of ἵστημι which you should learn: ἀνίστημι. It only has three principal parts, but does have the two separate aorist forms: ἀνίστημι, ἀναστήσω, ἀνέστησα / ἀνέστην (compare ἀνάστασις). This is the other of the two verbs used in talking about the resurrection, although it can also be used for ordinary circumstances.

> (1) Present active, future active, and first aorist active are transitive: "raise," "raise up."

> (2) Second aorist active and all middle forms are intransitive: "rise," "arise," "get up."

(4) ἀφίημι: Other —μι verbs occur less often in the GNT and/or have fewer principal parts.[1] Nevertheless, they deserve careful attention. The next one we will consider is ἀφίημι. This is a compound verb (ἀπό + ἵημι), but the basic verb does not appear in the GNT. The stem vowel fluctuates between *eta* and *epsilon*. Be careful with the many meanings, since they are not all interchangeable: "cancel"; "forgive," "pardon"; "leave"; "let," "allow"; "send away." Principal parts:

ἀφίημι, ἀφήσω, ἀφῆκα, ---, ἀφέωμαι, ἀφέθην

---

[1] For the summaries of this and the following verbs, I am indebted to Hewett (pp. 126 and 130-131).

The future active, aorist active (note the *kappa*), and aorist passive / future passive are regularly formed. Even though a first person singular form is given for the fifth principal part, in actuality only a third person plural (ἀφέωῖνται) is in use.

The present tense displays a mixture of –μι verb and –ω verb forms. The forms given here are the only ones which appear.

```
* * * * * * * * * * * * * * * * * * * * * * * * * * * * * * *
*          Present Active Indicative        Present M/P Indicative    *
*                                                                     *
*          Singular      Plural          Singular        Plural       *
*                                                                     *
*  1ˢᵗ   ἀφίημι       ἀφίομεν          ἀφίεμαι        ---           *
*  2ⁿᵈ   ἀφεῖς        ἀφίετε           ---            ---           *
*  3ʳᵈ   ἀφίησι(ν)    ἀφίουσι(ν)       ἀφίεται        ἀφίονται /    *
*                                                     ἀφίενται      *
* * * * * * * * * * * * * * * * * * * * * * * * * * * * * * *
```

The only imperfect form in use is a third person singular: ἤφιε.

(5) ἀπόλλυμι: The next verb is ἀπόλλυμι. There are ***separate meanings for active and middle forms***. ***Active***: "destroy," "lose," "kill." / ***Middle***: "be lost," "perish," "be ruined," "die." The future active has two forms, one with contract endings. Again there is a mix of –μι verb (using the stem vowel *upsilon*) and –ω verb forms. The perfect active appears only as a participle (see Chapter 32). Principal parts:

ἀπόλλυμι, ἀπολέσω (ἀπολῶ), ἀπώλεσα, ἀπόλωλα, ---, ---
[Apollyon, the angel of the bottomless pit (Rev. 9:11)]

There are not a lot of forms of this verb in use. This is a summary of those forms.

```
* * * * * * * * * * * * * * * * * * * * * * * * * *
*                    Singular              Plural         *
*                                                         *
*  Present Active:  3ʳᵈ ἀπολλύει      ----               *
*                                                         *
*  Present M/P:  1ˢᵗ ἀπόλλυμαι        ἀπολλύμεθα         *
*                3ʳᵈ ἀπόλλυται        ἀπόλλυνται         *
*                                                         *
* * * * * * * * * * * * * * * * * * * * * * * * * *
```

```
* * * * * * * * * * * * * * * * * * * * * * *
*                Singular              Plural     *
*                                                 *
*  Imperfect M/P: 3rd   ----        ἀπώλλυντο      *
*                                                 *
*  Future Active: 1st  ἀπολῶ                       *
*                 3rd  ἀπολέσει                    *
*                                                 *
*  Future Middle: 2nd   ----        ἀπολεῖσθε      *
*                 3rd  ἀπολεῖται     ἀπολοῦνται     *
*                                                 *
*  First Aorist Active: 1st  ἀπώλεσα               *
*                       3rd  ἀπώλεσε(ν)            *
*                                                 *
*  Second Aorist Middle: 3rd  ἀπώλετο   ἀπώλοντο    *
*                                                 *
* * * * * * * * * * * * * * * * * * * * * * *
```

(6) δείκνυμι: The verb δείκνυμι ("show") is well on the way to ceasing to be a –μι verb at all; only the present active first person and third person singular show –μι verb characteristics. There are only a few forms in use. The aorist passive appears only in participle form. Here are the principal parts:

δείκνυμι (δεικνύω), δείξω, ἔδειξα, ---, ---, ἐδείχθην [apodeictic]

Here are the indicative forms you will see:

```
* * * * * * * * * * * * * * * * * * *
*  Present Active:  1st s.  δείκνυμι       *
*                   2nd s.  δεικνύεις      *
*                   3rd s.  δείκνυσι(ν)    *
*                                          *
*  Future Active:  1st s. δείξω            *
*                  3rd s. δείξει           *
*                                          *
*  First Aorist Active:  1st s. ἔδειξα     *
*                        3rd s. ἔδειξε(ν)  *
*                                          *
* * * * * * * * * * * * * * * * * * *
```

(7) **φημί:** Our final verb, φημί ("say"), has only three forms in use. Note that the two present tense forms are enclitic.

```
✳ * * * * * * * * * * * * * * * ✳ ✳
*   Present Active: 3rd s.   φησί(ν)           *
*                   3rd pl.  φασί(ν)           *
*   Imperfect / Second Aorist Active:          *
*               3rd s. ἔφη ("he/she said")     *
*                                              *
* * * * * * * * * * * * * * * * * * *
```

VOCABULARY:

All the –μι verbs *and* their compounds introduced in the chapter.

μήτι – Used in questions to indicate either that a negative answer is expected or that the questioner is in some doubt about the answer. (This is a compound of μή, which can also be used in questions to anticipate a negative answer.) Such questions are often rhetorical.

μήτι οὗτός ἐστιν ὁ Χριστός;

This is not the Christ, is it? NASB [Negative answer expected.] / Can this be the Christ? RSV [Doubt about the answer expressed.] (John 4:29)

οὐχί Used in questions to indicate that an affirmative answer is expected. (You will also find οὐ alone used this way.)

Οὐχὶ δώδεκα ὧραί εἰσιν τῆς ἡμέρας;

Are there not twelve hours in the day [literally: "of the day"]? / There are twelve hours in the day, aren't there? (John 11:9a)

In addition to the –μι verbs discussed above, add the following two **deponents**. The present M/P and imperfect M/P are conjugated like –μι verbs, i.e., by adding the personal endings directly to the stem vowel.

κάθημαι, καθήσομαι, ---, ---, ---, --- – sit (literally and metaphorically for "be," "live") The second person singular present M/P is either κάθησαι or κάθη.

κεῖμαι, ---, ---, ---, ---, --- – lie (literally and metaphorically for "exist," "be")

PREPARING FOR THE EXAM:

(1) This exam covers several different kinds of material:

> 1) ***Relative pronouns*** and ***other relative words*** from Chapter 26.
> 2) ***Third declension neuter nouns*** and ***adjectives with some or all third declension forms*** from Chapter 27.
> 3) The ***fourth, fifth, and sixth principal parts*** of the verb from Chapters 28, 29, and 30.
> 4) The –μι ***verbs*** from Chapter 31.

Make sure that you spend enough time with each type of material to learn any new forms and to be aware of whatever else you need to know in order to work with the material.

(2) Familiarize yourself with any ***new terminology*** in recent chapters.

(3) ***Old quizzes*** are an excellent source of study material.

(4) For each chapter, think about ***what things have been stressed in class***. This is what you should expect to see on the test.

(5) Spend some time going back over the ***translation passages*** and working on your approach to translation.

(6) If you have not already done so, do the ***practice sentences*** (Chapter 27) and the ***verb parsing graph*** (Chapter 30).

Chapter 32
Participles: General Introduction / Participle Forms

PARTICIPLES: It is impossible to overestimate the importance of participles in the study of Greek. They are everywhere and appear in a seemingly infinite variety of forms. English has participles, too: a present participle, e.g., falling, dying, shining, and a past participle, e.g., fortified, prepared, fallen. These, like Greek participles, can be used as adjectives in phrases such as "the falling leaves," "the dying swan," "a shining star," "a fortified city," "a bride, prepared for her husband," and "the fallen hero." Here, however, the similarity ends, because, as we will see in Chapter 33, Greek participles are used in many ways which do not correspond at all to English usage. Before we can begin to look at participle uses, however, it is essential to be able to recognize the forms. Unless you can identify the form of a participle, it is not possible to determine how it is being used in a sentence. What follows is a summary of **basic information about participles**. Following that we will look at some specific examples.

1) A participle is a **verbal adjective**.

2) The **stem** of a participle comes from a **verb**.

3) The **endings** of a participle are **noun / adjective** endings. We will see **two patterns** emerge. The first pattern has third declension endings for masculine and neuter forms and first declension endings for feminine forms (the 3-1-3 pattern; compare the adjective πᾶς, πᾶσα, πᾶν). The second pattern has first declension feminine endings and second declension masculine and neuter endings (the 2-1-2 pattern: -ος, -η, -ον).

4) Like a verb, a participle has **tense and voice**.

5) Like a noun or adjective, a participle has **case, number, and gender**.

6) When asked to parse a participle, therefore, the following information should be given: **tense, voice, case, number, and gender (and, of course, first principal part)**.

7) Participles do not have mood *per se*, but for convenience, "participle" (abbreviated "part.") may be put in the mood column on a parsing graph.

8) The principal parts of the verb supply the **stems** used for participles.

> First principal part: present active participle
> present M/P participle
> Third principal part: first or second aorist active participle
> first or second aorist middle participle
> Fourth principal part: perfect active participle

Fifth principal part: perfect M/P participle
Sixth principal part: first or second aorist passive participle

9) There are no imperfect or pluperfect participles. There are future participles, but they are rare and not generally included in a basic presentation of participle forms. These would have the same stems as the indicative: second principal part for future active and middle and sixth principal part for future passive. The endings would be the same as the present active and present M/P participles.

10) The ***augment of the aorist tense is only used in the indicative***. This means that for participles, subjunctives, infinitives, and imperatives you must learn to recognize the ***aorist stems (third and sixth principal parts) without augment***. (You have had some experience doing this in forming the future passive from the sixth principal part. For help with some of the more common second aorist stems, see *Appendix C*.)

11) As we work through the forms, note the following parts of each participle: (1) the stem, (2) the endings, and (3) the letter(s) used to connect the endings to the stem. These will serve as your identifiers for the form.

12) The literal translations given for the participles are a ***starting point only***. Do *not* get too attached to them! Occasionally they will show up in your final translation, but more often they will be modified to express the specific function of the participle.

13) ***Verbs maintain their essential nature in the participles***. Deponent verbs will have middle and/or passive forms and active translations. Any special meanings for either the middle or passive will still be used for those forms. If the verb is not a deponent and there are no special meanings for middle or passive, then any M/P or passive participle will express the passive concept. If a verb has its direct object in the genitive or dative case, this will also be true of the participles (like verbs, participles can have direct objects).

14) The tenses continue to represent the same type of action as they did in the indicative. The present represents an on-going, continuous, or repeated action or something which is always happening or true. The aorist looks at the action as a whole (unitary action). The perfect emphasizes the present result of a past action or event. (The literal translation of the aorist and perfect participles may sound the same, but the view of the action is different.)

15) Outside of the indicative, verbal forms do not represent ***absolute time***. In the use of participles, however, tense *sometimes* represents ***relative time*** (relative to the main verb of the clause).

PRESENT ACTIVE PARTICIPLE:

(1) stem from first principal part
(2) connecting letters for masculine and neuter: ον (except nominative
    singular masculine, nominative and accusative singular neuter, and dative
    plural masculine and neuter) / connecting letters for feminine: –ουσ –
(3) third declension endings for masculine (compare ἄρχων) and neuter / first
    declension (-α, -ης) endings for feminine [3-1-3 pattern] *Note:* Feminine
    participles in the 3-1-3 pattern accent the ultima of the genitive plural,
    those in the 2-1-2 pattern do not.

```
* * * * * * * * * * * * * * * * * * * * * *
*                                          *
*    Present Active Participle of σῴζω: saving   *
*                                          *
*        M.            F.            N.     *
*                                          *
*                 Singular                 *
*                                          *
* N.  σῴζων       σῴζουσα      σῶζον        *
* G.  σῴζοντος    σῳζούσης     σῴζοντος     *
* D.  σῴζοντι     σῳζούσῃ      σῴζοντι      *
* A.  σῴζοντα     σῴζουσαν     σῶζον        *
*                                          *
*                  Plural                  *
*                                          *
* N.  σῴζοντες    σῴζουσαι     σῴζοντα      *
* G.  σῳζόντων    σῳζουσῶν     σῳζόντων     *
* D.  σῴζουσι(ν)  σῳζούσαις    σῴζουσι(ν)   *
* A.  σῴζοντας    σῳζούσας     σῴζοντα      *
*                                          *
* * * * * * * * * * * * * * * * * * * * * *
```

Other examples:

ἑτοιμάζων, ἑτοιμάζουσα, ἑτοιμάζον – preparing
ἀποστέλλων, ἀποστέλλουσα, ἀποστέλλον – sending out
ἐκβάλλων, ἐκβάλλουσα, ἐκβάλλον – casting out
στρέφων, στρέφουσα, στρέφον – turning [*transitive*]

PRESENT (ACTIVE) PARTICIPLE OF εἰμί: being [ontology]

```
* * * * * * * * * * * * * * * * * * * * * * * * * * * * * * * *
*              Singular                         Plural          *
*                                                               *
*     M.        F.        N.         M.        F.        N.      *
*                                                               *
*  N. ὤν       οὖσα      ὄν        ὄντες     οὖσαι     ὄντα      *
*  G. ὄντος    οὔσης     ὄντος     ὄντων     οὐσῶν     ὄντων     *
*  D. ὄντι     οὔσῃ      ὄντι      οὖσι(ν)   οὔσαις    οὖσι(ν)   *
*  A. ὄντα     οὖσαν     ὄν        ὄντας     οὔσας     ὄντα      *
*                                                               *
* * * * * * * * * * * * * * * * * * * * * * * * * * * * * * * *
```

PRESENT M/P PARTICIPLE:

(1) stem from first principal part
(2) connecting letters: *omicron* + –μεν–
(3) regular first (-η, -ης) / second declension adjective endings [2-1-2 pattern]

```
* * * * * * * * * * * * * * * * * * * * * * * * * * *
*         Present M/P Participle of σῴζω: being saved    *
*                                                        *
*         M.              F.              N.              *
*                                                        *
*                     Singular                           *
*                                                        *
*  N. σῳζόμενος       σῳζομένη        σῳζόμενον           *
*  G. σῳζομένου       σῳζομένης       σῳζομένου           *
*  D. σῳζομένῳ        σῳζομένῃ        σῳζομένῳ            *
*  A. σῳζόμενον       σῳζομένην       σῳζόμενον           *
*                                                        *
*                     Plural                             *
*                                                        *
*  N. σῳζόμενοι       σῳζόμεναι       σῳζόμενα            *
*  G. σῳζομένων       σῳζομένων       σῳζομένων           *
*  D. σῳζομένοις      σῳζομέναις      σῳζομένοις          *
*  A. σῳζομένους      σῳζομένας       σῳζόμενα            *
*                                                        *
* * * * * * * * * * * * * * * * * * * * * * * * * * *
```

Other examples.

> ἑτοιμαζόμενος, ἑτοιμαζομένη, ἑτοιμαζόμενον – being prepared
> ἐκβαλλόμενος, ἐκβαλλομένη, ἐκβαλλόμενον – being cast out
> στρεφόμενος, στρεφομένη, στρεφόμενον – turning [*intransitive*
>   meaning for passive forms]
> ἐρχόμενος, ἐρχομένη, ἐρχόμενον – coming [deponent]

FIRST AORIST ACTIVE PARTICIPLE:

(1) stem from first aorist third principal part (***without augment***)
(2) connecting letters for masculine and neuter: –αντ– (except nominative
    singular masculine, nominative and accusative singular neuter, and dative
    plural masculine and neuter) / connecting letters for feminine: –ασ–
(3) third declension endings for masculine and neuter / first declension endings
    for feminine (compare πᾶς, πᾶσα, πᾶν) [3-1-3 pattern]

```
*********************************
*                                                        *
*     First Aorist Active Participle of στρέφω:          *
*            having turned (transitive)                  *
*                                                        *
*     M.               F.               N.               *
*                                                        *
*                   Singular                             *
*                                                        *
* N.  στρέψας       στρέψασα        στρέψαν               *
* G.  στρέψαντος    στρεψάσης       στρέψαντος            *
* D.  στρέψαντι     στρεψάσῃ        στρέψαντι             *
* A.  στρέψαντα     στρέψασαν       στρέψαν               *
*                                                        *
*                   Plural                               *
*                                                        *
* N.  στρέψαντες    στρέψασαι       στρέψαντα             *
* G.  στρεψάντων    στρεψασῶν       στρεψάντων            *
* D.  στρέψασι(ν)   στρεψάσαις      στρέψασι(ν)           *
* A.  στρέψαντας    στρεψάσας       στρέψαντα             *
*                                                        *
*********************************
```

NOTE: The ***nominative singular masculine*** and the ***accusative plural feminine***
are notorious for causing confusion. The accusative plural feminine has ***one more
syllable:*** –ασ–. The nominative singular masculine form is more common.

Other examples:

σώσας, σώσασα, σῶσαν – having saved
ἑτοιμάσας, ἑτοιμάσασα, ἑτοιμάσαν – having prepared
ἀποστείλας, ἀποστείλασα, ἀποστεῖλαν – having sent out
ἐνέγκας, ἐνέγκασα, ἐνέγκαν – having brought [φέρω]

FIRST AORIST MIDDLE PARTICIPLE:

(1) stem from first aorist third principal part (***without augment***)
(2) connecting letters: *alpha* + –μεν–
(3) regular first (-η, -ης) / second declension adjective endings [2-1-2 pattern]

```
* * * * * * * * * * * * * * * * * * * * * * * * * *
*                                                    *
*           First Aorist Middle Participle of δέχομαι: *
*                     having received                *
*                                                    *
*        M.                F.                N.      *
*                                                    *
*                      Singular                      *
*                                                    *
* N.  δεξάμενος      δεξαμένη       δεξάμενον        *
* G.  δεξαμένου      δεξαμένης      δεξαμένου        *
* D.  δεξαμένῳ       δεξαμένη       δεξαμένῳ         *
* A.  δεξάμενον      δεξαμένην      δεξάμενον        *
*                                                    *
*                       Plural                       *
*                                                    *
* N.  δεξάμενοι      δεξάμεναι      δεξάμενα         *
* G.  δεξαμένων      δεξαμένων      δεξαμένων        *
* D.  δεξαμένοις     δεξαμέναις     δεξαμένοις       *
* A.  δεξαμένους     δεξαμένας      δεξάμενα         *
*                                                    *
* * * * * * * * * * * * * * * * * * * * * * * * * *
```

NOTE: In actual usage, you will most often encounter this form for deponents with a first aorist third principal part or verbs for which there is a special meaning for middle forms.

Other examples:

προσευξάμενος, προσευξαμένη, προσευξάμενον – having prayed
ἁψάμενος, ἁψαμένη, ἁψάμενον – having touched

FIRST AORIST PASSIVE PARTICIPLE:

(1) stem from first aorist sixth principal part (***without augment and without eta***)
(2) connecting letters for masculine and neuter: –*cντ*– (except nominative
 singular masculine, nominative and accusative singular neuter, and dative
 plural masculine and neuter) / connecting letters for feminine: –εισ–
(3) third declension endings for masculine and neuter / first declension (-α, -ης)
 endings for feminine [3-1-3 pattern]

```
* * * * * * * * * * * * * * * * * * * * * * * * *
*        First Aorist Passive Participle of ἐκβάλλω:        *
*                   having been cast out                    *
*                                                           *
*        M.              F.              N.                 *
*                                                           *
*                     Singular                              *
*                                                           *
*  N.  ἐκβληθείς      ἐκβληθεῖσα      ἐκβληθέν               *
*  G.  ἐκβληθέντος    ἐκβληθείσης     ἐκβληθέντος            *
*  D.  ἐκβληθέντι     ἐκβληθείσῃ      ἐκβληθέντι             *
*  A.  ἐκβληθέντα     ἐκβληθεῖσαν     ἐκβληθέν               *
*                                                           *
*                      Plural                               *
*                                                           *
*  N.  ἐκβληθέντες    ἐκβληθεῖσαι     ἐκβληθέντα             *
*  G.  ἐκβληθέντων    ἐκβληθεισῶν     ἐκβληθέντων            *
*  D.  ἐκβληθεῖσι(ν)  ἐκβληθείσαις    ἐκβληθεῖσι(ν)          *
*  A.  ἐβληθέντας     ἐκβληθείσας     ἐκβληθέντα             *
*                                                           *
* * * * * * * * * * * * * * * * * * * * * * * * *
```

Other examples:

σωθείς, σωθεῖσα, σωθέν – having been saved
ἐγερθείς, ἐγερθεῖσα, ἐγερθέν – having arisen / having been raised
πορευθείς, πορευθεῖσα, πορευθέν – having gone

SECOND AORIST ACTIVE PARTICIPLE:

(1) stem from second aorist third principal part (***without augment***)

(2) connecting letters for masculine and neuter: –οντ– except nominative
    singular masculine, nominative and accusative singular neuter, and dative
    plural masculine and neuter) / connecting letters for feminine: –ουσ–

(3) third declension endings for masculine and neuter / first declension (-α, -ης)
    endings for feminine [3-1-3 pattern]

```
* * * * * * * * * * * * * * * * * * * * * * *
*                                             *
*     Second Aorist Active Participle of ὁράω: *
*                  having seen                 *
*                                             *
*                   Singular                   *
*                                             *
*         M.            F.            N.        *
*                                             *
*   N.  ἰδών         ἰδοῦσα        ἰδόν         *
*   G.  ἰδόντος      ἰδούσης       ἰδόντος      *
*   D.  ἰδόντι       ἰδούσῃ        ἰδόντι       *
*   A.  ἰδόντα       ἰδοῦσαν       ἰδόν         *
*                                             *
*                    Plural                    *
*                                             *
*   N.  ἰδόντες      ἰδοῦσαι       ἰδόντα       *
*   G.  ἰδόντων      ἰδουσῶν       ἰδόντων      *
*   D.  ἰδοῦσι(ν)    ἰδούσαις      ἰδοῦσι(ν)    *
*   A.  ἰδόντας      ἰδούσας       ἰδόντα       *
*                                             *
* * * * * * * * * * * * * * * * * * * * * * *
```

Other examples:

ἐκβαλών, ἐκβαλοῦσα, ἐκβαλόν – having cast out

ἐλθών, ἐλθοῦσα, ἐλθόν – having come [ἔρχομαι]

εἰπών, εἰποῦσα, εἰπόν – having said / spoken [λέγω]

πεσών, πεσοῦσα, πεσόν – having fallen [πίπτω]

NOTE: *The connecting letters and endings of the second aorist active participle are the same as those of the present active participle. Obviously the stem is different and in some forms the accent is one syllable closer to the end of the word.*

SECOND AORIST MIDDLE PARTICIPLE:

(1) stem from second aorist third principal part (***without augment***)

(2) connecting letters: *omicron* + μεν

(3) regular first (-η, -ης) / second declension adjective endings [2-1-2 pattern]

The present M/P and the second aorist middle have the same connecting letters and endings. The stem must be carefully observed.

> γενόμενος, γενομένη, γενόμενον (The second aorist middle participle
>   of γίνομαι is the only one you will see with any regularity.)

SECOND AORIST PASSIVE PARTICIPLE:

(1) stem from second aorist sixth principal part (***without augment and without eta***)

(2) same endings as first aorist passive

(3) same connecting letters as first aorist passive

* *

Second Aorist Passive Participle of ἀποστέλλω:
having been sent out

	M.	F.	N.
		Singular	
N.	ἀποσταλείς	ἀποσταλεῖσα	ἀποσταλέν
G.	ἀποσταλέντος	ἀποσταλείσης	ἀποσταλέντος
D.	ἀποσταλέντι	ἀποσταλείσῃ	ἀποσταλέντι
A.	ἀποσταλέντα	ἀποσταλεῖσαν	ἀποσταλέν
		Plural	
N.	ἀποσταλέντες	ἀποσταλεῖσαι	ἀποσταλέντα
G.	ἀποσταλέντων	ἀποσταλεισῶν	ἀποσταλέντων
D.	ἀποσταλεῖσι(ν)	ἀποσταλείσαις	ἀποσταλεῖσι(ν)
A.	ἀποσταλέντας	ἀποσταλείσας	ἀποσταλέντα

* *

Other examples:

> στραφείς, στραφεῖσα, στραφέν – having turned [στρέφω – *intransitive*]
>
> φανείς, φανεῖσα, φανέν – having appeared [φαίνω]

PERFECT ACTIVE PARTICIPLE:

(1) stem from fourth principal part (***reduplication stays***)

(2) connecting letters for masculine and neuter: –οτ– (except nominative singular masculine, nominative and accusative singular neuter, and dative plural masculine and neuter) ***Note that this differs from other forms which use third declension endings in not having a nu.*** / connecting letters for feminine: –υι–

(3) third declension endings for masculine and neuter / first declension (-α, -ας) endings for feminine [3-1-3 pattern]

```
* * * * * * * * * * * * * * * * * * * * * * * * * * * * *
*        Perfect Active Participle of ἑτοιμάζω: having prepared   *
*                                                               *
*            M.              F.              N.                 *
*                                                               *
*                          Singular                            *
*                                                               *
*   N.   ἡτοιμακώς        ἡτοιμακυῖα      ἡτοιμακός            *
*   G.   ἡτοιμακότος      ἡτοιμακυίας     ἡτοιμακότος          *
*   D.   ἡτοιμακότι       ἡτοιμακυίᾳ      ἡτοιμακότι           *
*   A.   ἡτοιμακότα       ἡτοιμακυῖαν     ἡτοιμακός            *
*                                                               *
*                           Plural                             *
*                                                               *
*   N.   ἡτοιμακότες      ἡτοιμακυῖαι     ἡτοιμακότα           *
*   G.   ἡτοιμακότων      ἡτοιμακυιῶν     ἡτοιμακότων          *
*   D.   ἡτοιμακόσι(ν)    ἡτοιμακυίαις    ἡτοιμακόσι(ν)        *
*   A.   ἡτοιμακότας      ἡτοιμακυίας     ἡτοιμακότα           *
*                                                               *
* * * * * * * * * * * * * * * * * * * * * * * * * * * * *
```

Other examples:

> σεσωκώς, σεσωκυῖα, σεσωκός – having saved
>
> ἀπεσταλκώς, ἀπεσταλκυῖα, ἀπεσταλκός – having sent out
>
> ἐληλυθώς, ἐληλυθυῖα, ἐληλυθός – having come [ἔρχομαι]

εἰδώς, εἰδυῖα, εἰδός – knowing [οἶδα] (*Make a careful note of this*
*stem. In the **indicative** the stem ειδ represents the **aorist of***
ὁράω. *The same stem is used for the **participle, subjunctive, and***
infinitive of οἶδα.)
ἀπολωλώς, ἀπολωλυῖα, ἀπολωλός – lost [ἀπόλλυμι]

The perfect active participle of ἵστημι has both a regular form (ἑστηκώς,
ἑστηκυῖα, ἑστηκύς) and a contracted form (ἑστώς, ἑστῶσα, ἑστός). The
neuter nominative / accusative singular should also be (and sometimes is)
contracted to ἑστώς, but this is usually avoided in order to distinguish it from the
masculine.

```
* * * * * * * * * * * * * * * * * * *
*        Perfect Active Participle of ἵστημι          *
*           (Contracted Form): standing               *
*                                                     *
*                    Singular                         *
*                                                     *
*        M.            F.            N.               *
*                                                     *
* N. ἑστώς       ἑστῶσα        ἑστός                  *
* G. ἑστῶτος     ἑστώσας       ἑστῶτος                *
* D. ἑστῶτι      ἑστώσᾳ        ἑστῶτι                 *
* A. ἑστῶτα      ἑστῶσαν       ἑστός                  *
*                                                     *
*                     Plural                          *
*                                                     *
* N. ἑστῶτες     ἑστῶσαι       ἑστῶτα                 *
* G. ἑστώτων     ἑστωσῶν       ἑστώτων                *
* D. ἑστῶσι(ν)   ἑστώσαις      ἑστῶσι(ν)              *
* A. ἑστῶτας     ἑστώσας       ἑστῶτα                 *
*                                                     *
* * * * * * * * * * * * * * * * * * *
```

PERFECT M/P PARTICIPLE:

(1) stem from fifth principal part (**reduplication stays**)
(2) connecting letters: –μεν–
(3) regular first (-η, -ης) and second declension endings

Rejoice! You already know this one (Chapter 29). Remember that there is no connecting vowel and that the accent is always on the μεν syllable.

Examples:

    σεσωμένος, σεσωμένη, σεσωμένον – (having been) saved
    δεδομένος, δεδομένη, δεδομένον – (having been) given
    βεβλημένος, βεβλημένη, βεβλημένον – thrown
    πεπορευμένος, πεπορευμένη, πεπορευμένον – having gone

CONTRACT VERBS AND –μι VERBS: There are two categories of verbs which always require a little extra comment: contract verbs (in the present tense only) and –μι verbs (present active and M/P and aorist active and middle).

Contract verbs follow the regular rules for vowel contractions.

Epsilon contract verbs:

    present active masculine – ποιῶν, ποιοῦντος, etc.
    present active feminine – ποιοῦσα, ποιούσης, etc.
    present active neuter – ποιοῦν, ποιοῦντος, etc.
    present M/P – ποιούμενος, ποιουμένη, ποιούμενον

Alpha contract verbs:

    present active masculine – τιμῶν, τιμῶντος, etc.
    present active feminine – τιμῶσα, τιμώσης, etc.
    present active neuter – τιμῶν, τιμῶντος, etc.
    present M/P – τιμώμενος, τιμωμένη, τιμώμενον

Omicron contract verbs:

    present active masculine – πληρῶν, πληροῦντος, etc.
    present active feminine – πληροῦσα, πληρούσης, etc.
    present active neuter – πληροῦν, πληροῦντος, etc.
    present M/P – πληρούμενος, πληρουμένη, πληρούμενον

(1) δίδωμι

```
* * * * * * * * * * * * * * * * * * * * * * * *
*            Present Active Participle of δίδωμι           *
*                                                          *
*                        Singular                          *
*                                                          *
*            M.            F.            N.               *
*                                                          *
*   N.  διδούς        διδοῦσα       διδόν               *
*   G.  διδόντος      διδούσης      διδόντος            *
*   D.  διδόντι       διδούσῃ       διδόντι             *
*   A.  διδόντα       διδοῦσαν      διδόν               *
*                                                          *
*                         Plural                           *
*   N.  διδόντες      διδοῦσαι      διδόντα             *
*   G.  διδόντων      δισουσῶν      διδόντων            *
*   D.  διδοῦσι(ν)    διδούσαις     διδοῦσι(ν)          *
*   A.  διδόντας      διδούσας      διδόντα             *
*                                                          *
* * * * * * * * * * * * * * * * * * * * * * * *
```

Present M/P Participle: διδόμενος, διδομένη, διδόμενον

δίδωμι, τίθημι, and ἀφίημι have a different second aorist stem for the aorist active and, in the case of τίθημι, middle participles (and other non-indicative forms) from the one used for their indicative forms. For δίδωμι the stem is δ + the variable vowels ο / ου. The aorist active participle looks exactly like the present active participle without the δι.

Second Aorist Active Participle: δούς, δοῦσα, δόν (genitive singular: δόντος, δούσης, δόντος)

No aorist middle participles of δίδωμι appear in the GNT. For the remaining –μι verbs, if a present active or M/P or an aorist active or middle participle is not listed, this is either because the form does not appear in the GNT or because the form does not have unique –μι verb characteristics.

The second aorist active participle of **γινώσκω** follows the pattern of the aorist active participle of δίδωμι: γνούς, γνοῦσα, γνόν (genitive singular: γνόντος, γνούσης, γνόντος).

(2) τίθημι

The present active participle of τίθημι is an often mistaken form, since the stem includes a *theta* and the vowel(s), accent, and endings look exactly like those of the ***aorist passive participle***. The τι is the distinguishing feature, since this only appears on present (and imperfect indicative) forms.

```
* * * * * * * * * * * * * * * * * * * * * * *
*          Present Active Participle of τίθημι        *
*                                                     *
*                      Singular                       *
*                                                     *
*          M.            F.            N.             *
*                                                     *
* N.  τιθείς       τιθεῖσα       τιθέν               *
* G.  τιθέντος     τιθείσης      τιθέντος            *
* D.  τιθέντι      τιθείσῃ       τιθέντι             *
* A.  τιθέντα      τιθεῖσαν      τιθέν               *
*                                                     *
*                       Plural                        *
* N.  τιθέντες     τιθεῖσαι      τιθέντα             *
* G.  τιθέντων     τιθεισῶν      τιθέντων            *
* D.  τιθεῖσι(ν)   τιθείσαις     τιθεῖσι(ν)          *
* A.  τιθέντας     τιθείσας      τιθέντα             *
*                                                     *
* * * * * * * * * * * * * * * * * * * * * * *
```

Present M/P Participle: τιθέμενος, τιθεμένη, τιθέμενον

The second aorist active and middle stem for participles and other non-indicative forms of τίθημι is θ + the variable vowels ε / ει. The aorist forms look exactly like the present forms without the τι.

Second Aorist Active Participle: θείς, θεῖσα, θέν (genitive singular: θέντος, θείσης, θέντος)

Second Aorist Middle Participle: θέμενος, θεμένη, θέμενον

(3) ἀφίημι

The present active and second aorist active participles of ἀφίημι use the same endings as the present and aorist active participles of τίθημι. The aorist stem is ἀφ + ε / ει. This means that there is only a difference of one letter, the *iota*, between the present and aorist.

Present Active Participle: ἀφιείς, ἀφιεῖσα, ἀφιέν (genitive singular.
   ἀφιέντος, ἀφιείσης, ἀφιέντος)

Second Aorist Active Participle: ἀφείς, ἀφεῖσα, ἀφέν (genitive singular:
   ἀφέντος, ἀφείσης, ἀφέντος)

(4) ἵστημι

Both the present active participle and the **second** aorist active participle are formed using the vowel *alpha*. Thus there is only the *iota* to distinguish between the present and second aorist active forms. Remember that the present active participle will use the transitive meaning ("putting," "setting," etc.), whereas the second aorist will use the intransitive meaning ("having stood").

```
* * * * * * * * * * * * * * * * * * * * * *
*          Present Active Participle of ἵστημι          *
*                                                        *
*                      Singular                          *
*                                                        *
*         M.            F.            N.                 *
*                                                        *
*   N.  ἱστάς       ἱστᾶσα       ἱστάν            *
*   G.  ἱστάντος    ἱστάσης      ἱστάντος         *
*   D.  ἱστάντι     ἱστάση       ἱστάντι          *
*   A.  ἱστάντα     ἱστᾶσαν      ἱστάν            *
*                                                        *
*                       Plural                           *
*   N.  ἱστάντες    ἱστᾶσαι      ἱστάντα          *
*   G.  ἱστάντων    ἱστασῶν      ἱστάντων         *
*   D.  ἱστᾶσι(ν)   ἱστάσαις     ἱστᾶσι(ν)        *
*   A.  ἱστάντας    ἱστάσας      ἱστάντα          *
*                                                        *
* * * * * * * * * * * * * * * * * * * * * *
```

Second Aorist Active: στάς, στᾶσα, στάν (genitive singular: στάντος, στάσης, στάτος)

There is also a present M/P participle, though like the indicative, you will see it more in compounds: ἱστάμενος, ἱσταμένη, ἱστάμενον. It would have the intransitive meaning "standing," but this is taken over largely by the perfect.

The compound **ἀνίστημι** (as is typical of compounds) uses the same forms.

Present Active Participle: ἀνιστάς, ἀνιστᾶσα, ἀνιστάν (genitive singular: ἀνιστάντος, ἀνιστάσης, ἀνιστάντος) – transitive: "raising"

Second Aorist Active Participle: ἀναστάς, ἀναστᾶσα, ἀναστάν (genitive singular: ἀναστάντος, ἀναστάσης, ἀναστάντος) – intransitive: "having risen"

The second aorist active of compounds of **βαίνω** uses the same endings and accent pattern as the present and second aorist active of ἵστημι and ἀνίστημι for their participles:

> ἀναβάς, ἀναβᾶσα, ἀναβάν (genitive singular: ἀναβάντος, ἀναβάσης, ἀναβάντος)
> καταβάς, καταβᾶσα, καταβάν (genitive singular: καταβάντος, καταβάσης, καταβάντος)

(5) ἀπόλλυμι

Present M/P Participle: ἀπολλύμενος, ἀπολλυμένη, ἀπολλύμενον ("perishing")

PARTICIPLE FORMATION CHART: The chart on the next page will help for most *omega* verbs (exceptions are noted in the text). Do not, however, use it as a substitute for studying the paradigms. Remember that –μι verbs do not always play by the rules and sometimes borrow forms from other patterns, so give them a little extra attention. The connecting letters for contract verbs in the present tense will show the vowel contractions.

Participle Formation Chart

Participle	Stem	Connecting letters	Endings
Present Active	1st principal part	M. / N. $-o\nu\tau-$	3rd declension
		[nom. sing. masc. $-\omega\nu$]	
		[nom. / acc. sing. neut. $-o\nu$]	
		[dat. pl. masc. / neut. $-o\nu\sigma\iota(\nu)$]	
		F. $-o\nu\sigma-$	1st declension (-α, -ης)
Present M/P	1st principal part	$-o\mu\epsilon\nu-$	1st (-η, -ης) / 2nd declension
1st Aorist Active	3rd principal part (no augment)	M. / N. $-\alpha\nu\tau-$	3rd declension
		[nom. sing. masc. $-\alpha s$]	
		[nom. / acc. sing. neut. $-\alpha\nu$]	
		[dat. pl. masc. / neut. $-\alpha\sigma\iota(\nu)$]	
		F. $-\alpha\sigma-$	1st declension (-α, -ης)
1st Aorist Middle	3rd principal part (no augment)	$-\alpha\mu\epsilon\nu-$	1st (-η, -ης) / 2nd declension
2nd Aorist Active	3rd principal part (no augment)	M. / N. $-o\nu\tau-$	3rd declension
		[nom. sing. masc. $-\acute{\omega}\nu$]	
		[nom. / acc. sing. $-\acute{o}\nu$]	
		[dat. pl. masc. / neut. $-o\hat{\upsilon}\sigma\iota(\nu)$]	
		F. $-o\nu\sigma-$	1st declension (-α, -ης)
2nd Aorist Middle	3rd principal part (no augment)	$-o\mu\epsilon\nu-$	1st (-η, -ης) / 2nd declension
Aorist Passive	6th principal part (no augment and no eta)	M. / N. $-\epsilon\nu\tau-$	3rd declension
		[nom. sing. masc. $\epsilon\acute{\iota}s$]	
		[nom. / acc. sing. neut. $\acute{\epsilon}\nu$]	
		[dat. pl. masc. / neut. $-\epsilon\hat{\iota}\sigma\iota(\nu)$]	
		F. $-\epsilon\iota\sigma-$	1st declension (-α, -ης)
Perfect Active	4th principal part	M. / N. $-o\tau-$ (no nu)	3rd declension
		[nom. sing. masc. $-\acute{\omega}s$]	
		[nom. / acc. sing. neut. $-\acute{o}s$]	
		[dat. pl. masc. / neut. $-\acute{o}\sigma\iota(\nu)$]	
		F. $-\upsilon\iota-$	1st declension (-α, -ας)
Perfect M/P	5th principal part	$-\mu\epsilon\nu-$	1st (-η, -ης) / 2nd declension

PREPARING FOR THE QUIZ:

(1) On the one hand, there is a huge amount of material in this chapter. But, on the other hand, you already know most of the pieces, i.e., the verb principal parts and the noun / adjective endings. Begin by going back through the chapter carefully and ***observing the patterns***. Use both the paradigms in the chapter and the chart of form information.

(2) Work on the exercises carefully. Make a careful note of the ***information you must give to identify a participle***. As you do the identifications in Parts III, IV, and V, try to give as much information as you can without checking the answer key. Then check the key to see how you are doing. If you are consistently missing something, go back to that part of the chapter and figure out why.

(3) ***Identifying the aorist stems without the augment*** is a challenge at first. Remember that the other new forms you will be leaning also have this characteristic, so it is good to get used to it as soon as possible. Use the guide to aorist stems to help you.

(4) Note that several of the forms of the ***present participle of*** εἰμί are on the *Accents and Breathing Marks That Matter* list.

Chapter 33
Participle Uses

PARTICIPLE USED. Participles in Greek present the student with a unique challenge, because they are used in a wide variety of ways, *most of which do not correspond at all to English participle usage.* Great care must be used to

(1) Identify all aspects of the participle (tense, voice, case, number, and gender).

(2) Determine the *function* of the participle and its *relationship* to the other words in the sentence. These other words include the written or unwritten word with which the participle agrees (in case, number, and gender), the main verb of the clause, and any objects, adverbs, or prepositional phrases which go with the participle.

(3) *Use all the necessary English words to convey the idea expressed by the participle.*

Both the second and third points require considerable practice, because the precise meaning of the participle is often elusive and can only be ascertained by a careful analysis of the context in which it appears.

The examples which follow will serve to illustrate the primary participle uses. *Study them carefully and refer to them while you work on the translation passages.* Keep in mind that, although the participle is always in the *form* of an adjective, the uses are categorized according to the type of information which the participle conveys. (As we go through the uses, you may notice that many of them correspond to various subordinate clauses which you have already learned. I am often asked why the writers did not just stick to these other clauses and forget about the participles. The answer is that the participles were available, they are very versatile and concise, and the writers simply liked to use them.) In writing this chapter and the ones which follow, I have made an effort to co-ordinate the material as much as possible with *Greek Grammar Beyond the Basics,* since that is the recommended grammar book for advanced work. With all but one exception, I have used Wallace's categories, in order to make the transition from beginning to advanced work easier. If you wish to read his somewhat more detailed explanation of participle uses, see pp. 612-655. (Note that a few of the uses have not been included in this introductory material.)

ADJECTIVAL PROPER: The participle functions in essentially the same way as a modifying adjective. The two most common word orders are:

(1) article / modifier (in this case a participle) / noun [First attributive position. See Chapter 14 for information on the attributive position.]

τοῦ φαινομένου ἀστέρος   the <u>appearing</u> star   (Matthew 2:7)

(2) article / noun / article / modifier [Second attributive position. This is used quite often for participles.]

> τὸ ὕδωρ τὸ <u>ζῶν</u>   the <u>living</u> water (John 4:11b)

Also possible is: noun / modifier or modifier / noun (without an article)

> ὕδωρ <u>ζῶν</u>   <u>living</u> water (John 4:10)

The three preceding examples may be translated using the literal starting point translation for the present participles. Very often, however, additional information is associated with the participle. Since it comes from a verb, a participle may have a direct object or an indirect object of its own or may be modified by adverbs or prepositional phrases. These extra words make it impossible to give a literal translation of the participial phrase (the participle itself and any other words associated with it) in English.   For this reason, ***the best translation of an adjectival proper participle is often as a relative clause***. For example, consider the phrase ὁ πατήρ σου ὁ <u>βλέπων</u> ἐν τῷ κρύπτῳ (Matthew 6:4b). A literal translation would be "your seeing in secret Father." This obviously will not work, and so a relative clause is used instead: "your Father <u>who sees</u> in secret."

> τῆς χάριτος τῆς <u>δοθείσης</u> μοι
>
> the grace <u>which was given</u> to me (Romans 12:3)
>
> τὸν πατέρα τὸν <u>πέμψαντα</u> αὐτόν
>
> the Father <u>who sent</u> him (John 5:23b)
>
> κολυμβήθρα ἡ <u>ἐπιλεγομένη</u> ῾Εβραϊστὶ Βηθζαδά
>
> a pool <u>which is called</u> in Hebrew Bethesda (John 5:2)

Notice that the first two examples have aorist participles. These are translated with an English past tense. Although participles do not have *absolute* time, they frequently express a time *relative* to that of the main verb(s) of the clause. A present participle represents something going on at the same time as the main verb or something which is always happening or true. An aorist participle represents something which happened before the main verb. A perfect participle also represents something which happened before the main verb, but emphasizes the present result of what has happened. If you are translating the participle as any kind of subordinate clause, you should keep these time relationships in mind and adjust your translation accordingly, as illustrated in the examples. A present participle going on at the same time as an aorist (or imperfect) main verb is often translated with what sounds like an imperfect. An aorist or perfect participle which took place before an aorist main verb is often best translated with what sounds like a pluperfect (i.e., using "had").

It is also possible for a participle to be used as a predicate adjective. As with regular predicate adjectives, these will never be preceded by an article. [See Chapter 14 on the predicate position.]

> $Z\hat{\omega}\nu$ γὰρ ὁ λόγος τοῦ θεοῦ.   For the word of God is living. (Hebrews 4:12)

NOTE: *Only the attributive adjectival proper participle and the use which follows (substantive) have a definite article preceding them in normal use. Not every example of these two uses has an article, but only these two can. Thus the presence of a definite article serves as a contextual clue to these two uses.*

SUBSTANTIVE: Just as regular adjectives can be made into noun substitutes (ὁ ἀγαθός, οἱ δίκαιοι), so too can participles. As with the adjectival proper participle, the best translation is usually a ***relative clause***: "he who," "the one(s) who," "those who," "the thing (s) which," etc. The substantive participle, like a noun, can function as subject, direct object, etc. Most, although not all, substantive participles have a definite article (see note above).

> Οὗτοί εἰσιν οἱ ἐρχόμενοι ἐκ τῆς θλίψεως τῆς μεγάλης.

> These are the ones who / those who come out of the great tribulation. (Revelation 7:14b)

> ἔλεγον οὖν οἱ ᾽Ιουδαῖοι τῷ τεθεραπευμένῳ...

> Therefore the Jews were saying to him who / the one who / the man who was (had been) healed... (John 5:10)

> μακαρία ἡ πιστεύσασα.

> Blessed is she who believed. (Luke 1:45)

Occasionally a substantive participle in the present tense loses some of its verbal aspect and is translated as a noun, e.g., ὁ ἄρχων ("the one who rules" or just "the ruler").

ὁ βαπτίζων – the Baptizer, the Baptist (Mark 6:14)
ὁ σπείρων – the sower (Mark 4:14)

Here is a sentence which illustrates both the adjectival proper and the substantival uses of the participle:

<u>ὁ μὴ τιμῶν</u> τὸν υἱὸν οὐ τιμᾷ τὸν πατέρα τὸν <u>πέμψαντα</u> αὐτόν.

<u>The one who does not honor</u> the Son does not honor the Father <u>who sent</u>
   him. (John 5:23b)

NOTE: The negating word ("not") for participles, and in fact, all verb forms except the indicative, is μή.   Furthermore, all compounds of οὐ can also be written with μή, e.g., μηδέ ("nor," "not even"), μηδείς, μηδεμία, μηδέν ("no one," "nothing"), μηδέποτε ("never"), μηδέπω ("not yet"), and μηκέτι ("no longer," "no more"). See Chapter 27 for the corresponding paradigm of οὐδείς.

(1) ὁ τιμῶν is a present active nominative singular masculine participle being used as a substantive which serves as the subject of the sentence and is modified by μή. "He who does not honor..."
(2) τὸν υἱὸν is the direct object of the participle τιμῶν. "He who does not honor the Son..."
(3) τιμᾷ is the main verb of the sentence. Since it is indicative, it is modified by οὐ. "He who does not honor the Son does not honor..."
(4) τὸν πατέρα is the direct object of οὐ τιμᾷ. "He who does not honor the Son does not honor the Father..."
(5) (τὸν) πέμψαντα is an adjectival proper participle in the second attributive position modifying πατέρα. "He who does not honor the Son does not honor the Father who sent..."
(6) αὐτόν is an accusative singular masculine personal pronoun used as the direct object of the participle πέμψαντα. "He who does not honor the Son does not honor the Father who sent him."

And that is a fairly straightforward sentence!

COMPLEMENTARY: A participle is frequently used in the ***predicate position, without an article***, to give additional information which completes the thought begun by the main verb. This can be a "subject complement" or an "object complement." The lexical category to which the ***main verb***, not the participle, belongs is the key to identifying this participial use.

(1) A subject complement is found, *in agreement with the subject* (written or understood), after verbs of ***ceasing, completing, or continuing***.

ὡς δὲ ἐπαύσατο λαλῶν...   And when he (had) finished <u>speaking</u>...
(Luke 5:4)

(2) An object complement is found, *in agreement with the direct object*, after verbs of ***perception and cognition***. [Note that, although these are generally easy to translate, the category seems to defy classification. Every grammar book seems to call this use something different. (Wallace, for example, lists it with adjectival proper participles in the predicate position.) In translating complementary participles you get to leave present active participles (and those translated as present active) in the "-ing" form.]

καὶ εἶδεν δύο πλοῖα <u>ἑστῶτα</u> παρὰ τὴν λίμνην.

And he saw two boats <u>standing</u> beside the lake. (Luke 5:2a)

ADVERBIAL (CIRCUMSTANTIAL): While still in grammatical agreement with another word in the sentence (often the pronoun subject of the verb), a participle may give some kind of ***adverbial information***. In many instances the best translation of an adverbial participle is a ***subordinate clause***. Adverbial participles are especially challenging, because ***the specific adverbial idea being conveyed is in no way inherent in the participle itself, but must be determined by a careful examination of the context***. Of particular importance is determining the relationship between the action of the participle and that of the main verb of the clause in which it appears. While there are many situations where this is clear, there are other situations where some ambiguity exists, and still others where more than one of the adverbial situations may exist side by side. This last situation, of course, cannot be translated, but can inform exegesis. You need to think carefully about which adverbial idea *best* represents the participle (i.e., what idea the writer wished to emphasize), not only about what is possible. The following examples illustrate the adverbial ideas conveyed by adverbial participles. Note carefully the words in parentheses which are used to translate the adverbial ideas and the ways in which subordinate clauses are constructed from the participles. Adverbial participles *never* have an article.

(1) *Adverbial Time* ("while," "as," "when," "after"): The participle indicates the time frame associated with the main verb. "While" and "as" are more common with present participles; "when" and "after" with aorist participles. "When" seems to be common in translating what I call "immediate reaction situations," "after" when the time frame is important, and "while" or "as" for simultaneous happenings.

Περιπατῶν δὲ παρὰ τὴν θάλασσαν τῆς Γαλιλαίας εἶδεν δύο ἀδελφούς.

And <u>while / as he was walking</u> by the Sea of Galilee, he saw two brothers. (Matthew 4:18a)

Ὕστερον δὲ <u>ἀνακειμένοις</u> αὐτοῖς τοῖς ἔνδεκα ἐφανερώθη.

And later he appeared to the eleven themselves <u>while they were reclining at table</u>. (Mark 16:14)

<u>Ἀναστάς</u> δε...ἐφάνη πρῶτον Μαρίᾳ τῇ Μαγδαληνῇ.

And <u>after he had risen</u>...he appeared first to Mary Magdalene. (Mark 16:9)

<u>ἰδόντες</u> δὲ τὸν ἀστέρα ἐχάρησαν.

And <u>when they saw</u> the star, they rejoiced. (Matthew 2:10)

<u>ἀκούσας</u> δὲ ὁ βασιλεὺς Ἡρῴδης ἐταράχθη.

But <u>when</u> Herod the king <u>heard</u> [this] he was troubled. (Matthew 2:3)

The last two examples illustrate what I have labeled "immediate reaction situations." Someone sees or hears something and immediately reacts to it in some way. Often the immediate reaction participles have an underlying element of cause, but they are generally translated with "when." Note that in immediate reaction situations translated by "when," aorist temporal participles do not generally shift the time frame, whereas in other clauses using the conjunctions "when" or "after" they often do.

(2) *Adverbial Cause* ("because," "since"): The participle gives the reason or cause for the action of the main verb.

Ἰωσὴφ δὲ ὁ ἀνὴρ αὐτῆς, δίκαιος ὢν καὶ <u>μὴ θέλων</u> αὐτὴν
δειγματίσαι, ἐβουλήθη λάθρα ἀπολῦσαι αὐτήν.

But Joseph her husband, <u>because he was</u> a righteous man and did not want
to disgrace her, desired to divorce her secretly. (Matthew 1:19)

Πλανᾶσθε <u>μὴ εἰδότες</u> τὰς γραφάς.

You are mistaken <u>because you do not know / understand</u> the Scriptures.
(Matthew 22:29)

(3) *Adverbial Means* ("by"): The participle indicates the means by which the
action of the main verb is accomplished.

Ἥμαρτον <u>παραδοὺς</u> αἷμα ἀθῷον.

I sinned by <u>betraying</u> innocent blood. (Matthew 27:4a)

σῶσον σεαυτὸν <u>καταβὰς</u> ἀπὸ τοῦ σταυροῦ.

Save yourself <u>by coming down</u> from the cross. (Mark 15:30)

*Note that in both of these examples the aorist participle does not signify time
before the main verb, but represents a simultaneous unitary activity.* In the first
example, the participle could have been translated "when I betrayed," but
adverbial means is a better choice.

(4) *Adverbial Manner* (Often a present participle in the "–ing" form or some
other description of the emotion or attitude involved): The participle indicates the
manner associated with the action of the main verb. The participle is often one of
emotion or attitude.

ἐπορεύοντο <u>χαίροντες</u>.　　They went on their way <u>rejoicing</u>. (Acts
　　5:41)

Μαρία δὲ εἱστήκει πρὸς τῷ μνημείῳ ἔξω <u>κλαίουσα</u>. [This is one
　　of a very small number of instances of πρός with the dative case.]

But Mary was standing outside at the tomb <u>weeping</u>. (John 20:11a)

(5) *Adverbial Concession* ("although"): The main verb is true *regardless of* or *in
spite of* the action or state of the participle.

γνόντες τὸν θεὸν οὐχ ὡς θεὸν ἐδόξασαν.

<u>Although they knew</u> God, they did not honor Him as God. (Romans 1:21)

πάντα δὲ τὰ μέλη τοῦ σώματος πόλλα <u>ὄντα</u> ἕν ἐστιν σῶμα.

And all the members of the body, <u>although they are</u> many, are one body.
(1 Corinthians 12:12)

(6) *Adverbial Condition* ("if"): The participle indicates a condition which must be fulfilled in order for the action of the main verb to take place.

καὶ πάντα ὅσα ἂν αἰτήσητε ἐν τῇ προσευχῇ <u>πιστεύοντες</u> λήμψεσθε.

And all the things which you ask for in prayer you will receive <u>if you believe / have faith</u>. (Matthew 21:22)

θερίσομεν <u>μὴ ἐκλυόμενοι</u>.

We shall reap <u>if we do not become weary</u>. (Galatians 6:9)

(7) *Adverbial Purpose* ("to," "in order to," "for the purpose of"): The participle indicates the purpose of the action of the main verb.

πορεύομαι εἰς Ἰερουσαλὴμ <u>διακονῶν</u> τοῖς ἁγίοις.

I am going to Jerusalem <u>to minister</u> to the saints. (Romans 15:25)

νομικός τις ἀνέστη <u>ἐκπειράζων</u> αὐτόν.

A certain lawyer got up <u>to test</u> him. (Luke 10:25)

(8) *Adverbial Result*: The participle indicates the actual outcome or result of the action of the main verb. Use the phrase "with the result of / that" to test whether the participle indicates result, although those words won't actually appear in the translation. The translation often is just the "–ing" form of the verb, so the exegete must be especially careful to analyze the relationship between the two verbal actions.

πατέρα ἴδιον ἔλεγεν τὸν θεὸν ἴσον ἑαυτὸν <u>ποιῶν</u> τῷ θεῷ.

He was calling God his own Father, [with the result of] <u>making</u> himself equal to God. (John 5:18)

ATTENDANT CIRCUMSTANCE: This is a very common use of the participle. It looks exactly like an adverbial participle and, indeed, is in the broad category of adverbial uses of the participle. Rather than representing an action which is dependent upon the main verb in any of the previously described ways, however, it simply represents another action which takes place along with the main verb. Frequently the two things happen very close together and often the action of the participle is a sort of necessary prelude to the action of the main verb, e.g., "he got up (participle) and left the room (main verb)." The participle is translated along with the main verb (usually indicative or imperative) by using *the same form as the main verb and connecting the two with "and." Note carefully that the translator must add the word "and"; it is not actually there in the text.* Although the two verbs are thus translated, there is still somewhat more emphasis on the main verb; it is usually a more important action in terms of the context than the action of the participle. (Attendant circumstance participles are especially common in narrative passages.)

<u>ἀπελθὼν</u> δεῖξον σεαυτὸν τῷ ἱερεῖ.

<u>Go and</u> show yourself to the priest. (Luke 5:14)

καὶ <u>ἀναστάντες</u> ἐξέβαλον αὐτὸν ἔξω τῆς πόλεως.

And <u>they rose up and</u> drove him out of the city. (Luke 4:29)

<u>Συλλαβόντες</u> δὲ αὐτὸν ἤγαγον καὶ εἰσήγαγον εἰς τὴν οἰκίαν τοῦ ἀρχιερέως.

Then they <u>seized</u> him <u>and</u> led him [away] and brought him into the high priest's house. (Luke 22:54a)

NOTES:

(1) It is often quite difficult to determine whether to use an adverbial time translation or an attendant circumstance one. Sometimes it helps to consider whether one action necessarily leads to another ("when he finds it he rejoices") or whether the two just happen together ("they fell down and worshipped him"). The first two examples above would not work well as adverbial time; that would put too much emphasis on the "set up" participle. In the first, the participle is clearly part of the command. To translate "When you go" or "After you have

gone" does not convey that idea. Likewise, it is too verbose in the second example, to translate, "And after they rose / had risen up." The third example, however, might possibly be translated as adverbial time: "And when / after they had arrested him, they led him away and brought him to the house of the high priest." The translator needs to decide whether to simply regard the three verbal actions as just happening one after another or to emphasize that the second two happened *after* the first had taken place. The adverbial time translation also gives a bit more importance to the action of "arresting" or "seizing" Jesus. With practice, it gets easier to tell which one to choose. ***The important thing is not to get so attached to either one that you always choose it and forget or ignore the other.***

(2) There are also some participles which are just very loosely attached to the main verb as an "attendant activity" but do not technically fall into Wallace's somewhat narrower definition of the attendant circumstance participle. If you run into such a participle and, in spite of your best efforts, cannot categorize it anywhere else, this is probably the category to which you will have to default. These will generally be translated with the "–ing" form of the verb or connected to the main verb by "and."

> καὶ ἰδοὺ ὤφθη αὐτοῖς Μωϋσῆς καὶ Ἡλίας <u>συλλαλοῦντες</u> μετ' αὐτοῦ.

> And behold, Moses appeared to them and Elijah, <u>talking</u> with him.
> (Matthew 17:3)

> καὶ φωνὴ ἐγένετο ἐκ τῆς νεφέλης <u>λέγουσα</u>...

> And a voice came [literally: "happened"] out of the cloud <u>saying / and said</u>... (Luke 9:35)

REDUNDANT / PLEONASTIC: The participle of a ***verb of speaking*** (or some other kind of mental or spoken communication) is used along with ***another speaking verb***. There are two main patterns, which have essentially become formulas. Sometimes one or the other verb is omitted in translation, since one of the two is technically redundant.

(1) The first of the two most common patterns uses the aorist passive participle of ἀποκρίνομαι (even in circumstances where no actual question has been asked). The usual translation of the formula is "answered and said."

καὶ ἀποκριθεὶς πᾶς ὁ λαὸς εἶπεν, Τὸ αἷμα αὐτοῦ ἐφ' ἡμᾶς καὶ ἐπὶ τὰ τέκνα ἡμῶν.

And all the people <u>answered</u> and said, "His blood be on us and on our children."

And all the people <u>answered</u>… (Matthew 27:25)

(2) The second formula involves the present active participle of λέγω. The usual translation of the participle is "saying" or "and said."

Εἶπεν δὲ παραβολὴν πρὸς αὐτοὺς <u>λέγων</u>, Ἀνθρώπου τινὸς πλουσίου εὐφόρησεν ἡ χώρα.

And he told to them a parable, <u>saying</u>, "The land of a certain rich man produced good crops." (Luke 12:16)

GENITIVE ABSOLUTE: Translations of a genitive absolute will *sound exactly like* the translations of the adverbial participle (frequently, but not always, a time clause). *It is a separate grammatical use*, **however, and should be identified as such**. It consists of a noun or pronoun in the genitive case and a genitive participle without an article in agreement with the noun or pronoun. Occasionally the noun / pronoun is missing. These words are not in the genitive case for any of the usual reasons, but **simply because they are a genitive absolute**, hence the genitive absolute is grammatically independent from the rest of the sentence. **When constructing a subordinate clause from a genitive absolute, make the noun or pronoun the subject and the participle the verb.** If the participle is active in meaning, the noun or pronoun is doing or did it; if the participle is a true passive, it is being done or was done to the noun or pronoun.

ἔτι <u>αὐτοῦ λαλοῦντος</u> ἰδοὺ νεφέλη φωτεινὴ ἐπεσκίασεν αὐτούς.

<u>While he was</u> still <u>speaking</u>, behold a bright cloud overshadowed them. (Matthew 17:5a)

καὶ <u>ἐκβληθέντος τοῦ δαιμονίου</u> ἐλάλησεν ὁ κωφός.

And <u>after the demon had been cast out</u>, the dumb man spoke. (Matthew 9:33a)

μὴ ἔχοντος δὲ αὐτοῦ ἀποδοῦναι ἐκέλευσεν αὐτὸν ὁ κυριός
πραθῆναι.

And <u>because he was not able</u> [literally: "did not have (the means)"] to
repay, the master ordered that he be sold as a slave. (Matthew
18:25)

PERIPHRASTIC: The participle is used with a verb of being (usually εἰμί) to
form the equivalent of a finite verb. (A finite verb is one in which the person is
indicated by the endings.) Wallace provides this convenient chart (p. 648).

<u>Finite Verb (of εἰμί)</u> +	<u>Participle</u> =	<u>Finite Tense Equivalent</u>
Present	Present	Present
Imperfect	Present	Imperfect
Future	Present	Future
Present	Perfect	Perfect
Imperfect	Perfect	Pluperfect

Ἦσαν...ἀναβαίνοντες εἰς Ἱεροσόλυμα, καὶ ἦν προάγων αὐτοὺς ὁ
Ἰησοῦς.

<u>They were going up</u> to Jerusalem, and Jesus <u>was going before</u> them.
(Mark 10:32a)

Unlike the future indicative, the future periphrastic has a progressive aspect and
translation.

ἀπὸ τοῦ νῦν ἀνθρώπους <u>ἔσῃ ζωγρῶν.</u>

From now on <u>you will be catching</u> people. (Luke 5:10c)

The Nicene Creed

The following is the Greek text of the creed commonly called "The Nicene Creed," although in fact it is the wording adopted by the Council of Constantinople in 381, which reaffirmed the Christology of the original wording adopted at the Council of Nicea (325), but expanded the part dealing with the Holy Spirit, added the final three clauses (about the Church, baptism and the resurrection of the dead), and eliminated the "anathemas" at the end of the original version.

Note that there is no Greek phrase corresponding to the Latin "filioque" ("and [from] the Spirit") in the clause concerning the "procession" of the Holy Spirit. This phrase was first added by the Third Council of Toledo in Spain (589), and became normative in the West when it was endorsed by Pope Nicholas I in 867. The "filioque" was one of the major causes of the so-called "Great Schism" between the East and West in 1054, which still persists today in the separate Roman Catholic (western) and Orthodox (eastern) branches of the Church.

Participles are underlined.

Πιστεύω εἰς ἕνα θεόν, πατέρα παντοκράτορα, ποιητὴν οὐρανοῦ καὶ
    γῆς, ὁρατῶν τε πάντων καὶ ἀοράτων.
Καὶ εἰς ἕνα κύριον, Ἰησοῦν Χριστόν, τὸν υἱὸν τοῦ θεοῦ τὸν
    μονογενῆ, τὸν ἐκ τοῦ πατρὸς <u>γεννηθέντα</u> πρὸ πάντων τῶν
    αἰώνων, [θεὸν ἐκ θεοῦ,] φῶς ἐκ φωτός, θεὸν ἀληθινὸν ἐκ θεοῦ
    ἀληθινοῦ, <u>γεννηθέντα</u> οὐ <u>ποιηθέντα</u>, ὁμοούσιον τῷ πατρί, δι᾽
    οὗ πάντα ἐγένετο, τὸν δι᾽ ἡμᾶς ἀνθρώπους καὶ διὰ τὴν
    ἡμετέραν σωτηρίαν <u>κατελθόντα</u> ἐκ τῶν οὐρανῶν καὶ
    <u>σαρκωθέντα</u> ἐκ πνεύματος ἁγίου καὶ Μαρίας τῆς παρθένου καὶ
    <u>ἐνανθρωπήσαντα</u>, <u>σταυρωθέντα</u> τε ὑπὲρ ἡμῶν ἐπὶ Ποντίου
    Πιλάτου, καὶ <u>παθόντα</u> καὶ <u>ταφέντα</u>· καὶ <u>ἀναστάντα</u> τῇ τρίτῃ
    ἡμέρᾳ κατὰ τὰς γραφάς, καὶ <u>ἀνελθόντα</u> εἰς τοὺς οὐρανούς, καὶ
    <u>καθεζόμενον</u> ἐν δεξιᾷ τοῦ πατρός· καὶ πάλιν <u>ἐρχόμενον</u> μετὰ
    δόξης κρῖναι <u>ζῶντας</u> καὶ νεκρούς, οὗ τῆς βασιλείας οὐκ ἔσται
    τέλος.
[Καὶ] εἰς τὸ πνεῦμα ἅγιον, τὸν κύριον καὶ τὸ <u>ζῳοποιοῦν</u>, τὸ ἐκ τοῦ
    πατρὸς <u>ἐκπορευόμενον</u>, τὸ σὺν πατρὶ καὶ υἱῷ
    <u>συμπροσκυνούμενον</u> καὶ <u>συνδοξαζόμενον</u>, τὸ <u>λαλῆσαν</u> διὰ τῶν
    προφητῶν.
Καὶ εἰς μίαν ἁγίαν, καθολικήν, καὶ ἀποστολικὴν ἐκκλησίαν.

Ὁμολογῶ ἓν βάπτισμα εἰς ἄφεσιν ἁμαρτιῶν.
Προσδοκῶ ἀνάστασιν νεκρῶν καὶ ζωὴν τοῦ μέλλοντος αἰῶνος.

[᾿Αμήν.]

UNDERSTANDING THE CHAPTER AND PREPARING FOR THE QUIZ:
We have now moved into a whole new area of translation work. Participles are extremely complex and it is not really possible to "master" all of them in the context of a first year course. Nevertheless, as you work on the assigned passages and the class work passages over the next several days you can do the following things.

(1) Learn the ***correct terminology*** for the different participle uses.

(2) Learn the various ***contextual clues*** (definite article, certain kinds of verbs, etc.) which can assist you in making the decision regarding the participle use.

(3) Establish in your mind the ***process*** to be used in identifying and translating the various uses.

(4) Familiarize yourself with the ***extra words*** which must sometimes be added in order to correctly translate certain participle uses. Make sure you know how to move from the literal participle translations to the ones illustrated in the chapter.

(5) Study the ***examples*** in the chapter carefully so that you can match whatever participle you are working on to the correct pattern.

(6) ***Don't guess!!*** Doing the above five things should eliminate guesswork. You need to be prepared to defend your decision regarding participle use and translation by referring to the material (both the explanations and the examples) in the chapter.

(7) Answer the ***review questions*** following each day's translation work. These will help you determine whether or not you understand the material.

Chapter 34

THE SUBJUNCTIVE MOOD: The subjunctive represents *another mood* of the verb. It is highly nuanced and defies attempts to define it in simple terms. To get some idea of the nature of the subjunctive, however, consider the following two statements. "The subjunctive conveys the idea that the speaker regards what is expressed by the verb as a *possibility*, *supposition*, or *desire* rather than as a fact" (Young, p. 137). "[T]he subjunctive is used to grammaticalize *potentiality*. It normally does so in the realm of *cognitive probability*, but may also be used for *cognitive possibility* (overlapping with the optative) or *volitional intentionality* (overlapping with the imperative)" (Wallace, p. 463). From an analysis of these definitions we discover that the subjunctive deals with what someone thinks might happen or is likely to happen, what could happen, or what someone wants or doesn't want to have happen. A more succinct statement is that the subjunctive *expresses contingency*, something in some way less than certain, though frequently regarded as probable.

Only two tenses are used to any extent: ***present and aorist***. (The perfect subjunctive of οἶδα is also used, since this is translated as a present. Other perfect subjunctives appear as periphrastics: a perfect participle with the subjunctive of εἰμί.) Though there is no future subjunctive, many subjunctive uses reflect a ***future orientation***, since they deal with actions or states which, if they occur, will occur in the future. Verb tenses in the subjunctive involve ***only aspect***. The present denotes an on-going, continuous, or repeated activity or something which is always happening or true. The aorist denotes the act as a whole (unitary action), whether viewed from the perspective of its beginning, its totality, or its completed state. ***Time is not an element of the subjunctive. The aorist subjunctive, therefore, has nothing to do with past time and you must keep this in mind when translating.*** In translation one often does not hear any difference between the present and the aorist subjunctive, but the difference is there in the Greek and should be kept in mind when doing exegesis.

Although there are a number of subjunctive uses, they are by and large easier to recognize and translate than participles. There are a variety of contextual clues to help you out and you should make yourself aware of these. Some subjunctive uses have specific "red flag" words to let you know that a subjunctive is coming and, in some cases, identify the use for you. Other uses only employ specific forms of the verb. As you study the examples, note these identification clues and also pay careful attention to the translation patterns. (Don't try to make up your own patterns; use the ones you are given.) Sometimes the translation does not sound "subjunctive" at all; at other times the translation can be nuanced by using the helping verb "should." Do not use "may" and "might" except in translating purpose clauses. The material presented in this chapter and Chapter 35 does not cover every possible use of the subjunctive, but it covers those you are likely to encounter.

μή and its compounds (see Chapter 33) are used to negate the subjunctive.

SUBJUNCTIVE FORMS: Before beginning our study of subjunctive uses, however, we need to see what the forms look like. This is radically different from the participle picture, since only two sets of endings cover almost all forms. These are the two sets of endings.

```
* * * * * * * * * * * * * * * * * * * * * * * * * * * * *
*      Present Active, Aorist Active,      Present M/P and Aorist Middle   *
*            and Aorist Passive                                             *
*                                                                          *
*        Singular      Plural              Singular      Plural            *
*                                                                          *
*    1ˢᵗ   –ω          –ωμεν                 –ωμαι         –ώμεθα           *
*    2ⁿᵈ   –ῃς         –ητε                  –ῃ            –ησθε            *
*    3ʳᵈ   –ῃ          –ωσι(ν)               –ηται         –ωνται           *
*                                                                          *
* * * * * * * * * * * * * * * * * * * * * * * * * * * * *
```

If we compare these endings to the two sets used for the indicative we find that in each place where the present has ε the subjunctive has η, where the indicative has ει the subjunctive has η, and where the indicative has ο the subjunctive has ω. In the first set of endings, the third plural uses ω in place of ου. **Note:** The aorist passive subjunctive endings are accented with a circumflex.

Note the following overlaps in endings: (1) The ending of the first person singular in the first set of subjunctive endings is identical to the ending of the present and future active indicative first person singular. (2) The ending of the second person singular in the second set is identical to the ending of the present M/P and future middle indicative second person singular. (3) Note also that the third person singular in the first set is identical to the second person singular in the second set. This creates the potential for some overlapping forms. These will be noted as we go through the paradigms. These do not present as much difficulty as one might think they would, because there are often contextual clues to help make the distinction.

While, on the one hand, the small number of possible endings is good news, on the other hand it means that you must pay ***very careful attention to the stem***.

Remember that, as was the case with participles, aorist forms (third and sixth principal parts) will be *without augment*.

No literal translations are given with these paradigms, because *the translation of the subjunctive always depends on how it is being used*

```
* * * * * * * * * * * * * * * * * * * * * * * * * * * * * *
*         Present Active and Present M/P Subjunctive of πέμπω       *
*                                                                   *
*      Singular        Plural          Singular        Plural       *
*                                                                   *
*   1ˢᵗ πέμπω      πέμπωμεν        πέμπωμαι      πεμπώμεθα    *
*   2ⁿᵈ πέμπῃς     πέμπητε         πέμπῃ         πέμπησθε     *
*   3ʳᵈ πέμπῃ      πέμπωσι(ν)      πέμπηται      πέμπωνται    *
*                                                                   *
* * * * * * * * * * * * * * * * * * * * * * * * * * * * * *
```

(1) Note that the **first person singular** is the same for the **present active indicative** and the **present active subjunctive**.

(2) Note that the **second person singular** *is the same for the* **present M/P indicative** *and the* **present M/P subjunctive***. There is also an overlap between the* **present active subjunctive third person singular** *and the* **present M/P subjunctive second person singular***.*

```
* * * * * * * * * * * * * * * * * * * * * * * * * * * * * *
*      First Aorist Active and First Aorist Middle Subjunctive of πέμπω  *
*                                                                   *
*      Singular        Plural          Singular        Plural       *
*                                                                   *
*   1ˢᵗ πέμψω      πέμψωμεν        πέμψωμαι      πεμψώμεθα    *
*   2ⁿᵈ πέμψῃς     πέμψητε         πέμψῃ         πέμψησθε     *
*   3ʳᵈ πέμψῃ      πέμψωσι(ν)      πέμψηται      πέμψωνται    *
*                                                                   *
* * * * * * * * * * * * * * * * * * * * * * * * * * * * * *
```

(1) Note that, *if* the unaugmented aorist active stem is the same as the future active stem, the **future active indicative first person singular** and the **aorist active subjunctive first person singular** will be identical. This will be the case for all regularly formed first aorists. You must be especially careful with the first aorist of liquid stem verbs, since the unaugmented stems can be tricky and can even, on occasion, look exactly like the present stem (e.g., κρίνω and ἐγείρω).

(2) Note that, in practical terms, you are only likely to see the aorist middle subjunctive for deponents and verbs which have a special meaning for middle forms. Overlapping forms exist between the ***aorist active subjunctive third person singular*** and the ***aorist middle subjunctive second person singular***.

(3) ***If*** the future middle and unaugmented aorist middle stems are the same, there is a third potential overlapping form: ***future middle indicative second person singular***.

```
* * * * * * * * * * * * * * * * * * * * * * *
*                                           *
*    First Aorist Passive Subjunctive of πέμπω   *
*                                           *
*          Singular          Plural         *
*                                           *
*   1ˢᵗ    πεμφθῶ         πεμφθῶμεν          *
*   2ⁿᵈ    πεμφθῇς        πεμφθῆτε           *
*   3ʳᵈ    πεμφθῇ         πεμφθῶσι(ν)        *
*                                           *
* * * * * * * * * * * * * * * * * * * * * * *
```

Note the circumflex accent on the endings. This accent is a useful marker to distinguish the aorist passive subjunctive from other aorist passive forms.

```
* * * * * * * * * * * * * * * * * * * * * * * * * * *
* Second Aorist Active Subjunctive   Second Aorist Middle Subjunctive *
*         of λέγω                         of γίνομαι        *
*                                                    *
*   Singular      Plural          Singular      Plural    *
*                                                    *
* 1ˢᵗ εἴπω       εἴπωμεν         γένωμαι       γενώμεθα   *
* 2ⁿᵈ εἴπῃς      εἴπητε          γένῃ          γένησθε    *
* 3ʳᵈ εἴπῃ       εἴπωσι(ν)       γένηται       γένωνται   *
*                                                    *
* * * * * * * * * * * * * * * * * * * * * * * * * * *
```

The second aorist middle, like the first aorist middle, will normally be found only for deponents and verbs which have a special meaning for middle forms. Since verbs with a second aorist often have an irregular future form as well, some of the potential overlapping forms which affect the first aorist will not be a concern here. The only potential overlap would be between the ***second aorist active subjunctive third person singular*** and the ***second aorist middle subjunctive second person singular*** for verbs with both active and middle forms in use.

```
******************
*  Second Aorist Passive Subjunctive  *
*           οἱ στρέφω                  *
*                                      *
*      Singular        Plural          *
*                                      *
*  1st  στραφῶ      στραφῶμεν          *
*  2nd  στραφῇς     στραφῆτε           *
*  3rd  στραφῇ      στραφῶσι(ν)        *
*                                      *
******************
```

εἰμί: The present subjunctive of εἰμί is just the present active endings with accents and breathing marks! Note that several of the subjunctive forms of εἰμί appear on the *Accents and Breathing Marks That Matter* list.

```
*************
*  Present (Active)   *
*  Subjunctive of εἰμί *
*                     *
*   Singular  Plural  *
*                     *
*  1st  ὦ      ὦμεν   *
*  2nd  ῇς     ἦτε    *
*  3rd  ῇ      ὦσι(ν) *
*                     *
*************
```

CONTRACT VERBS: *Epsilon* contract verbs in the present tense have the usual subjunctive endings, but a different accent, reflecting the vowel contractions.

```
********************************
*   Present Active and M/P Subjunctive of ζητέω   *
*                                                 *
*   Singular   Plural        Singular   Plural    *
*                                                 *
* 1st ζητῶ    ζητῶμεν       ζητῶμαι   ζητώμεθα    *
* 2nd ζητῇς   ζητῆτε        ζητῇ      ζητῆσθε     *
* 3rd ζητῇ    ζητῶσι(ν)     ζητῆται   ζητῶνται    *
*                                                 *
********************************
```

Alpha contract verbs, as a result of the contractions, wind up looking ***exactly the same in the present indicative and the present subjunctive (both active and M/P)***. *Omicron* contract verbs have the same forms in the subjunctive and indicative for first person, second person, and third person singular active and second person singular M/P.

```
* * * * * * * * * * * * * * * * * * * * * * * * * * * * * * *
*              Present Active and M/P Subjunctive of ἀγαπάω              *
*                                                                        *
*       Singular      Plural            Singular       Plural            *
*                                                                        *
*  1ˢᵗ  ἀγαπῶ         ἀγαπῶμεν          ἀγαπῶμαι       ἀγαπώμεθα          *
*  2ⁿᵈ  ἀγαπᾷς        ἀγαπᾶτε           ἀγαπᾷ          ἀγαπᾶσθε           *
*  3ʳᵈ  ἀγαπᾷ         ἀγαπῶσι(ν)        ἀγαπᾶται       ἀγαπῶνται          *
*                                                                        *
*                                                                        *
*              Present Active and M/P Subjunctive of δικαιόω              *
*                                                                        *
*                                                                        *
*  1ˢᵗ  δικαιῶ        δικαιῶμεν         δικαιῶμαι      δικαιώμεθα         *
*  2ⁿᵈ  δικαιοῖς       δικαιῶτε          δικαιοῖ         δικαιῶσθε          *
*  3ʳᵈ  δικαιοῖ        δικαιῶσι(ν)       δικαιῶται       δικαιῶνται         *
*                                                                        *
* * * * * * * * * * * * * * * * * * * * * * * * * * * * * * *
```

–μι VERBS: Even here the usual subjunctive endings prevail, though there are a few exceptions. ***Note:*** If a form does not appear in the paradigms, there is no example of it in the GNT.

The first –μι verb to be considered is *τίθημι*.

```
*  *  *  *  *  *  *  *  *  *  *  *  *  *  *  *  *  *  *  *  *  *  *  *  *  *  *  *  *
*                                    τίθημι                                      *
*                                                                                *
*           Present Active          Second Aorist           Second Aorist        *
*            Subjunctive         Active Subjunctive      Middle Subjunctive       *
*                                                                                *
*        Singular    Plural     Singular  Plural        Singular    Plural       *
*                                                                                *
*   1st  τιθῶ      τιθῶμεν       θῶ      θῶμεν         θῶμαι      θώμεθα          *
*   2nd  τιθῇς     τιθῆτε        θῇς     θῆτε          θῇ         θῆσθε           *
*   3rd  τιθῇ      τιθῶσι(ν)     θῇ      θῶσι(ν)       θῆται      θῶνται          *
*                                                                                *
*  *  *  *  *  *  *  *  *  *  *  *  *  *  *  *  *  *  *  *  *  *  *  *  *  *  *  *  *
```

(1) Note that the same situation applies here as it did with the participles. The present active and second aorist active subjunctive use the endings normally associated with the aorist passive subjunctive. Don't let this fool you!

(2) Since the sixth principal part (ἐτέθην) is regular, that subjunctive would have a regular formation: τεθῶ.

ἵστημι:

```
*  *  *  *  *  *  *  *  *  *  *  *  *  *  *  *  *  *  *  *  *  *  *  *  *  *  *  *
*      Present Active and Second Aorist Active Subjunctive of ἵστημι          *
*                                                                             *
*        Singular      Plural            Singular         Plural              *
*                                                                             *
*   1st  ἱστῶ        ἱστῶμεν            στῶ            στῶμεν                  *
*   2nd  ἱστῇς       ἱστῆτε             στῇς           στῆτε                   *
*   3rd  ἱστῇ        ἱστῶσι(ν)          στῇ            στῶσι(ν)                *
*                                                                             *
*  *  *  *  *  *  *  *  *  *  *  *  *  *  *  *  *  *  *  *  *  *  *  *  *  *  *  *
```

(1) Remember that the present active has the transitive meaning "set," etc. The second aorist active has the intransitive meaning "stand."

(2) Note that the accent for this verb also is a circumflex on the ending.

(3) Since the first aorist active and the aorist passive indicative are regular, they will also have regular subjunctive forms: first aorist active – στήσω (note the overlap with future active indicative) and first aorist passive – σταθῶ.

The second aorist active subjunctive of **ἀφίημι**, the second aorist active subjunctive of **βαίνω** and its compounds, and the *perfect* active subjunctive of **οἶδα** follow this same accent pattern:

```
* * * * * * * * * * * * * * * * * * * * * * * * * * * *
*        Second Aorist Active           Second Aorist Active       *
*       Subjunctive of ἀναβαίνω         Subjunctive of ἀφίημι      *
*                                                                  *
*                                                                  *
*       Singular       Plural          Singular       Plural       *
*                                                                  *
*  1ˢᵗ  ἀναβῶ          ἀναβῶμεν          ἀφῶ            ἀφῶμεν      *
*  2ⁿᵈ  ἀναβῇς         ἀναβῆτε           ἀφῇς           ἀφῆτε       *
*  3ʳᵈ  ἀναβῇ          ἀναβῶσι(ν)        ἀφῇ            ἀφῶσι(ν)    *
*                                                                  *
* * * * * * * * * * * * * * * * * * * * * * * * * * * *
```

```
           * * * * * * * * * * * *
           * Perfect Active Subjunctive *
           *         of οἶδα          *
           *                          *
           *    Singular    Plural    *
           *                          *
           * 1ˢᵗ  εἰδῶ      εἰδῶμεν   *
           * 2ⁿᵈ  εἰδῇς     εἰδῆτε    *
           * 3ʳᵈ  εἰδῇ      εἰδῶσι(ν) *
           *                          *
           * * * * * * * * * * * *
```

δίδωμι has a somewhat different pattern with omega throughout, but still with the circumflex accent on the endings and the iota subscripts in the second person and third person singular. The aorist passive would be regular: δοθῶ.

There are several variations on the third person singular aorist active subjunctive of δίδωμι: δοῖ, δώῃ, and δώσῃ. There are also variant readings which have the first plural (δώσωμεν) and the third plural (δώσωσιν), suggesting that δωσ– was coming to be seen as an alternate stem.

	Singular	Plural	Singular	Plural
1st	διδῶ	διδῶμεν	δῶ	δῶμεν
2nd	διδῷς	διδῶτε	δῷς	δῶτε
3rd	διδῷ	διδῶσι(ν)	δῷ	δῶσι(ν)

Note that the second aorist active of γινώσκω follows the same pattern:

Second Aorist Active Subjunctive of γινώσκω

	Singular	Plural
1st	γνῶ	γνῶμεν
2nd	γνῷς	γνῶτε
3rd	γνῷ / γνοῖ	γνῶσι(ν)

SUBJUNCTIVE CLAUSES INTRODUCED BY ἵνα: We will look at one category of subjunctive uses in this chapter and the rest of the uses in Chapter 35. Approximately one third of all the subjunctives in the GNT occur in subordinate clauses introduced by ἵνα (occasionally ὅπως). The majority of these uses parallel those of the infinitive (Chapters 36 and 37), which is why the translation often, but not always, *sounds like an infinitive*. The use of ἵνα clauses in place of infinitives increased significantly during the Koine period. The use of the word ἵνα is a contextual clue to a subjunctive use, but one must still distinguish between the variety of ἵνα clauses.

PURPOSE CLAUSE: This is the most frequent use for a ἵνα clause. The focus is on the intention of the action of the main verb. The purpose clause answers the question "Why?" in relation to the action of the main verb. Sometimes an English infinitive is sufficient to translate a purpose clause. If that is not possible, the clause is introduced by "in order that" or just "that." The helping verbs used in translating purpose clauses are "may" and "might." The decision about which to use causes far more difficulty than it should. If the **main verb** indicates a **present or future context**, use "may" in the purpose clause. If the **main verb** indicates a **past context**, use "might."

> Κύριε, δός μοι τοῦτο τὸ ὕδωρ, <u>ἵνα μὴ διψῶ μηδὲ διέρχωμαι</u> ἐνθάδε ἀντλεῖν.

> Sir, give me this water, <u>that I may not be thirsty nor come by</u> here to draw. (John 4:15)

> οὐ γὰρ ἀπέστειλεν ὁ θεὸς τὸν υἱὸν εἰς τὸν κόσμον <u>ἵνα κρίνῃ</u> τὸν κόσμον ἀλλ' <u>ἵνα σωθῇ</u> ὁ κόσμος δι' αὐτοῦ.

> For God did not send the Son into the world <u>to judge / that he might judge / in order that he might judge</u> the world, but <u>that / in order that</u> the world <u>might be saved</u> through him. (John 3:17)

SUBSTANTIVAL / NOUN CLAUSES: The **entire ἵνα clause** functions in place of a noun. It answers the question "What?" rather than "Why?" There are four basic uses: (1) subject, (2) predicate nominative, (3) direct object, and (4) apposition.

(1) *Subject*: The verb is generally an "impersonal" one (one translated with "it", e.g., "it is better," "it is expedient," "it is profitable") or the third person singular of εἰμί with a neuter singular adjective. The ἵνα clause, not "it," is the subject, telling **what** is better, expedient, etc. This impersonal verb is the contextual clue indicating a subject ἵνα clause.

> συμφέρει ὑμῖν <u>ἵνα</u> εἷς ἄνθρωπος <u>ἀποθάνῃ</u> ὑπὲρ τοῦ λαοῦ καὶ μὴ ὅλον ἔθνος <u>ἀπόληται.</u>

> It is expedient / better for you <u>that</u> one man <u>die / should die</u> for the people and [<u>that</u>] the whole nation <u>not perish</u>. (John 11:50)

(2) *Predicate Nominative*: The ἵνα clause functions as a predicate nominative following ἐστί(ν) and a noun subject. This sentence structure is the contextual clue to the predicate nominative ἵνα clause.

Ἐμὸν βρῶμά ἐστιν ἵνα ποιήσω τὸ θέλημα τοῦ πέμψαντός με καὶ τελειώσω αὐτοῦ τὸ ἔργον.

My food is to do / that I do / that I should do the will of him who sent me and [to] complete/ [that I] complete / [that I should] complete his work. (John 4:34)

(3) *Direct Object*: The ἵνα clause follows a verb of commanding, asking, urging, praying, proclaiming, etc. The clause gives the *content* of the request, command, prayer, etc. (This is sometimes called a "content" clause.) The nature of the introductory verb is the contextual clue to the direct object ἵνα clause.

Καὶ ἐξελθόντες ἐκήρυξαν ἵνα μετανοῶσιν.

And they went out and preached that [people] should repent. (Mark 6:12)

Εἰ υἱὸς εἶ τοῦ θεοῦ, εἰπὲ τῷ λίθῳ τούτῳ ἵνα γένηται ἄρτος.

If you are the Son of God, tell / command this stone to become / that it should become bread. (Luke 4:3)

NOTES:

(1) The direct object ἵνα clause is the one most likely to be mistaken for a purpose clause. It would be possible, for example, to translate the first example above: "And they went out and preached in order that [people] might repent." When we compare this with the direct object translation, however, it seems reasonably clear that it is the content of the preaching rather than the purpose of the preachers which is under discussion.

(2) Some grammar books distinguish a separate category of ἵνα clauses following verbs of wishing, planning, arranging, etc. (This category is called "complementary" because it parallels the use of the complementary infinitive, underlining the close relationships between the infinitive and ἵνα clauses and between the complementary and direct object categories.) Others consider this too fine a distinction and feel that such clauses can just as easily be considered direct object (content) clauses, giving the content of the wish, plan, arrangement, etc.

καὶ καθῶς θέλετε ἵνα ποιῶσιν ὑμῖν οἱ ἄνθρωποι ποιεῖτε αὐτοῖς ὁμοίως.

> And just as you wish <u>that</u> people <u>would do</u> to you / people <u>to do</u> to you, do likewise to them. (Luke 6:31)

(4) *Apposition*: The ἵνα clause answers the question "What?" with regard to the noun to which it is in apposition. It is possible to use the word "namely" in the translation. This type of clause appears primarily in Johannine writings.

> αὕτη ἐστὶν ἡ ἐντολὴ ἡ ἐμή, <u>ἵνα ἀγαπᾶτε</u> ἀλλήλους καθὼς ἠγάπησα ὑμᾶς.

> This is my commandment, [namely] <u>that you love / should love</u> one another just as I loved you. (John 15:12)

NOTE: It is common to confuse the appositional ἵνα clause with the predicate nominative use. Note carefully that in the type of sentence which uses an appositional ἵνα clause there is already a predicate nominative, in this case "my commandment." It is the predicate nominative to which the ἵνα clause is in apposition.

EPEXEGETICAL CLAUSE: A ἵνα clause can be used after **certain nouns or adjectives** to explain or clarify that word. The following words are among those sometimes followed by an epexegetical clause: ἐξουσία ("power/authority to do something"), χρεία ("need for someone to do something / that someone should do something"), ἄξιος ("worthy to do something"), and ὥρα ("hour for something to happen / when something will happen or someone will do something"). These words serve as the contextual clue to the identification of an epexegetical ἵνα clause.

> οὐ χρείαν ἔχεις <u>ἵνα τίς σε ἐρωτᾷ.</u>

> You do not have a need <u>for</u> anyone <u>to question</u> you. (John 16:30a)

Note the accent on τίς. Remember that when two (or more) words which would normally not have an accent come in sequence, each except the last acquires an accent. The example cited here could get you into real trouble if you are not aware of this, since you would assume that τίς is interrogative and then become frustrated trying to fit it into the sentence.

> ἦλθεν αὐτοῦ ἡ ὥρα <u>ἵνα μεταβῇ</u> ἐκ τοῦ κόσμου τούτου πρὸς τὸν πατέρα.

His hour had come to go / cross over from this world to the Father   (Or
"...when he would go..." (John 13:1)

NOTE: ἵνα clauses can also be used to indicate result and as a substitute for the imperative, but these are not common. See John 9:2 for an obvious example of a result clause.

UNDERSTANDING THE CHAPTER AND PREPARING FOR THE QUIZ:

(1) Begin by studying the *subjunctive forms* and doing the form exercise. Subjunctive forms are not especially difficult, but you do need to recognize the endings and take care to distinguish the present from the aorist stem.

(2) Re-read the section on *ἵνα clauses* and study the examples and translation patterns. Note especially the *contextual clues* which will help in distinguishing some of the ἵνα clauses from the others, since they will all look alike in context.

(3) Note the word ὅπως which sometimes substitutes for ἵνα. It does not alter the translation.

(4) Carefully prepare the passages assigned for homework.

(5) After completing all translation work, do the *Chapter 34 Review*.

Chapter 35
Uses of the Subjunctive (Part 2)

USES OF THE SUBJUNCTIVE: This chapter introduces the other subjunctive uses, apart from the various ἵνα clauses (Chapter 34).   Subjunctive uses are broadly divided into two categories: independent uses and use in dependent (subordinate) clauses. We will begin with *four independent uses*. Remember to watch for various contextual clues. Remember also the distinction between the present and aorist subjunctive: not time, but *aspect* or kind of action.

HORTATORY: The name of this use comes from the Latin word *hortari* ("to urge" or "to encourage"). The *first person plural* subjunctive is used to urge someone else to join with the speaker in doing something. The usual English translation is "let us…" (On five occasions a first person singular is used: "let me…").   Although this subjunctive is easy to translate once it is identified, it is probably the hardest to spot in context unless it is negated, since there are no other contextual clues except the subjunctive verb in the first person plural.

> Ἀγαπητοί, <u>ἀγαπῶμεν</u> ἀλλήλους.

> Beloved, <u>let us love</u> one another. (1 John 4:7)

The present tense is used here, because the love is to be on-going. In the next example the aorist subjunctive is used, because the verbal actions are seen as a whole without any indication regarding duration.

> εἰ νεκροὶ οὐκ ἐγείρονται, <u>Φάγωμεν καὶ πίωμεν</u>, αὔριον γὰρ ἀποθνῄσκομεν.

> If the dead are not raised, <u>let us eat</u> and [<u>let us</u>] <u>drink</u>, for tomorrow we
>> die. (1 Corinthians 15:32b)

DELIBERATIVE: The deliberative subjunctive asks a *real or rhetorical question*. *First person singular or plural* is the most common verb form, although second and third person are found (especially in indirect discourse). Since the *future indicative* can also be used for deliberative questions, either "should" or "shall" is appropriate for use in translation. In the first example a question is asked to which an answer is expected. The only real contextual clue to this use is the fact that it *is* a question, either direct or indirect. That, plus the fact that a first person subjunctive verb form is most common should point in the direction of a deliberative question.

> ἔξεστιν δοῦναι κῆνσον Καίσαρι ἢ οὔ; <u>δῶμεν</u> ἢ <u>μὴ δῶμεν;</u>

Is it lawful to pay tax to Caesar or not? <u>Should / Shall we pay</u> or <u>should / shall we not pay</u>? (Mark 12:14c and d)

Other times a question is raised to which an answer is not really expected (rhetorical) or the subjunctive represents the subject debating about what to do.

ἐπιμένωμεν τῇ ἁμαρτίᾳ, ἵνα ἡ χάρις πλεονάσῃ;

<u>Should / Shall we continue</u> in sin, that grace may abound? (Romans 6:1b)

τί εἴπω ὑμῖν;

What <u>should / shall I say</u> to you? (1 Corinthians 11:22c)

In the following example the deliberative subjunctive is embedded in the sentence as an *indirect* question:

οὐ γὰρ ᾔδει τί ἀποκριθῇ.

For he did not know what <u>he should say / answer</u>. (Mark 9:6) ["Say" is usually used here rather than "answer," since no question has been asked. The direct question would have been, "What should I say / answer?"]

EMPHATIC NEGATION: The ***combined negative*** οὐ μή is used with the ***aorist subjunctive*** (also, though less frequently, with the ***future indicative***) to express an emphatic future negation. These two elements are the contextual clue to recognition of this subjunctive use. This is actually more forceful than οὐ with the indicative; it negates even the possibility of something happening. Often some extra word or phrase (e.g., "never," "certainly," "surely") is added to the translation to express this emphasis, though this is not always done. Emphatic negation is found primarily (though not exclusively) in sayings of Jesus and in quotations from the Septuagint. Frequently there is a soteriological theme in these statements.

καὶ τὸν ἐρχόμενον πρὸς ἐμὲ οὐ μὴ ἐκβάλω ἔξω.

And the one who comes to me <u>I will surely not cast out</u>. (John 6:37)

PROHIBITION: μή (or one of its compounds) is used with the ***aorist subjunctive (typically second person)*** to forbid the occurrence of an action. ("Just don't do it!") This combination of words is the contextual clue to the subjunctive expressing prohibition. Other commands and prohibitions will be considered in Chapter 38.

<u>μὴ φοβηθῇς</u> παραλαβεῖν Μαρίαν τὴν γυναῖκά σου.

<u>Do not be afraid</u> to take Mary as your wife. (Matthew 1:20a)

<u>Μὴ ἀδικήσητε</u> τὴν γῆν μήτε τὴν θαλάσσαν μήτε τὰ δένδρα, ἄχρι σφραγίσωμεν τοὺς δούλους τοῦ θεοῦ ἡμῶν ἐπὶ τῶν μετώπων αὐτῶν.

<u>Do not harm</u> the earth or the sea or the trees, until we seal / have sealed the servants of our God upon their foreheads. (Revelation 7:3) [The second subjunctive used in this sentence is in an ***indefinite temporal clause*** (see below).]

The remainder of the subjunctive uses (including the ἵνα clauses) appear in ***dependent (subordinate) clauses*** of one sort or another.

THIRD CLASS CONDITIONS: As mentioned previously, the classification of conditional sentences in Greek is a complicated matter. One generally acknowledged system classifies them according to the "if" word used and the tense and mood of the two clauses. (See Chapters 11 and 16 for first class and second class conditions.) Third class conditions have ἐάν ("if" – a combination of εἰ and ἄν, an untranslated particle expressing contingency, also used in second class conditions) ***and the subjunctive in the protasis (the "if" clause) and any tense / any mood in the apodosis (the "then" clause)***. The word ἐάν and the subjunctive in the protasis are the contextual clues to the identification of a third class condition. One very common pattern, the primary classical one, is called the ***future more probable***. This suggests that the protasis will likely occur and has a ***future indicative*** in the apodosis. Also included as a third class condition, because it uses the subjunctive in the protasis, is a type of condition using the ***present indicative*** in the apodosis and known as ***present general***. Present general conditions are used to state general principles, usually without comment on likelihood of fulfillment.

NOTES:

(1) Other possibilities exist for the third class condition. It may indicate what could possibly occur in the future or what is only hypothetical and will not occur

(2) Some grammar books list the present general condition as a fifth class condition, but because of the use of ἐάν and the subjunctive, we will keep it in the third class condition category.

(3) Since the protasis looks alike in both cases, you will have to use the verb tense in the apodosis to distinguish between these two sub-categories of third class conditions.

Present general third class condition:

> ἐάν τις περιπατῇ ἐν τῇ ἡμέρᾳ, οὐ προσκόπτει.

> If anyone walks in the day, he does not stumble. (John 11:9b)

Future more probable third class condition:

> ἐὰν ἀγαπᾶτε με, τὰς ἐντολὰς τὰς ἐμὰς τηρήσετε.

> If you love me, you will keep my commandments. (John 14:15)

INDEFINITE RELATIVE CLAUSE: The *structure* of sentences involving an indefinite relative clause is similar to that of the third class conditions. Instead of just ἐάν, however, they use the subjunctive after ὃς ἄν / ἐάν or ὅστις ἄν / ἐάν (the two words together are translated "whoever"). The neuter can also be used and is translated "whatever." These words are the contextual clue to identification. The construction implies a generic or uncertain subject or object.

> καὶ ὃς ἐὰν δέξηται ἓν παιδίον τοιοῦτο ἐπὶ τῷ ὀνόματί μου, ἐμὲ δέχεται.

> And whoever receives one such little child in my name, receives me.
> (Matthew 18:5)

INDEFINITE TEMPORAL CLAUSE: Indefinite temporal (time) clauses are formed by using the subjunctive with the conjunction ὅταν *(ὅτε + ἄν)* meaning "when" or "whenever" or various words meaning "until" (e.g., ἕως, ἄχρι / ἄχρις, μέχρι / μέχρις, often followed by οὗ, which does not change the meaning, and possibly accompanied by ἄν). These words are the contextual clue. A present subjunctive is used with ὅταν when the main clause and the subordinate clause are contemporaneous and usually indicates an action which is seen as being repeated. An aorist subjunctive is used when the action of the subordinate clause takes place before that of the main clause.

Ὅταν δὲ νηστεύητε, μὴ γίνεσθε ὡς οἱ ὑποκριταὶ σκυθρωποί.

And <u>when(ever) you fast</u>, do not be gloomy like the hypocrites. (Matthew 6:16a)

ὁ υἱὸς τοῦ ἀνθρώπου ἐπαισχυνθήσεται αὐτόν, ὅταν ἔλθῃ ἐν τῇ δόξῃ τοῦ πατρὸς αὐτοῦ μετὰ τῶν ἀγγέλων τῶν ἁγίων.

The Son of Man will be ashamed of him, <u>when he comes</u> in the glory of his Father with the holy angels. (Mark 8:38)

οὐ μὴ παρέλθῃ ἡ γενεὰ αὕτη μέχρις οὗ ταῦτα πάντα γένηται.

This generation will surely not pass away <u>until</u> all these things <u>take place</u>. (Mark 13:30) [This passage also includes an example of emphatic future negation.]

UNDERSTANDING THE CHAPTER AND PREPARING FOR THE QUIZ:

(1) Re-read the chapter, paying close attention to the various *contextual clues* which help to identify each subjunctive use and to the *translation patterns* to be employed in translating the various uses.

(2) Go over all translation passages and practice *identifying the subjunctive uses*.

(3) Answer the *review questions*. If there are any that you can't answer, check the chapter again.

Chapter 36

INFINITIVES: The infinitive is a ***verbal noun***. Like a verb, it has ***tense*** and ***voice***. Although it does not display any noun characteristics in and of itself (i.e., it does not change form for case, number, and gender), it sometimes appears with a ***neuter singular definite article*** (the so-called ***"articular Infinitive"***). It can also be modified by neuter singular adjectives.

There are four tenses of the infinitive, but only three are used to any extent: ***present, aorist, and perfect*** (the other is future). As with the subjunctive, the tense of an infinitive does not represent absolute time, although the infinitive can take on relative time value *in specific contexts.* As we have seen before, the present represents an on-going, continuous, or repeated action or something which is always happening or true, the aorist represents the action as a whole, and the perfect represents the continuation of a state or the existing results of an action.

The basic translation of both the present and aorist infinitives is "to…" (e.g., "to send" / "to be sent"). The basic translation of most perfect infinitives is "to have…" (e.g., "to have saved" / "to have been saved"). As was the case with participles, however, this basic translation will frequently be altered based on the specific function of the infinitive. Nor should it be forgotten that, although present and aorist infinitives may *sound alike*, they are, in fact, different in aspect. The categories of use presented in this chapter and in Chapter 37 cover the most frequent uses of the infinitive. Keep in mind that several of these categories parallel the uses of ἵνα clauses (see Chapter 34).

ACCUSATIVE SUBJECT OF THE INFINITIVE: If the subject of the infinitive is the same as that of the main verb, it does not need to be repeated. If a separate subject is expressed for the infinitive, it will usually be in the ***accusative case***. (***You should add this to your list of uses for the accusative case***.) If this leads to confusion with a predicate noun (also accusative to agree with the accusative subject), the same rules apply as when the verb is indicative: a pronoun, a proper name, or a noun with a definite article takes precedence as the subject (see Chapter 10). If it leads to confusion with an accusative direct object, logic and/or context will usually provide the solution.

ADDITIONAL VOCABULARY: There are several verbs which are frequently used with an infinitive. These should be added to your working vocabulary.

βούλομαι, ---, ---, ---, ---, ἐβουλήθην – wish, want; be willing

δεῖ – it is necessary; one must, one ought (This is the present active third person singular of δέω: "bind," used as an impersonal verb; imperfect: ἔδει.)

δύναμαι, δυνήσομαι, ---, ---, ---, ἐδυνήθην – be able, can (The present
   and imperfect are conjugated with *alpha* as the connecting vowel. This
   alpha often causes certain present or imperfect forms to be mistaken for
   first aorists; be forewarned! Note that ***there is no first aorist middle***.)

ἔξεστι(ν) – it is proper, it is permitted, it is lawful (This is the present active
   third person singular of an otherwise unused verb: ἔξειμι.)

θέλω, θελήσω, ἠθέλησα, ---, ---, --- – wish, want; will (The imperfect and
   aorist have *eta* as an augment, because the classical first principal part was
   ἐθέλω.)

μέλλω, μελλήσω, ---, ---, ---, --- – be about, be going; intend; *if* the context
   requires: be destined

ὀφείλω, ---, ---, ---, ---, --- – ought, must (with infinitive); owe

The negative μή and its compounds are used with the infinitive.

FORMS: There are not a lot of different infinitive forms, but a few of them are a
bit tricky.

Present active: First principal part + ειν *(λύειν, ἀποστέλλειν, βαπτίζειν)*

Present M/P: First principal part + ε + σθαι *(ἔρχεσθαι, ἐκπορεύεσθαι,
   διώκεσθαι)*

First aorist active: Third principal part [without augment] + αι *(ἀποστεῖλαι,
   ἀποστέλλω, καλέσαι, ποιῆσαι, κηρύξαι)*

The accent is always on the penult; a circumflex if this has a long vowel or
diphthong, an acute accent if it has a short vowel.   *Note*: This form is sometimes
confused with the aorist active nominative plural feminine participle. The latter
has *one more syllable*: λύσα<u>σα</u>ι, ἀποστείλα<u>σα</u>ι, καλέσα<u>σα</u>ι.

First aorist middle: Third principal part [without augment] + α + σθαι
   (δέξασθαι, ἄρξασθαι, αἰτήσασθαι)

First aorist passive: Sixth principal part [without augment] + ναι *(λυθῆναι,
   ἐγερθῆναι, βαπτισθῆναι, φοβηθῆναι)*

Second aorist active: Third principal part [without augment] + εῖν The accent is
   always a circumflex on the ultima. *(λαβεῖν, ἐλθεῖν, ἰδεῖν, εἰπεῖν)*.

Second aorist middle: Third principal part [without augment] + $\acute{\epsilon}$ + σθαι
   (γενέσθαι, περιβαλλέσθαι.)

Second aorist passive: Sixth principal part [without augment] + ναι (χαρῆναι,
   ἀποσταλῆναι, στραφῆναι.)

Perfect active: Fourth principal part [reduplication stays] + $\acute{\epsilon}$ + ναι
   (ἐληλυθέναι, πεποιηκέναι, εἰδέναι) Remember that this last example
is the infinitive of οἶδα and will have a *present tense* translation.

Perfect M/P: Fifth principal part [reduplication stays] + σθαι (σεσῶσθαι,
   δεδιώχθαι, γεγράφθαι) **Note:** The *sigma* combines with consonants in
   the same way as the second person plural of the perfect M/P indicative.

εἰμί: present (active) – εἶναι

CONTRACT VERBS (PRESENT ONLY):

epsilon contract verbs: ποιεῖν, ποιεῖσθαι
alpha contract verbs: ἀγαπᾶν, ἀγαπᾶσθαι
omicron contract verbs: πληροῦν, πληροῦσθαι   [Be careful; the present active
   infinitive is identical to the present active nominative / accusative
   singular neuter participle.]

-μι VERBS:[2] (Remember that any first aorist active, perfect, or aorist passive
infinitives are formed regularly.)

δίδωμι:
present active – διδόναι   present M/P – δίδοσθαι
second aorist active – δοῦναι

τίθημι:
present active – τιθέναι   present M/P – τίθεσθαι
second aorist active – θεῖναι   second aorist middle – θέσθαι

---

[2] Summary based on Hewett, p. 177.

ἵστημι:
present active – ἱστάναι   present M/P – ἵστασθαι
second aorist active – στῆναι

ἀπόλλυμι:
first aorist active – ἀπολέσαι   second aorist middle – ἀπολέσθαι

ἀφίημι: present active – ἀφιέναι
          second aorist active – ἀφεῖναι

δείκνυμι: present active – δεικνύειν

Note the following two irregular forms:

βαίνω: 2nd aorist active – βῆναι [Only in compounds: ἀναβῆναι, καταβῆναι.]

γινώσκω: 2nd aorist active – γνῶναι

Uses of the Infinitive (Part 1)

SUBJECT: An infinitive or an infinitive phrase can function as the ***subject of a verb***. This is especially common with impersonal verbs and ἐστίν. Two of the most frequently used impersonal verbs are δεῖ ("it is necessary") and ἔξεστι(ν) ("it is proper, permitted, lawful"). The presence of the impersonal verb is the contextual clue to a subject infinitive. The imperfect of δεῖ (ἔδει) is used to indicate something that "should have" taken place.

> ἐπηρώτων αὐτὸν εἰ <u>ἔξεστιν</u> ἀνδρὶ γυναῖκα <u>ἀπολῦσαι.</u>

> They began asking him if / whether <u>it was lawful</u> for a man <u>to divorce</u> a
>   woman / his wife. (Mark 10:2)

Notice that with ἔξεστι the person *for whom* something is (or is not) lawful, proper, etc. goes in the *dative case.*

> καὶ καθὼς Μωϋσῆς ὕψωσεν τὸν ὄφιν ἐν τῇ ἐρήμῳ, οὕτως
>   <u>ὑψωθῆναι δεῖ</u> τὸν υἱὸν τοῦ ἀνθρώπου.

> And just as Moses lifted up the serpent in the desert, so it is necessary that
> the Son of Man be lifted up. (John 3:14)

Note that the word "that" must be added. In this second passage, τὸν υἱὸν is an example of the accusative subject of an infinitive. The translation may be left in the more literal form of the accusative subject may be made the subject of "must" ["…the Son of Man must be lifted up."]

DIRECT OBJECT: Although true direct object infinitives are rare, the following two categories are classified by some grammarians as subcategories of the direct object category. The logic of this can be seen in that, for the most part, both of them answer the question "What?" in regard to the main verb with which they are connected.

COMPLEMENTARY: Often an infinitive is used to "complete" the thought begun in the main verb. The contextual clue to this use is the *main verb itself*. Among the most common are: ἄρχομαι, βούλομαι, δύναμαι, ἐπιτρέπω ("allow", "permit" – also ἀφίημι), ζητέω, θέλω, μέλλω, and ὀφείλω.

   οὐ δύναμαι ἐγὼ ποιεῖν ἀπ᾽ ἐμαυτοῦ οὐδέν.

   I cannot do / am not able to do anything on my own. (John 5:30a)

   λέγει αὐτῷ, Θέλεις ὑγιὴς γενέσθαι;

   He said to him, "Do you wish to become well?" (John 5:6)

INDIRECT DISCOURSE: The infinitive is used after a *verb of perception or communication* to express the substance of what is perceived or communicated. This use parallels that of a ὅτι clause and is often translated in the same way (*including the concept of time relative to the main verb*). There are many possible introductory verbs and the introductory verb itself is the contextual clue to identification. Among the most common are ἀκούω, δοκέω ("think"), ἐρωτάω (and its compounds), ἐλπίζω, κελεύω (and other verbs meaning "order" or "command"), κρίνω, λέγω, νομίζω ("think," "suppose"), and παρακαλέω ("encourage," "urge," etc.). *Note:* When an infinitive is used to express indirect discourse, there is no Greek word for "that." It must be included by the translator on the basis of recognizing the indirect discourse.

ἦλθον λέγουσαι καὶ ὀπτασίαν ἀγγέλων <u>ἑωρακέναι</u>, οἳ λέγουσιν
<u>αὐτὸν ζῆν</u>.

> They came saying / and said <u>that they had</u> also <u>seen</u> a vision of angels,
> who said <u>that he was alive</u>. (Luke 24:23)

We know from the form of the participle λέγουσαι that the "they" are women. In the first example of indirect discourse in this passage there is no separate subject expressed because it is the same as the subject of "came." In the second example there is a separate subject: αὐτόν.

Note: When testing to see if an infinitive is in indirect discourse, it is sometimes helpful to see if you can recover the direct statement, thought, command, etc. In this example the original statements would have been: "We have seen a vision of angels," and "He is alive."

καὶ ἤρξαντο παρακαλεῖν <u>αὐτὸν ἀπελθεῖν</u> ἀπὸ τῶν ὁρίων αὐτῶν.

> And they began to beg <u>him to depart</u> from their region. / And they began
> to beg <u>that he depart</u> from their region. (Mark 5:17)

NOTES:

(1) There is also a ***complementary infinitive*** in this sentence (παρακαλεῖν). The contextual clue is the verb ἤρξαντο ("began").

(2) The correct identification of αὐτόν is a bit tricky here. In the first translation it certainly sounds like "him" is the direct object of "beg." In the second, however, it is clear that it represents the subject of "depart." In fact, it is serving as both. Since, however, the ***accusative subject of the infinitive*** is new to you (and probably seems a little strange at this point) you will have to be careful not to forget about it in such situations. If you are unsure as to whether this is a possible answer, try out the translation using "that" to see if the word in the accusative case winds up as the subject of the verb in the infinitive form.

(3) In the parallel passage which appeared in the Chapter 34 Exercises (#2 in the Translation Passages), a substantival / noun clause is used as the direct object of "beg." This lends support to the idea that indirect discourse can be considered a subcategory of the ***direct object infinitive***.

ACCUSATIVE OF MEASURE (OR EXTENT OF TIME): The accusative indicates the duration or extent of the verbal action. It answers the question "For how long?" Sometimes the word "for" needs to be added to the translation. Wallace gives a useful summary of the genitive, dative, and accusative of time (pp. 202–203).

> καὶ ἀσπασάμενοι τοὺς ἀδελφοὺς ἐμείναμεν <u>ἡμέραν μίαν</u> παρ' αὐτοῖς.

> And after we had greeted the brethren, we stayed with them <u>for one day</u>.
> (Acts 21:7)

[**Note:** The accusative of measure also covers "extent of space." This answers the question "How far?" Example: "We went on <u>for ten more miles</u>." This use, however, is quite uncommon, whereas *extent of time* is fairly common.]

UNDERSTANDING THE CHAPTER AND PREPARING FOR THE QUIZ:

(1) As in the preceding units, the first thing to do is learn the ***forms***. Note especially those which have the potential to be confusing, e.g. the present active of *epsilon* contract verbs and the second aorist active, both of which end in εἶν.

(2) Then re-read the part of the chapter which introduces ***three infinitive uses***: ***subject, complementary,*** and ***indirect discourse.***

(3) First of all, you should work carefully through the ***homework passages***, using the answer key to help you recognize and translate the infinitive uses. Then, after the class work day, finish as many as possible of the ***remaining passages***. Obviously these give you experience in recognizing and translating the infinitive uses, but they also give you overall practice in translation. (Since some of them also include participles and/or subjunctives, they give you a good sense of what you may encounter as you move into more advanced work.)

(4) After all the translation work is finished, answer the ***review questions***. These are meant to be a final check on how well you know the new material.

(5) Note that this chapter gives you two additional uses for the accusative case: ***accusative subject of the infinitive*** and ***accusative of measure (or extent of time)***.

Chapter 37
Uses of the Infinitive (Part 2)

EPEXEGETICAL: An infinitive or infinitive phrase may be used to explain, clarify, or qualify a ***noun or adjective***. As was the case with epexegetical ἵνα clauses, the infinitive generally appears with certain kinds of words which serve as a contextual clue. Some of these words are those expressing fitness, authority (e.g., ἐξουσία), freedom, hope, need (e.g., χρεία), obligation, or readiness. There are, however, other examples involving nouns which arc harder to categorize.

> ἐξουσίαν ἔχω θεῖναι αὐτήν, καὶ ἐξουσίαν ἔχω πάλιν λαβεῖν αὐτήν.

> I have authority to lay it down, and I have authority to take it up again. (John 10:18b)

An epexegetical infinitive may also be preceded by τοῦ (the genitive singular neuter definite article). This is an idiomatic construction. It does not imply any specific genitive case use and does not affect the translation.

> ἐπλήσθησαν αἱ ἡμέραι τοῦ τεκεῖν αὐτήν.

> The days for her to give birth were fulfilled / came to an end. (Luke 2:6)

This second example is somewhat of an exception to the sort of words which are normally associated with the epexegetical infinitive. If we analyze the context, however, it is clear that the infinitive is giving additional clarifying information about the noun "days." [Note the ***accusative subject*** *of the infinitive*: αὐτήν.]

PURPOSE: The infinitive is used to indicate the purpose for the action of the main verb. In relationship to that verb, the purpose infinitive answers the question "Why?" This contextual relationship is the clue to a purpose infinitive. Most purpose infinitives can be translated with just "to" (the literal infinitive translation) or "in order to." Occasionally, however, you will need to translate with a full clause introduced by "that" or "in order that." Again, this use parallels that of a ἵνα clause. An infinitive of purpose can appear in several different constructions.

(1) The infinitive alone:

> ἰδοὺ ἐξῆλθεν ὁ σπείρων σπεῖραι.

> Behold, the sower went out to sow. (Mark 4:3b)

(2) τοῦ + infinitive: Here again the use of the article is idiomatic and is not translated. The parallel passage in Luke uses this construction for the infinitive of purpose.

> Ἐξῆλθεν ὁ σπείρων <u>τοῦ σπεῖραι</u> τὸν σπόρον αὐτοῦ.

The sower went out <u>to sow</u> his seed. (Luke 8:5a)

(3) εἰς τό or πρὸς τό + infinitive: Again the neuter singular article is used, here in the accusative case following one of the two prepositions. This also is idiomatic and the preposition and article are not translated.

> ἀπήγαγον αὐτὸν <u>εἰς τὸ σταυρῶσαι</u>.

They led him away <u>to crucify</u> [him]. (Matthew 27:31)

> ἐνδύσασθε τὴν πανοπλίαν τοῦ θεοῦ <u>πρὸς τὸ δύνασθαι ὑμας</u>
>   στῆναι πρὸς τὰς μεθοδείας τοῦ διαβόλου.

Put on the full armor of God <u>that you may be able</u> to stand against the
      tricks of the Devil. (Ephesians 6:11)

NOTES:

(1) There are *two infinitives* in the second passage; the first (δύνασθαι) is in a ***purpose*** construction and the second (στῆναι) is a ***complement*** (see Chapter 36) to the first.

(2) The first infinitive has its subject ("you") expressed. For this reason the translation has to use a clause introduced by "that" or "in order that." There is no specific word with this meaning; it is part of the nature of the purpose infinitive.

(3) Do not be fooled into thinking that δύνασθαι is an aorist middle infinitive. Remember that present and imperfect forms of this verb are conjugated using *alpha*.

For the preceding uses of the infinitive, as well as for those uses in Chapter 36, it is often (though not always) possible to keep the basic infinitive translation. For the following uses that will not be possible, so other translation patterns must be learned. These involve converting the infinitive and its accompanying material into some sort of ***subordinate clause***. An accusative subject of the infinitive becomes the subject of the subordinate clause.

RESULT: Result infinitive constructions overlap to a certain extent those used for purpose, sometimes making it difficult to distinguish one from the other. The most common way to express result with an infinitive, however, involves the introductory "red flag" word ὥστε. The appropriate translations for ὥστε in the context of a result infinitive are "so that," "so as to," or "with the result that."

> καὶ ἐγένετο ὡσεὶ νεκρός, <u>ὥστε τοὺς πολλοὺς λέγειν</u> ὅτι ἀπέθανεν.

> And he became like a dead person, <u>so that / with the result that many were saying</u> that he had died. (Mark 9:26b)

(1) Note the **accusative subject** *of the infinitive*: πολλούς.

(2) The result infinitive serves as the introductory verb for an indirect statement.

(3) ὥστε is not used exclusively with infinitives. See John 3:16 for the best known example of ὥστε with the indicative.

TIME: Infinitive time constructions are expressed by **prepositional phrases** as follows. The construction itself is the contextual clue to the use. Once again an accusative subject of the infinitive is common.

(1) ἐν τῷ + infinitive ("while" with a present infinitive, "when" with an aorist infinitive):

> ἐγένετο δὲ <u>ἐν τῷ εἶναι αὐτοὺς</u> ἐκεῖ ἐπλήσθησαν αἱ ἡμέραι τοῦ τεκεῖν αὐτήν.

> And it came to pass that <u>while they were</u> there, the days were fulfilled for her to give birth. (Luke 2:6)

> καὶ <u>ἐν τῷ γενέσθαι τὴν φωνὴν</u> εὑρέθη Ἰησοῦς μόνος.

> And <u>when the voice had occurred</u> Jesus was found alone. (Luke 9:36a)

Note: When the aorist infinitive occurs in this construction it is *sometimes* necessary to add "had" to the translation. We might wonder why the writer didn't use the construction listed below involving μετά ("after"). The answer is probably the same as that involving the temporal participle: if the time frame is not especially stressed or if there is very little separation between the two actions, "when" is preferred over "after."

(2) πρὸ τοῦ, πρίν, πρὶν ἤ + infinitive ("before"):

Κύριε, κατάβηθι πρὶν ἀποθανεῖν τὸ παιδίον μου.

Sir, come down <u>before my child dies.</u> (John 4:49)

Πρὸ τοῦ σε Φίλιππον φωνῆσαι ὄντα ὑπὸ τὴν συκὴν εἶδόν σε.

<u>Before Philip called</u> you, while you were under the fig tree, I saw you. (John 1:48b)

Note: In this sentence, both σε and *Φίλιππον* are accusative, so one must rely on context to determine which word is the subject of the infinitive and which is the direct object. In this case we know that it was Philip who called Nathanael and not the other way around.

(3) μετὰ τό + infinitive ("after"):

παρέστησεν ἑαυτὸν ζῶντα μετὰ τὸ παθεῖν αὐτόν.

He presented himself alive <u>after he suffered / had suffered.</u> (Acts 1:3)

CAUSE: (διὰ τό + infinitive – "because") – The infinitive phrase gives the reason or cause for the main verb. Again the construction itself is the contextual clue.

Ἀνέβη δὲ καὶ Ἰωσήφ...διὰ τὸ εἶναι αὐτὸν ἐξ οἴκου καὶ πατριᾶς Δαυίδ.

And Joseph also went up...<u>because he was</u> of the house and family of David. (Luke 2:4)

UNDERSTANDING THE CHAPTER AND PREPARING FOR THE QUIZ:

(1) Re-read the chapter and learn the *new uses*, the *contextual clues* to each, and the *ways they are to be translated*.

(2) Finish any remaining *translation passages* and answer the *review questions*.

Chapter 38
Imperative Mood: Forms and Uses

THE IMPERATIVE MOOD: The imperative is known as the *mood of intention.* It represents an attempt to bring about a desired action through the agency of another or to prevent an undesired action. There are only two tenses: present and aorist. Second person and third person forms are used; the first person slot is taken over by the hortatory subjunctive. Second person forms, for the most part, do not use the word "you." They just use to vocabulary word alone, e.g. "Save me." "Come here." There is no Greek punctuation mark corresponding to our exclamation mark, but that is sometimes appropriate to use with an imperative. Third person forms are translated with "let him / her / it…" and "let them…." As with other verb forms apart from the indicative, there is no augment on aorist forms. μή and its compounds are used for negation.

FORMS:

* *

	Present Active Imperative of βαπτίζω		Present M/P Imperative of of προσεύχομαι	
	Singular	*Plural*	*Singular*	*Plural*
2nd	βάπτιζε	βαπτίζετε	προσεύχου	προσεύχεσθε
3rd	βαπτιζέτω	βαπτιζέτωσαν	προσευχέσθω	προσευχέσθωσαν

* *

Note that the present tense **second person plural forms** are identical to the corresponding forms of the indicative.

* *

	First Aorist Active Imperative of δοξάζω		First Aorist Middle Imperative of ἐργάζομαι	
	Singular	*Plural*	*Singular*	*Plural*
2nd	δόξασον	δοξάσατε	ἔργασαι	ἐργάσασθε
3rd	δοξασάτω	δοξασάτωσαν	ἐργασάσθω	ἐργασάσθωσαν

* *

NOTE: The *first aorist active infinitive* and the *first aorist middle imperative second person singular* are *spelled* the same. If the form has only two syllables, they will also be *accented* the same, e.g. ἦρξαι. If the form has more than two syllables, the infinitive is always accented on the penult, whereas the imperative accent recedes to the antepenult, e.g. αἰτῆσαι (infinitive), αἴτησαι (imperative) The only verbs, however, which have both forms in normal use are ones with one meaning for active forms and another for middle forms, e.g. αἰτέω, ἄρχω, ἐνδύω, and φυλάσσω.

* *

	Second Aorist Active Imperative of ἐκβάλλω		Second Aorist Middle Imperative of γίνομαι	
	Singular	*Plural*	*Singular*	*Plural*
2nd	ἔκβαλε	ἐκβάλετε	γενοῦ	γένεσθε
3rd	ἐκβαλέτω	ἐκβαλέτωσαν	γενέσθω	γενέσθωσαν

* *

NOTE: There are five second person singular second aorist active forms which accent the ultima: εἰπέ, ἐλθέ, λαβέ, εὑρέ, ἰδέ.

* * * * * * * * * * * * * * * * * * * *

	First Aorist Passive Imperative of πορεύομαι	
	Singular	*Plural*
2nd	πορεύθητι	πορεύθητε
3rd	πορευθήτω	πορευθήτωσαν

* * * * * * * * * * * * * * * * * * * *

* *

	Second Aorist Passive Imperative of στρέφω and χαίρω			
	Singular	*Plural*	*Singular*	*Plural*
2nd	στράφητι	στράφητε	χάρηθι	χάρητε
3rd	στραφήτω	στραφήτωσαν	χαρήτω	χαρήτωσαν

* *

NOTE: If the penult of the *second person singular* aorist passive has a *theta* (all first aorists), *phi,* or *chi* before the *eta,* the ending is –τι. If, however, the penult has some other letter before the *eta,* the ending is –θι (χάρηθι, φάνηθι).

CONTRACT VERBS (PRESENT TENSE):

```
* * * * * * * * * * * * * * * * * * * * * * * * * * * * *
*           Present Active and Present M/P Imperative of αἰτέω      *
*                                                                   *
*       Singular      Plural          Singular       Plural         *
*                                                                   *
*   2nd  αἴτει        αἰτεῖτε         αἰτοῦ          αἰτεῖσθε        *
*   3rd  αἰτείτω      αἰτείτωσαν      αἰτείσθω       αἰτείσθωσαν     *
*                                                                   *
*          Present Active and Present M/P Imperative of πλανάω       *
*                                                                   *
*   2nd  πλάνα        πλανᾶτε         πλανῶ          πλανᾶσθε        *
*   3rd  πλανάτω      πλανάτωσαν      πλανάσθωω      πλανάσθωσαν     *
*                                                                   *
*          Present Active and Present M/P Imperative of φανερόω      *
*                                                                   *
*   2nd  φανέρου      φανεροῦτε       φανεροῦ        φανεροῦσθε      *
*   3rd  φανερούτω    φανερούτωσαν    φανερούσθω     φανερούσθωσαν   *
*                                                                   *
* * * * * * * * * * * * * * * * * * * * * * * * * * * * *
```

εἰμί – present (active) second person singular: ἴσθι
        present (active) third person singular and plural: ἔστω (ἤτω)   ἔστωσαν

–μι **VERBS:** The following forms appear in the GNT:[3]

δίδωμι – present active second person singular and plural: δίδου   δίδοτε
        second aorist active second person singular and plural: δός   δότε

τίθημι – second aorist active second person plural: θέτε
        second aorist middle second person plural: θέσθε

---

[3] Summary based on Hewett, p. 191.

ἵστημι – second aorist active second person singular and plural: στῆθι   στῆτε
[The compound ἀνίστημι also has a second person singular form.
ἀνάστα.]

ἀφίημι   second aorist active second person singular and plural. ἄφες   ἄφετε

Other second aorist forms are:

γινώσκω – second person singular and plural: γνῶθι   γνῶτε
third person singular: γνώτω

ἀναβαίνω – second person singular and plural: ἀνάβα   ἀνάβατε

καταβαίνω – second person singular: κατάβηθι

In James 1:19, the word ἴστε may be a second person plural imperative of οἶδα.

Uses of the Imperative

COMMAND: Although there are a variety of nuances possible, the most basic function is to give a ***command***. The ***aorist tense*** commands the action as a whole (Just do it!). The ***present tense*** is used to emphasize that what is commanded is to be an on-going or repeated process. (Keep on doing it! Do it all the time! Make it a habit / life-style! Start doing and continue to do it!)

ἀκολούθει μοι.

Follow me! (Mark 2:14a)

Ἄρον τὸν κράβαττον καὶ περιπάτει.

Take up your pallet and walk. (John 5:11)

ὁ ἔχων ὦτα ἀκουέτω.

He who has ears, let him hear! / Let the one who has ears hear! (Matthew 11:15)

NOTES:

(1) When a command is in the second person, the word "you" is generally not used unless an emphatic pronoun subject is involved.

$\underline{\Delta \acute{o}\tau \epsilon}$ αὐτοῖς ὑμεῖς φαγεῖν.

You <u>give</u> them [something] to eat! (Mark 6:37a)

(2) The third person imperatives are translated with "let him/her/it…" and "let them…." This should not be confused with the idea of permission (although occasionally permission is implied). It is more like saying "he/she/it/they must."

ἕκαστος ἡμῶν τῷ πλησίον <u>ἀρεσκέτω</u>.

<u>Let</u> each of us <u>[him] strive to please</u> his neighbor. (Romans 15:2)

PROHIBITION: The forbidding of an action amounts to a negative command or *prohibition*. The use of μή or a compound of it turns the ***present imperative*** into a prohibition. There are two aspects to such prohibitions.

(1) The prohibition may be used to halt an action already in progress. It says, in effect, "Stop…."

<u>μὴ ποιεῖτε</u> τὸν οἶκον τοῦ πατρός μου οἶκον ἐμπορίου.

<u>Stop making</u> my Father's house a market-house! / <u>Do not make</u>… (John 2:16)

The formula μὴ φοβοῦ / μὴ φοβεῖσθε is typically used to re-assure those who are already afraid.

(2) The other use of a present tense prohibition is to give a general precept. (Don't ever do this! Don't get in the habit or continue in the habit of doing it! Don't make it part of your life-style!)

<u>Μὴ θησαυρίζετε</u> ὑμῖν θησαυροὺς ἐπὶ τῆς γῆς.

<u>Do not store up</u> for yourselves treasures on earth. (Matthew 6:19)

Note that the personal pronoun "you" here takes on the quality of a reflexive.

Remember that a summary prohibition is generally expressed not by the imper-ative, but by μή and the aorist subjunctive.

REQUEST OR ENTREATY: A distinction is sometimes made between a command and a *request* or *entreaty*. The form is the same and the translation sounds the same. The difference is in attitude; generally a superior person is being addressed or the speaker is pleading with another. This is common in prayers. It is the equivalent of saying "Please…"

ἠρώτων αὐτὸν οἱ μαθηταὶ λέγοντες, ῾Ραββί, φάγε.

The disciples were urging him saying, "Rabbi, [please] eat." (John 4:31)

All of the imperatives in the Lord's Prayer would go in this category:

ἁγιασθήτω (aorist passive 3 s. ἁγιάζω)
ἐλθέτω (2nd aorist active 3 s. ἔρχομαι)
γενηθήτω (aorist passive 3 s. γίνομαι)
δός (2nd aorist active 2 s. δίδωμι)
ἄφες (2nd aorist active 2 s. ἀφίημι)
ῥῦσαι (1st aorist middle 2 s. ῥύομαι)

Note that the one prohibition in the Lord's Prayer is a summary prohibition. For that reason, it is expressed by the aorist *subjunctive* and not the aorist imperative: μὴ εἰσενέγκῃς (1st aorist active 2 s. εἰσφέρω).

UNDERSTANDING THE CHAPTER AND PREPARING FOR THE EXAM:

(1) Go over all the *forms* and do the form and translation exercise.

(2) Make sure you understand the difference between a *command in the present tense* and a *command in the aorist*.

(3) Learn the two possible nuances of a *present tense prohibition*.

(4) Make note of the fact that an imperative addressed to a person in a superior position may be referred to as a *request or entreaty*.

(5) Do the *review* which follows the exercises.

Appendix A
Principal Parts List

The following list gives the principal parts for all verbs covered in the introductory course. For vocabulary meanings, see the individual chapters (number given in parentheses) and/or a lexicon. A dotted line indicates either that no form of that principal part appears in the Greek New Testament or that no principal part exists. Thus you do not need to concern yourself with them at this time. If you encounter such a verb form outside of the GNT, you should have enough knowledge about how Greek verbs work to track it down.

NOTES:

(1) For some verbs there are both first and second aorist forms. Usually this is a result of "regularizing" the second aorist forms. Alternate forms are listed in parentheses, as are other alternate forms which occasionally occur.

(2) In compiling this list, I have consulted several sources (Bowne, Metzger, and Vance) in addition to the Danker lexicon. While there is considerable agreement among them, there are also some discrepancies. If you find a form which is not listed here, you should be able to use your knowledge of Greek principal parts to figure it out.

(3) On occasion, I have listed in brackets a principal part for an uncompounded verb, even though that principal part only appears in the GNT in compounds. This will enable you to recognize the form if / when you encounter such compounds.

(4) Some principal parts only appear in the GNT as participles.

(5) Remember that some –μι verbs use a different stem for their non-indicative aorist active and/or middle forms.

(6) The list in the workbook is arranged in columns and has space for adding definitions and other notes. It would probably be better to use that one for your study and save this one for reference.

ἀγαπάω *(22)*, ἀγαπήσω, ἠγάπησα, ἠγάπηκα, ἠγάπημαι, ἠγαπήθην
ἀγοράζω *(2)*, ---, ἠγόρασα, ---, ἠγόρασμαι, ἠγοράσθην
ἄγω *(6)*, ἄξω, ἤγαγον, ---, [ἦγμαι], ἤχθην
αἴρω *(29)*, ἀρῶ, ἦρα, ἦρκα, ἦρμαι, ἤρθην
αἰτέω *(20)*, αἰτήσω, ᾔτησα, ᾔτηκα, [ᾔτημαι], ---
ἀκολουθέω *(20)*, ἀκολουθήσω, ἠκολούθησα, ἠκολούθηκα, ---, ---
ἀκούω *(2)*, ἀκούσω (ἀκούσομαι), ἤκουσα, ἀκήκοα, ---, ἠκούσθην

ἁμαρτάνω *(9)*, ἁμαρτήσω, ἥμαρτον (ἡμάρτησα), ἡμάρτηκα,   , ---

ἀναβαίνω *(28)*, ἀναβήσομαι, ἀνέβην, ἀναβέβηκα, ---, ---

ἀνίστημι *(11)*, ἀναστήσω, ἀνέστησα / ἀνέστην, ---, ---, --- **[Note:** The
two aorists are not just alternate forms, but have separate meanings.]

ἀνοίγω *(11)*, ἀνοίξω, ἀνέῳξα (ἤνοιξα, ἠνέῳξα), ἀνέῳγα, ἀνέῳγμαι
(ἤνοιγμαι, ἠνέῳγμαι), ἀνεῴχθην (ἠνοίχθην, ἠνεῴχθην, ἠνοίγην)

ἀπαγγέλλω *(30)*, ἀπαγγελῶ, ἀπήγγειλα, ---, ---, ἀπηγγέλην **[Note:**
Some of the other compounds of ἀγγέλλω have a fifth principal part
stem: ἤγγελμαι.]

ἀπέρχομαι *(13)*, ἀπελεύσομαι, ἀπῆλθον, ἀπελήλυθα, ---, ---

ἀποδίδωμι *(31)*, ἀποδώσω, ἀπέδωκα, ---, ---, ἀπεδόθην

ἀποθνῄσκω *(11)*, ἀποθανοῦμαι, ἀπέθανον, ---, ---, ---

ἀποκρίνομαι *(30)*, ---, ἀπεκρινάμην, ---, ---, ἀπεκρίθην

ἀποκτείνω *(30)*, ἀποκτενῶ, ἀπέκτεινα, ---, ---, ἀπεκτάνθην

ἀπόλλυμι *(31)*, ἀπολέσω (ἀπολῶ), ἀπώλεσα, ἀπόλωλα, ---, ---

ἀπολύω *(11)*, ἀπολύσω, ἀπέλυσα, ---, ἀπολέλυμαι, ἀπελύθην

ἀποστέλλω *(28)*, ἀποστελῶ, ἀπέστειλα, ἀπέσταλκα, ἀπέσταλμαι,
ἀπεστάλην

ἅπτω *(18)*, ---, ἧψα, ---, ---, ---

ἄρχω *(6,18)*, ἄρξω, ἦρξα, ---, --- , ---

ἀφίημι *(31)*, ἀφήσω, ἀφῆκα, ---, ἀφέωμαι, ἀφέθην

βάλλω *(9)*, βαλῶ, ἔβαλον (ἔβαλα), βέβληκα, βέβλημαι, ἐβλήθην

βαπτίζω *(2)*, βαπτίσω, ἐβάπτισα, ---, βεβάπτισμαι, ἐβαπτίσθην

βλέπω *(6)*, βλέψω, ἔβλεψα, ---, ---, ---

βούλομαι *(36)*, ---, ---, ---, ---, ἐβουλήθην

γεννάω *(22)*, γεννήσω, ἐγέννησα, γεγέννηκα, γεγέννημαι, ἐγεννήθην

γίνομαι *(13)*, γενήσομαι, ἐγενόμην, γέγονα, γεγένημαι, ἐγενήθην

γινώσκω *(4)*, γνώσομαι, ἔγνων, ἔγνωκα, ἔγνωσμαι, ἐγνώσθην

γράφω *(6)*, γράψω, ἔγραψα, γέγραφα, γέγραμμαι, ἐγράφην

δεῖ *(36)* [Impersonal verb, third person singular of δέω.]

δείκνυμι (δεικνύω) *(31)*, δείξω, ἔδειξα, ---, [δέδειγμαι], ἐδείχθην

δέχομαι *(13)*, [δέξομαι], ἐδεξάμην, ---, δέδεγμαι, ἐδέχθην

διδάσκω *(4)*, διδάξω, ἐδίδαξα, ---, ---, ἐδιδάχθην

δίδωμι *(31)*, δώσω, ἔδωκα, δέδωκα, δέδομαι, ἐδόθην

διέρχομαι *(13)*, διελεύσομαι, διῆλθον, διελήλυθα, ---, ---

δικαιόω *(22)*, δικαιώσω, ἐδικαίωσα, ---, δεδικαίωμαι, ἐδικαιώθην

διώκω *(6)*, διώξω, ἐδίωξα, ---, δεδίωγμαι, ἐδιώχθην

δοξάζω *(2)*, δοξάσω, ἐδόξασα, ---, δεδόξασμαι, ἐδοξάσθην

δύναμαι *(36)*, δυνήσομαι, ---, ---, ---, ἠδυνήθην
ἐγγίζω *(28)*, ἐγγιῶ, ἤγγισα, ἤγγικα, ---, ---
ἐγείρω *(29)*, ἐγερῶ, ἤγειρα, ---, ἐγήγερμαι, ἠγέρθην
εἰμί *(10)*, ἔσομαι, ---, ---, ---, ---
εἰσέρχομαι *(13)*, εἰσελεύσομαι, εἰσῆλθον (εἰσῆλθα), εἰσελήλυθα,
        ---, ---
ἐκβάλλω *(11)*, ἐκβαλῶ, ἐξέβαλον, ἐκβέβληκα, ---, ἐξεβλήθην
ἐκπορεύομαι *(13)*, ἐκπορεύσομαι, ---, ---, ---, ---, ---
ἐλπίζω *(2)*, ἐλπιῶ, ἤλπισα, ἤλπικα, ---, ---
ἐξέρχομαι *(13)*, ἐξελεύσομαι, ἐξῆλθον (ἐξῆλθα), ἐξελήλυθα, ---, ---
ἔξεστι *(36)* [Impersonal verb, third person singular of the unused ἔξειμι.]
ἐπιτίθημι *(31)*, ἐπιθήσω, ἐπέθηκα, ---, ---, ---
ἐπιτιμάω *(22)*, ---, ἐπετίμησα, ---, ---, ---
ἐργάζομαι *(15)*, ---, ἠργασάμην, ---, εἴργασμαι, ---
ἔρχομαι *(13)*, ἐλεύσομαι, ἦλθον (ἦλθα), ἐλήλυθα, ---, ---
ἐρωτάω *(22)*, ἐρωτήσω, ἠρώτησα, ---, ---, ---
ἐσθίω *(2)*, φάγομαι, ἔφαγον, ---, ---, ---
ἑτοιμάζω *(6)*, ἑτοιμάσω, ἡτοίμασα, ἡτοίμακα, ἡτοίμασμαι, ἡτοιμάσθην
εὑρίσκω *(4)*, εὑρήσω, εὗρον (εὗρα), εὕρηκα, ---, εὑρέθην
εὔχομαι *(13)*, [εὔξομαι], εὐξάμην, ---, ---, ---
ἔχω *(2)*, ἕξω, ἔσχον, ἔσχηκα, ---, ---
ζάω *(22)*, ζήσω (ζήσομαι), ἔζησα, ---, ---, ---
ζητέω *(20)*, ζητήσω, ἐζήτησα, ---, ---, ἐζητήθην
θέλω *(36)*, θελήσω, ἠθέλησα, ---, ---, ---
θεραπεύω *(4)*, θεραπεύσω, ἐθεράπευσα, ---, τεθεράπευμαι,
        ἐθεραπεύθην
[θνήσκω]*(11)*, ---, ---, τέθνηκα, ---, ---
ἵστημι (ἱστάνω) *(31)*, στήσω, ἔστησα / ἔστην, ἔστηκα, ---, ἐστάθην
        [**Note**: The two aorists are not just alternate forms, but have separate
        meanings.]
καθαρίζω *(29)*, καθαριῶ, ἐκαθάρισα, ---, κεκαθάρισμαι, ἐκαθαρίσθην
κάθημαι *(31)*, καθήσομαι, ---, ---, ---, ---
καλέω *(20)*, καλέσω, ἐκάλεσα, κέκληκα, κέκλημαι, ἐκλήθην
καταβαίνω *(28)*, καταβήσομαι, κατέβην, καταβέβηκα, ---, ---
καταλείπω *(11)*, καταλείψω, κατέλιπον (κατέλειψα), ---,
        καταλέλειμμαι, κατελείφθην
κεῖμαι *(31)*, ---, ---, ---, ---, ---
κελεύω *(4)*, ---, ἐκέλευσα, ---, ---, ---

κηρύσσω *(4)*, κηρύξω, ἐκήρυξα, ---, ---, ἐκηρύχθην

κλαίω *(6)*, κλαύσω, ἔκλαυσα, ---, ---, ---

κράζω *(6)*, κράξω, ἔκραξα, κέκραγα, ---, ---

κρίνω *(25)*, κρινῶ, ἔκρινα, κέκρικα, κέκριμαι, ἐκρίθην

κωλύω *(2)*, , ἐκώλυσα, ---, ---, ἐκωλύθην

λαλέω *(20)*, λαλήσω, ἐλάλησα, λελάληκα, λελάλημαι, ἐλαλήθην

λαμβάνω *(9)*, λήμψομαι, ἔλαβον, εἴληφα, εἴλημμαι, [ἐλήμφθην]

λέγω *(2)*, ἐρῶ, εἶπον (εἶπα), εἴρηκα, εἴρημαι, ἐρρέθην (ἐρρήθην)

λείπω *(11)*, [λείψω], ἔλιπον, ---, [λέλειμμαι], [ἐλείφθην]

λυπέω *(20)*, ---, ἐλύπησα, λελύπηκα, λελύπημαι, ἐλυπήθην

λύω *(2)*, [λύσω], ἔλυσα, ---, λέλυμαι, ἐλύθην

μανθάνω *(9)*, ---, ἔμαθον, μεμάθηκα, ---, ---

μαρτυρέω *(20)*, μαρτυρήσω, ἐμαρτύρησα, μεμαρτύρηκα, μεμαρτύρημαι, ἐμαρτυρήθην

μέλλω *(36)*, μελλήσω, ---, ---, ---, ---

μένω *(25)*, μενῶ, ἔμεινα, μεμένηκα, ---, ---

μιμνῄσκομαι *(18)*, ---, ---, ---, μέμνημαι, ἐμνήσθην [**Note**: Active compounds have future and aorist stems: μνήσω, ἔμνησα.]

μισέω *(20)*, μισήσω, ἐμίσησα, μεμίσηκα, μεμίσημαι, ---

νικάω *(22)*, νικήσω, ἐνίκησα, νενίκηκα, ---, ---

οἶδα *(28)* [Perfect tense form translated as present (pluperfect ᾔδειν).]

ὁράω *(22)*, ὄψομαι, εἶδον (εἶδα), ἑώρακα (ἑόρακα), ---, ὤφθην

ὀφείλω *(36)*, ---, ---, ---, ---, ---

παραδίδωμι *(31)*, παραδώσω, παρέδωκα, παραδέδωκα, παραδέδομαι, παρεδόθην

παραλαμβάνω *(11)*, παραλήμψομαι, παρέλαβον, ---, ---, παρελήμφθην

παρέρχομαι *(13)*, παρελεύσομαι, παρῆλθον, παρελήλυθα, ---, ---

πάσχω *(9)*, ---, ἔπαθον, πέπονθα, ---, ---

πείθω *(6,18)*, πείσω, ἔπεισα, πέποιθα, πέπεισμαι, ἐπείσθην

πειράζω *(4)*, πειράσω, ἐπείρασα, ---, πεπείρασμαι, ἐπειράσθην

πέμπω *(2)*, πέμψω, ἔπεμψα, ---, ---, ἐπέμφθην

περιπατέω *(20)*, περιπατήσω, περιεπάτησα, περιπεπάτηκα, ---, ---

πίνω *(2)*, πίομαι, ἔπιον, πέπωκα, ---, [ἐπόθην]

πίπτω *(9)*, πεσοῦμαι, ἔπεσον (ἔπεσα), πέπτωκα, ---, ---

πιστεύω *(4)*, πιστεύσω, ἐπίστευσα, πεπίστευκα, πεπίστευμαι, ἐπιστεύθην

πλανάω *(22)*, πλανήσω, ἐπλάνησα, ---, πεπλάνημαι, ἐπλανήθην

πληρόω *(22)*, πληρώσω, ἐπλήρωσα, πεπλήρωκα, πεπλήρωμαι,
    ἐπληρώθην
ποιέω *(20)*, ποιήσω, ἐποίησα, πεποίηκα, πεποίημαι, ἐποιήθην
πορεύομαι *(13)*, πορεύσομαι, ---, ---, πεπόρευμαι, ἐπορεύθην
πράσσω *(4)*, πράξω, ἔπραξα, πέπραχα, πέπραγμαι, ἐπράχθην
προσέρχομαι *(13)*, προσελεύσομαι, προσῆλθον (προσῆλθα),
    προσελήλυθα, ---, ---
προσεύχομαι *(13)*, προσεύξομαι, προσηυξάμην, ---, ---, ---
προσφέρω *(11)*, ---, προσήνεγκα (προσήνεγκον), προσενήνοχα, ---,
    προσηνέχθην
σκανδαλίζω *(6, 18)*, ---, ἐσκανδάλισα, ---, ἐσκανδάλισμαι,
    ἐσκανδαλίσθην
σταυρόω *(22)*, σταυρώσω, ἐσταύρωσα, ---, ἐσταύρωμαι, ἐσταυρώθην
στρέφω *(6,18)*, [στρέψω], ἔστρεψα, ---, [ἔστραμμαι], ἐστράφην
συνάγω *(11,18)*, συνάξω, συνήγαγον (συνῆξα), ---, συνῆγμαι, συνήχθην
συνέρχομαι *(13)*, συνελεύσομαι, συνῆλθον (συνῆλθα), συνελήλυθα,
    ---, ---
σῴζω *(2)*, σώσω, ἔσωσα, σέσωκα, σέσῳ(σ)μαι, ἐσώθην
τάσσω *(11)*, [τάξω], ἔταξα, τέταχα, τέταγμαι, [ἐτάγην (ἐτάχθην)]
τελέω *(20)*, τελέσω, ἐτέλεσα, τετέλεκα, τετέλεσμαι, ἐτελέσθην
τηρέω *(20)*, τηρήσω, ἐτήρησα, τετήρηκα, τετήρημαι, ἐτηρήθην
τίθημι *(31)*, θήσω, ἔθηκα, τέθεικα, τέθειμαι, ἐτέθην
τιμάω *(22)*, τιμήσω, ἐτίμησα, ---, τετίμημαι, ---
ὑποτάσσω *(11,18)*, ---, ὑπέταξα, ---, ὑποτέταγμαι, ὑπετάγην
φαίνω *(30)*, φανοῦμαι, ἔφανα, ---, ---, ἐφάνην
φανερόω *(22)*, φανερώσω, ἐφανέρωσα, πεφανέρωκα, πεφανέρωμαι,
    ἐφανερώθην
φέρω *(11)*, οἴσω, ἤνεγκα (ἤνεγκον), [ἐνήνοχα], ---, ἠνέχθην
φεύγω *(9)*, φεύξομαι, ἔφυγον, [πέφευγα], ---, ---
φημί *(31)*, ---, ἔφην, ---, ---, ---
φιλέω *(20)*, ---, ἐφίλησα, πεφίληκα, ---, ---
φοβέομαι *(20)*, ---, ---, ---, ---, ἐφοβήθην [**Note**: One compound which
    appears in the GNT has active forms.]
φυλάσσω *(4)*, φυλάξω, ἐφύλαξα, πεφύλαχα, ---, ἐφυλάχθην
χαίρω *(30)*, χαρήσομαι, ---, ---, ---, ἐχάρην

Appendix B
Accents and Breathing Marks That Matter

αἰ   nominative plural feminine definite article (Chapter 7)
αἵ   nominative plural feminine relative pronoun (Chapter 26)

ἀλλά   conjunction: "but" (Chapter 2)
ἄλλα   nominative / accusative plural neuter adjective: "other" (Chapter 19)

αὐταί   nominative plural feminine personal / intensive pronoun (Chapter 19)
αὗται   nominative plural feminine demonstrative pronoun: "these" (Chapter 21)

αὐτή   nominative singular feminine personal / intensive pronoun (Chapter 19)
αὕτη   nominative singular feminine demonstrative pronoun: "this" (Chapter 21)

εἶ   present active indicative second person singular of εἰμί: "you are" (Chapter 10)
εἰ   conjunction: "if," "whether" (Chapter 11 / Chapter 25)

εἰς   preposition: "into" (Chapter 3)
εἷς   nominative singular masculine numeral: "one" (Chapter 12)

ἐν   preposition: "in" (Chapter 5)
ἕν   nominative / accusative singular neuter numeral: "one" (Chapter 12)

ἐξ   preposition: "from," "out of" (Chapter 5)
ἕξ   indeclinable numeral: "six" (Chapter 12)

ἕξω   future active indicate of ἔχω (Chapter 6)
ἔξω   adverb / preposition with genitive: "outside" / "outside of"

ἡ   nominative singular feminine definite article (Chapter 7)
ἤ   conjunction: "either," "or," "than" (Chapter 9 / Chapter 27)
ἥ   nominative singular feminine relative pronoun (Chapter 26)
ᾗ   dative singular feminine relative pronoun (Chapter 26)
ᾖ   present active subjunctive third person singular of εἰμί (Chapter 34)

ἦν   imperfect active indicative third person singular of εἰμί: "he/she/it was," "there was" (Chapter 10)
ἥν   accusative singular feminine relative pronoun (Chapter 26)

ἦς   imperfect active indicative second person singular of εἰμί: "you were" (Chapter 10)

ἧς   genitive singular feminine relative pronoun (Chapter 26)

ᾖς   present active subjunctive second person singular of εἰμί (Chapter 34)

ὁ   nominative singular masculine definite article (Chapter 3)

ὅ   nominative / accusative singular neuter relative pronoun (Chapter 26)

οἱ   nominative plural masculine definite article (Chapter 3)

οἵ   nominative plural masculine relative pronoun (Chapter 26)

ὅν   accusative singular masculine relative pronoun (Chapter 26)

ὄν   present participle nominative / accusative singular neuter of εἰμί (Chapter 32)

οὐ   negative: "not" (Chapter 2)

οὗ   genitive singular masculine / neuter relative pronoun **and** relative conjunction "where" (Chapter 26)

οὕς   accusative plural masculine relative pronoun (Chapter 26)

οὖς   nominative / accusative singular neuter: "ear" (Chapter 27)

πότε   interrogative: "when" (Chapter 23)

ποτε, ποτέ   indefinite: "sometime," etc. (Chapter 23)

ποῦ   interrogative: "where" (Chapter 23)

που   indefinite: "somewhere" (Chapter 23)

πῶς   interrogative: "how" (Chapter 23)

πως   indefinite: "somehow" (Chapter 23)

τίς, τί   interrogative pronoun, also adverb: "why" (Chapter 23)

τις, τι   indefinite pronoun (Chapter 23)

ᾧ   dative singular masculine / neuter relative pronoun (Chapter 26)

ὦ   present active subjunctive first person singular of εἰμί (Chapter 34) [Also an interjection: "O!"]

ὧν   genitive plural masculine / neuter relative pronoun (Chapter 26)
ὤν   present participle nominative singular masculine of εἰμί (Chapter 32)

ὦσί(ν)   dative plural neuter: "ear" (Chapter 27)
ὦσι(ν)   present active subjunctive third person plural of εἰμί (Chapter 34)

A few liquid stem verbs have the same stem in the present and future, but the future has *epsilon* contract endings, e.g. μένω, μενῶ and κρίνω, κρινῶ. Thus the only difference between the two tenses is the accent. (Chapter 25)

Both *the first aorist active infinitive (Chapter 36) and the first aorist middle imperative second person singular (Chapter 38)* end in –αι. (The –αι is considered short for accent placement.) If the word has only two syllables, these two forms will look exactly alike. If the word has more than two syllables, however, there will be a difference. The first aorist active infinitive is always accented on the penult, regardless of how many syllables the word has, e.g. ἐνδῦσαι: "to clothe" [someone else], φυλάξαι: "to protect." The first aorist middle imperative second person singular has a recessive accent, e.g. ἔνδυσαι: "clothe yourself," "put on," φύλαξαι: "be on guard against." **Note:** In actual usage, this issue will generally only arise for verbs which have one meaning for active forms and another for middle forms.

See *Appendix D* for accent issues involving the first aorist optative third person singular.

You may come across some other words which can have identical forms with different accents or breathing marks. I have not attempted to collect them all. Watch carefully when checking a lexicon. Here are a couple of examples:

ὀδούς   nominative singular masculine: "tooth"
ὁδούς   accusative plural second declension feminine: "roads"

ὄρος, ὄρους   nominative / accusative singular and genitive singular neuter: "mountain"
ὅρος, ὅρους   nominative singular and accusative plural masculine: "boundary"

In most of these instances, one or both forms are not especially common. The main issues occur with definite articles, prepositions, pronouns, the subjunctive of εἰμί, and other little words.

Appendix C
Guide to Unaugmented Aorist Stems

One of the big challenges in learning verb forms apart from the indicative is recognizing the aorist stems. This is not too difficult for regular first aorist active and middle forms and for most aorist passives (for that reason most of these are not included in the list). Many second aorist active forms, however, are hard to get used to. Here are some of the most common second (or otherwise unusual) aorist stems you will encounter; all are active (and middle if a middle is in use) unless otherwise noted.

This chart shows you what the aorist stem looks like after any prefix, augment, connecting vowel(s), and personal endings have been removed.

ἀρ	αἴρω [First aorist.]
ἰδ	ὁράω
πι	πίνω
σχ	ἔχω
βαλ	βάλλω
γεν	γίνομαι [Aorist middle.]
εἰπ	λέγω
ἐλθ	ἔρχομαι
εὑρ	εὑρίσκω
λαβ	λαμβάνω
λιπ	λείπω
μαθ	μανθάνω
παθ	πάσχω
πεσ	πίπτω
φαγ	ἐσθίω
φαν	φαίνω [First aorist active *and* second aorist passive.]
φυγ	φεύγω
χαρ	χαίρω [Second aorist passive.]
ἐνεγκ	φέρω [First aorist.]

The –μι verbs are a bit trickier. The indicative has a first aorist active. Non-indicative forms, however, use a different stem (identified as a *second* aorist, though the endings differ from the typical second aorist). We find the stem vowel fluctuating in the same way that it does in the indicative.

ε / ει	ἵημι	[Remember that ἵημι only appears in the GNT in compounds, so you will see the prepositional prefix before the vowel(s).]

δ + ο / ου	δίδωμι
θ + ε / ει	τίθημι
στ + α / η	ἵστημι [Second aorist active.]

While not –μι verbs themselves, the following two verbs display many of the same characteristics in the aorist.

β + α / η	βαίνω [Only compounds in the GNT.]
γν + ο / ω / ου	γινώσκω

[These verbs use the typical subjunctive endings in the aorist, except for δίδωμι and γινώσκω which use *omega* throughout. See the subjunctive chapter for specific forms and accents.]

Appendix D
The Optative Mood

There is one additional mood in Greek which I have never found time to include in the basic course. It is called the optative. There are fewer than 70 optatives in the GNT and about one fourth of them occur in a particular formula: μὴ γένοιτο ("May it not / never be!" Sometimes freely translated, "God forbid!" or "By no means!" or "Certainly not!"). The optative is used when the speaker "wishes to portray an action as *possible*" (Wallace, p. 480). It is generally thought of as the mood which is farthest removed from reality.

The optative which you are most likely to encounter is the optative used "to express an *obtainable wish* or a *prayer*" (called by Wallace the "Voluntative Optative," p. 481). Here are a couple of examples:

> ὑμᾶς δὲ ὁ κύριος <u>πλεονάσαι</u> καὶ <u>περισσεύσαι</u> τῇ ἀγάπῃ εἰς ἀλλήλους.

> And <u>may</u> the Lord <u>cause</u> you <u>to increase and abound</u> in love toward one another. (1 Thessalonians 3:12)

> Ὁ δὲ κύριος <u>κατευθύναι</u> ὑμῶν τὰς καρδίας εἰς τὴν ἀγάπην τοῦ θεοῦ καὶ εἰς τὴν ὑπομονὴν τοῦ Χριστοῦ.

> And <u>may</u> the Lord <u>direct</u> your hearts into the love of God and into the steadfastness of Christ. (2 Thessalonians 3:5)

> ὁ δὲ θεὸς τῆς ἐλπίδος <u>πληρώσαι</u> ὑμᾶς πάσης χαρᾶς καὶ εἰρήνης ἐν τῷ πιστεύειν.

> And <u>may</u> the God of hope <u>fill</u> you with all joy and peace in believing. (Romans 15:13)

For other uses of the optative, you can consult Wallace, pp. 483-484.

Only present and aorist forms occur in the GNT, though future and perfect forms do exist. They have the usual aspect, the present representing a continuous action or something which is always happening or true and the aorist representing the action as a whole. As with other non-indicative moods, the aorist has no augment.

Here are a few paradigms to illustrate the various endings:

* *

	Present Active Optative of θέλω		Present M/P Optative of βούλομαι	
	Singular	*Plural*	*Singular*	*Plural*
1st	θέλοιμι	θέλοιμεν	βουλοίμην	βουλοίμεθα
2nd	θέλοις	θέλοιτε	βούλοιο	βούλοισθε
3rd	θέλοι	θέλοιεν	βούλοιτο	βούλοιντο

	First Aorist Active Optative of φυλάσσω		First Aorist Middle Optative of εὔχομαι	
1st	φυλάξαιμι	φυλάξαιμεν	εὐξαίμην	εὐξαίμεθα
2nd	φυλάξαις	φυλάξαιτε	εὔξαιο	εὔξαισθε
3rd	φυλάξαι	φυλάξαιεν	εὔξαιτο	εὔξαιντο

* *

Both the –οι and the –αι are considered *long* for accent placement. Thus there are some accent issues relating to identically spelled forms. Since the ***first aorist active infinitive*** is always accented on the penult, if this syllable is *short* it will create an identical form with the ***first aorist active optative third person singular*** (φυλάξαι, καλέσαι). If the first aorist active infinitive has a *long* vowel or diphthong in the penult, however, then this syllable will have a circumflex accent (πιστεῦσαι, τηρῆσαι), whereas the optative will continue to have an acute accent on the penult (πιστεύσαι, τηρήσαι). If we involve middle forms, then there are three forms which will be spelled alike: the ***first aorist active infinitive*** (short penult: φυλάξαι, long penult: ἐνδῦσαι), the ***first aorist middle imperative second person singular*** (short penult: φύλαξαι, long penult: ἔνδυσαι, ἦρξαι), and the ***first aorist active optative third person singular*** (short penult: φυλάξαι, long penult: ἐνδύσαι).

```
*  *  *  *  *  *  *  *  *  *  *  *  *  *  *  *  *  *  *  *  *  *  *  *  *  *  *  *  *  *  *
*          Second Aorist Active              Second Aorist Middle           *
*           Optative of ἐσθίω                  Optative of γίνομαι          *
*                                                                           *
*       Singular        Plural             Singular        Plural          *
*                                                                           *
*  1ˢᵗ  φάγοιμι        φάγοιμεν           γενοίμην       γενοίμεθα          *
*  2ⁿᵈ  φάγοις         φάγοιτε            γένοιο         γένοισθε          *
*  3ʳᵈ  φάγοι          φάγοιεν            γένοιτο        γένοιντο          *
*                                                                           *
*  *  *  *  *  *  *  *  *  *  *  *  *  *  *  *  *  *  *  *  *  *  *  *  *  *  *  *  *  *  *  *
```

```
        *  *  *  *  *  *  *  *  *  *  *  *  *  *  *  *  *  *  *  *
        *      First Aorist Passive Optative of λογίζομαι      *
        *                                                      *
        *          Singular                Plural             *
        *                                                      *
        *    1st  λογισθείην          λογισθείημεν            *
        *    2ⁿᵈ  λογισθείης          λογισθείητε             *
        *    3ʳᵈ  λογισθείη           λογισθείησαν            *
        *                                                      *
        *  *  *  *  *  *  *  *  *  *  *  *  *  *  *  *  *  *  *  *
```

Other forms which appear in the GNT are the present M/P of δύναμαι, spelled as in the present and imperfect indicative with *alpha* (δυναίμην, δύναιντο), the present active third person singular of εἰμί (εἴη), and the aorist active third person singular δίδωμι (δῴη).

Text Vocabulary

The definitions given here are the ones given in the individual chapters. For more extensive definitions and other information about specific words, students and teachers are encouraged to consult either the dictionary attached to the UBS text of the New Testament or the Danker lexicon. Verb principal parts are not included here as they are provided in a separate list. Other words are presented in typical lexicon fashion. The numbers following each word indicate the chapter in which that vocabulary word is first introduced.

ἀγαθός, -ή, -όν (14) – good

ἀγαπάω (22) – love

ἀγάπη, -ης, f. (7) – love

ἅγιος, -α, -ον (14) – holy, sacred; *as a plural substantive*: holy ones, saints

ἀγόρα, -ας, f. (8) – market place

ἀγοράζω (2) – buy

ἄγω (6) – lead, bring

ἀδελφός, -οῦ, m. (3) – brother

ἀδικία, -ας, f. (8) – wrongdoing; wickedness, unrighteousness, injustice

αἷμα, -τος, n. (27) – blood

αἴρω (29) – take up, lift up; take away, remove

αἰτέω (20) – ask, ask for; *middle*: same translation as active

αἰών, -ῶνος, m. (24) – age; eternity

αἰώνιος, -ον (14) – eternal, everlasting

ἀκολουθέω (20) – follow

ἀκούω (2) – hear, listen (to) [*genitive direct object* (sometimes)]

ἀλήθεια, -ας, f. (8) – truth

ἀληθής, -ές (27) – true, truthful; real

ἀλλά (2) – but

ἀλλήλων (21) – each other, one another

ἄλλος, -η, -ο (19) – other, another

ἁμαρτάνω (9) – sin

ἁμαρτία, -ας, f. (8) –sin

ἄν (16) – *untranslatable particle expressing contingency in certain constructions*

ἀναβαίνω (28) – go up, come up, ascend

ἀνάστασις, -εως, f. (24) – resurrection

ἀνήρ, ἀνδρός, m. (24) – man; husband

ἄνθρωπος, -ου, m. (5) – person, man; mankind

ἀνίστημι (31) – raise, raise up; *middle and second aorist active*: rise, arise, get up

ἀνοίγω (11) – open

ἄξιος, -α, -ον (14) – worthy

ἀπαγγέλλω (30) – report, tell; announce, proclaim

ἀπέρχομαι (13) – go away, depart

ἀπό (5) – *preposition with genitive*: from, away from

ἀποδίδωμι (31) – give back, return; pay

ἀποθνῄσκω (11) – die

ἀποκρίνομαι (30) – answer

ἀποκτείνω (30) – kill

ἀπόλλυμι (31) – destroy; lose; kill; *middle*: be lost, perish, be ruined; die

ἀπολύω (11) – release, set free; send away

ἀποστέλλω (28) – send; send out, send away

ἅπτω (18) – light, kindle; *middle* (18): touch, take hold of [*genitive direct object*]

ἄρτος, -ου, m. (3) – bread; *plural*: loaves

ἀρχή, -ῆς, f. (7) – beginning; ruling power, authority, ruler

ἀρχιερεύς, -έως, m. (24) – high priest

ἄρχω (6) – rule [*genitive direct object*]; *middle* (18): begin

ἄρχων, -οντος, m. (24) – ruler

ἀσθένεια, -ας, f. (8) – sickness; weakness

αὐτός, -ή, -ό (19) – he, she, it; self, of oneself, very; *preceded by article*: same

ἀφίημι (31) – cancel; forgive, pardon; leave; let, allow; send away

ἄχρι / ἄχρις (35) – until [*also* ἄχρι οὗ]

βάλλω (9) – throw

βαπτίζω (2) – baptize

βασιλεία, -ας, f. (8) – kingdom

βασιλεύς, -έως, m. (24) – king

βιβλίον, -ου, n. (12) – book

βλέπω (6) – look (on / at); see

βούλομαι (36) – wish, want; be willing

γάρ (4) – for

γεννάω (22) – beget, be *or* become the father of; bear, give birth to; *passive*: be born

γένος, -ους, n. (27) – race, nation, family; descendants; sort, kind

γίνομαι (13) – be made, be created; come about, happen; become

γινώσκω (4) – know, come to know

γραμματεύς, -έως, m. (24) – scribe

γράφω (6) – write

γυνή, γυναικός, f. (24) – woman; wife

δαιμόνιον, -ου, n. (12) – demon

δι᾿ (6)   and, but, so, now, *sometimes paired with* μεν, *possibly translated* on the
  other hand

δεῖ (36)   it is necessary, one must, one ought [*third person singular of* δέω]

δείκνυμι (31)   show

δέκα (12)   ten

δένδρον, -ου, n. (12) – tree

δέχομαι (13) – receive, accept; welcome

διά (14) – *preposition with genitive*: through, by means of; *preposition with
  accusative*: on account of, because of

διάκονος, -ου, m. (5) – servant, minister; deacon

διδάσκαλος, -ου, m. (5) – teacher

διδάσκω (4) – teach

δίδωμι (31) – give

διέρχομαι (13) – go through, cross

δίκαιος, -α, -ον (14) – righteous; just, right

δικαιοσύνη, -ης, f. (7) – righteousness; justice

δικαιόω (22) – justify, vindicate, treat as righteous

διώκω (6) – persecute; pursue, seek after

δόξα, -ης, f. (8) – glory

δοξάζω (2) – glorify

δοῦλος, -ου, m. (5) – slave, servant

δύναμαι (36) – be able, can

δύναμις, -εως, f. (24) – power, might; work of power, mighty work, miracle

δύο (12, 27) – two [*dative plural*: δυσί(ν)]

δῶρον, -ου, n. (12) – gift

ἐάν (35) – if

ἑαυτοῦ, -ῆς, -οῦ (19) – himself, herself, itself; *plural*: ἑαυτῶν – ourselves,
  yourselves, themselves

ἐγγίζω (28) – come near, draw near approach; *perfect*: be at hand

ἐγείρω (29) – raise, raise up; wake; *passive*: get up, rise, arise; awaken

ἐγώ (19) – I; *plural*: ἡμεῖς – we

ἔθνος, -ους, n. (27) – nation; Gentile

εἰ (11) – if; (25) whether

εἰμί (10) – be, exist

εἰρήνη, -ης, f. (7) – peace

εἰς (3) – *preposition with accusative*: into

εἷς, μία, ἕν (12, 27) – one

εἰσέρχομαι (13) – go in(to), enter

ἐκ, ἐξ (5) – *preposition with genitive*: from, out of

ἕκαστος, -η, -ον (19) – each

ἐκβάλλω (11) – cast out, drive out; send out, take out

ἐκεῖ (21) – there (in that place *or* to that place)

ἐκεῖνος, -η, -ο (21) – that; *plural*: these

ἐκπορεύομαι (13) – go out, come out, proceed

ἐλπίζω (2) – hope, hope (for)

ἐλπίς, ἐλπίδος, f. (24) – hope

ἐμαυτοῦ, -ῆς (19) – myself

ἐμός, -ή, -όν (21) – my

ἐν (5) – *preposition with dative*: in, on; by

ἐννέα (12) – nine

ἐντολή, -ῆς, f. (7) – command, commandment

ἕξ (12) – six

ἐξέρχομαι (13) – go out, proceed

ἔξεστι (36) – it is proper, it is permitted, it is lawful [*third person singular of the otherwise unused* ἔξειμι]

ἐπί (16) – *preposition with genitive*: on, upon; before, in the presence of; in the time of; *preposition with dative*: on, at; near; *preposition with accusative*: on, upon; against; to

ἐπιτίθημι (31) – lay on / upon, put on

ἐπιτιμάω (22) – rebuke; warn [*dative direct object*]

ἑπτά (12) – seven

ἐργάζομαι (15) – work; do

ἔργον, -ου, n. (12) – work, deed

ἔρημος, -ου, f. (16) – deserted place, uninhabited region, desert

ἔρχομαι (13) – come [occasionally "go" This is more common in compounds.]

ἐρωτάω (22) – ask (either question or request)

ἐσθίω (2) – eat

ἕτερος, -α, -ον (19) – the other (of two); other, another

ἔτι (23) – still, yet

ἑτοιμάζω (6) – prepare, make ready

ἔτος, -ους, n. (27) – year

εὐαγγέλιον, -ου, n. (12) – good news, gospel

εὑρίσκω (4) – find

εὔχομαι (13) – pray

ἔχω (2) – have, possess, hold

ἕως (35) – until [also ἕως οὗ and ἕως ὅτου]

ζάω (22) – live

ζητέω (20) – seek, search for, look for; strive for, try to obtain; investigate

ζωή, -ῆς, f. (7) – life

ἤ (9) – or, either...or; (27) than

ἥλιος, -ου, m. (5) – sun

ἡμέρα, -ας, f. (8) – day

ἡμέτερος, -α, -ον (21) – our

θάλασσα, -ης, f. (8) – sea

θάνατος, -ου, m. (5) – death

θέλημα, -τος, n. (27) – will

θέλω (36) – wish, want; will

θεός, οῦ, m. (3) – god; God

θεραπεύω (4) – heal

θησαυρός, -οῦ, m. (3) – treasure; treasury

θλίψις, -εως, f. (24) – tribulation

θύρα, -ας, f. – door

ἱερεύς, -έως, m. (24) – priest

ἱερόν, -οῦ, n. (12) – temple

ἱμάτιον, -ου, n. (12) – coat, robe (outer garment); garment, clothing

ἵνα (34) – that, in order that; so that

ἵστημι (31) – put, place, set; establish; *middle, passive, and second aorist active*:
      stand; stand still; stop; *perfect with present force*: stand

καθαρίζω (29) – cleanse, make clean, purify

κάθημαι (31) – sit, sit down; live; be

καθώς (26) – as, just as

καί (2) – and; (9) both...and; (12) also, even

καιρός, -οῦ, m. (21) – time (viewed as an occasion), appointed time, proper time,
      season

κακός, -ή, -όν (14) – bad, evil, wrong

καλέω (20) – call, name; invite

καλός, -ή, -όν (14) – good; honorable; fine, beautiful

καρδία, -ας, f. (8) – heart

καρπός, -οῦ, m. (3) – fruit

κατά (8) – *preposition with genitive*: against; *preposition with accusative*:
      according to, in accordance with

καταβαίνω (28) – go down, come down, descend

καταλείπω (11) – leave, leave behind

κεῖμαι (31) – lie; be

κελεύω (4) – order, command

κεφαλή, -ῆς, f. (7) – head

κηρύσσω (5) – proclaim, preach

κλαίω (6) – weep, weep for

κόσμος, -ου, m. (3) – world

κράζω (6) – call out, cry out

κρίνω (25) – judge, pass judgment; condemn

κρίσις, -εως, f. (24) – judgment

κύριος, -ου, m. (5) – lord, master; Lord

κωλύω (2) – hinder, prevent

λαλέω (20) – talk, speak

λαμβάνω (9) – take; receive

λαός, -οῦ, m. (3) – people; nation

λέγω (2) – say, speak, tell

λείπω (11) – leave

λόγος, -ου, m. (3) – word; Word

λυπέω (20) – grieve [*transitive*], vex; offend, insult; *passive*: grieve [*intransitive*], be sad, be sorrowful, be distressed

λύπη, -ης, f. (7) – grief, pain

λύω (2) – loose, untie; free, set free, release; break, annul; destroy

μαθητής, -οῦ, m. (16) – disciple

μακάριος, -α, -ον (14) blessed, happy, fortunate

μανθάνω (9) – learn

μαρτυρέω (20) – bear witness, testify

μάρτυς, μάρτυρος, m. (24) – witness; martyr

μέγας, μεγάλη, μέγα (27) – great, large

μείζων, -ον (27) – greater

μέλλω (36) – be about (to), be going (to); intend; be destined

μέλος, -ους, n. (27) – member, part, limb (of the body, whether literal or figurative)

μέν (6) – *particle often paired with* δέ *and not translated;* on the one hand

μένω (25) – stay, remain, abide

μέρος, -ους, n. (27) – part (often geographical or quantitative)

μετά (12) – *preposition with genitive*: with, among; *preposition with accusative*: after

μέχρι / μέχρις (35) – until [*also* μέχρι οὗ]

μή (33) – not; *used in questions to indicate that a negative answer is expected*

μηδέ (33) – nor, and not, not even

μηδείς, μηδεμία, μηδέν (33) – no one, nothing

μηδέποτε (33) – never

μηδέπω (33) – not yet

μηκέτι (33) – no longer, no more

μήτηρ, μητρός, f. (24) – mother

μήτι (31) – *used in questions to indicate either that a negative answer is expected or that the questioner has some doubt about the answer*

μιμνήσκομαι (18) – remember [*genitive direct object*]

μισέω (20) – hate

ναός, -οῦ, m. (3) – temple, sanctuary

νεκρός, -ά, όν (14) – dead; *as a substantive*: dead body, corpse

νέος, -α, -ον (14) – new; young

νεφέλη, -ης, f. (7) – cloud

νικάω (22) – conquer, overcome

νόμος, -ου, m. (3) – law

νῦν (13) – now

νύξ, νυκτός, f. (24) – night

ὁ, ἡ, τό (3, 7, 12) – *definite article*: the

ὁδός, -ου, f. (16) – way, road; way, way of life

ὅθεν (26) – from there, from which, whence

οἶδα (28) – [*perfect*] know

οἶκος, -ου, m. (5) – house

οἶνος, -ου, m. (5) – wine

οἷος, -η, -ον (26) – such as, as, of what sort

ὀκτώ (12) – eight

ὄνομα, -τος, n. (27) – name

ὅπου (26) – where

ὅπως (34) – that, in order that

ὁράω (22) – see; *passive*: appear

ὀργή, -ῆς, f. (7) – anger, wrath

ὄρος, -ους, n. (27) – mountain

ὅς, ἥ, ὅ (26) – who, which, that

ὅς, ἥ, ὅ ἄν / ἐάν (35) – whoever, whatever

ὅσος, -η, -ον (26) – as much as, as many as; all…who, all…which (that); all those who, all the things which, everything which; as great, as far, as long

ὅστις, ἥτις, ὅ τι (26) – whoever, everyone who, all who (whichever, everything which); who, which, that

ὅστις, ἥτις, ὅ τι ἄν / ἐάν (35) – whoever, whatever

ὅταν (35) – when, whenever

ὅτε (26) – when

ὅτι (15) – because, since; (20) that

οὐ, οὐκ, οὐχ (2) – not; (31) *used in questions to indicate that an affirmative answer is expected* [*also* οὐχί]

οὗ (26) – where

οὐδέ (13) – and not, nor (neither...nor)

οὐδείς, οὐδεμία, οὐδέν (13, 27) – no one, nothing

οὐδέποτε (23) – never

οὐκέτι (23) – no longer

οὖν (4) – therefore, then

οὔπω (23) – not yet

οὐρανός, -οῦ, m. (3) – sky; heaven

οὖς, ὠτός, n. (27) – ear

οὗτος, αὕτη, τοῦτο (21) – this; *plural:* these

οὕτως (22) – thus, in this way

ὀφείλω (36) – ought, must; owe

ὄχλος, -ου, m. (3) – crowd

πάλιν (13) – again

παρά (25) – *preposition with genitive:* from; *preposition with dative:* with, near, at the side of; in the sight of, in the judgment of; *preposition with accusative:* by, beside; along; than, more than; rather than

παραδίδωμι (31) – hand over, deliver; betray; hand down

παραλαμβάνω (11) – receive, accept; take with, take along

παρέρχομαι (13) – pass away, go by

πᾶς, πᾶσα, πᾶν (27) – each, every; all; whole

πάσχω (9) – suffer

πατήρ, πατρός, m. (24) – father

πείθω (6) – persuade, convince; *passive* (18): obey, pay attention to [*dative direct object*]; be persuaded, believe; *perfect active* (28): depend on, trust in, rely on; be convinced; be certain, be sure; *perfect passive* (29): be convinced, be confident; be certain

πειράζω (4) – try; test, tempt

πέμπω (2) – send

πέντε (12) – five

περιπατέω (20) – go about, walk; live, conduct oneself

πίνω (2) – drink

πίπτω (9) – fall, fall down

πιστεύω (4) – believe; trust [*dative direct object*]; believe in (πιστεύω εἰς)

πίστις, -εως, f. (24) – faith, belief, trust

πλανάω (22) – lead astray, mislead, deceive; *passive*: go astray, wander; be mistaken, be misled, be deceived

πλείων, -ον (27) – more

πλῆθος, -ους, n. (27) – multitude

πληρόω (22) – fulfill; fill; bring to completion

πλοῖον, -ου, n. (12) – boat

πνεῦμα, -τος, n. (27) – spirit; wind; breath

πόθεν (23) – from where?, whence?

ποιέω (20) – do, make

ποῖος, -η, -ον (23) – what kind of?, what sort of?, which?, what?

πόλις, -εως, f. (24) – city

πολύς, πολλή, πολύ (27) – much, many

πονηρός, -ά, -όν (14) – evil, wicked

πορεύομαι (13) – go; travel

πόσος, -η, -ον (23) – how great?, how much?; *plural*: how many?

πότε (23) – when?

ποτε, ποτέ (23) – sometime, anytime, once, ever

πότερον (25) – whether; *paired with* ἤ: whether…or

ποῦ (23) – where?

που (23) – somewhere, anywhere

πούς, ποδός, m. (24) – foot

πράσσω (4) – do, accomplish; act

πρίν / πρὶν ἤ (37) – before

πρό (37) – *preposition with genitive*: before

πρός (3) – *preposition with accusative*: to, toward

προσέρχομαι (13) – go to, approach

προσεύχομαι (13) – pray

προσφέρω (11) – bring to; offer, present

πρόσωπον, -ου, n. (12) – face

προφήτης, -ου, m. (16) – prophet

πῦρ, πυρός, n. (27) – fire

πῶς (23) – how?

πως (23) – somehow, anyhow

σάρξ, σαρκός, f. (24) – flesh

σεαυτοῦ, -ῆς (19) – yourself

σημεῖον, -ου, n. (12) – sign; miraculous sign, miracle

σκανδαλίζω (6) – cause to sin, cause to give up one's faith; offend, shock;
   passive (18): fall away, fall into sin, give up one's faith

σκότος, -ους, n. (27) – darkness

σός, -ή, -όν (21) – your (s.)

σοφία, -ας, f. (8) – wisdom

σοφός, -ή, -όν (14) – wise

σπέρμα, -τος, n. (27) – seed; offspring, descendants

σταυρόω (22) –crucify

στόμα, -τος, n. (27) – mouth

στρατιώτης, -ου, m. (16) – soldier

στρέφω (6) – turn [*transitive*]; *passive*: turn [*intransitive*], turn around

σύ (19) – you (s.); *plural*: ὑμεῖς – you (pl.)

συμφέρει (34) – it is better, it is to one's advantage, it is helpful / good / useful

σύν (5) – *preposition with dative*: with

συνάγω (11) – gather [*transitive*]; bring together; *passive* (18): come together,
   gather, assemble [*intransitive*]

συνέρχομαι (13) – go with, accompany; come together (with)

σῴζω (2) – save

σῶμα, -τος, n. (27) – body

σωτήρ, -ῆρος, m. (24) – savior

τάσσω (11) – arrange; order, appoint

τέκνον, -ου, n. (12) – child

τελέω (20) – finish, complete, end

τέλος, -ους, n. (27) – end; goal

τέσσαρες, τέσσαρα / τέσσερα (12, 27) – four

τηρέω (20) – keep; observe, obey, keep (laws, commandments)

τίθημι (31) – put, place, lay, set; lay down; lay aside

τιμάω (22) – honor

τίς, τί (23) – who?, what?, which?, what sort of? [*also*: τί – why?]

τις, τι (23) – someone, something; anyone, anything; some, a certain

τοιοῦτος, τοιαύτη, τοιοῦτον/ο (21) – such, of such a kind

τοσοῦτος, τοσαύτη, τοσοῦτον/ο (21) – so large, so great, so much; *plural*: so
   many)

τότε (22) – then, at that time

τρεῖς, τρία (12, 27) – three

ὕδωρ, ὕδατος, n. (27) – water

υἱός, -οῦ, m. (3) – son

ὑμέτερος, -α, -ον (21)   your (pl.)

ὑπέρ (15)   *preposition with genitive*: for, for the sake of, on behalf of;
    preposition with accusative: over and above, beyond

ὑπό (17)   *preposition with genitive*: by; *preposition with accusative*: under,
    below

ὑποτάσσω (11)   subject, subordinate, place in subjection to; *passive* (18): be
    subject to, submit to, obey [*dative direct object*]

φαίνω (30) – shine, give light; *passive*: appear, be or become visible

φανερόω (22) – show, reveal, make known; *passive*: be revealed, become known

φέρω (11) – bring, carry; bear, endure

φεύγω (9) – flee

φημί (31) – say

φιλέω (20) – love

φίλος, -ου, m. (3) – friend

φοβέομαι (20) – fear, be afraid (of); reverence (with God as object)

φυλάσσω (4) – guard; keep; protect; *middle* (18): be on one's guard (against),
    avoid, look out for, beware of

φωνή, -ῆς, f. (7) – voice; sound

φῶς, φωτός, n. (27) – fire

χαίρω (30) – rejoice; *passive*: rejoice

χάρις, -ιτος, f. (24) – grace

χείρ, χειρός, f. (24) – hand

χρόνος, -ου, m. (21) – time, period of time

χώρα, -ας, f. (8) – country, region

ψυχή, -ῆς, f. (7) – soul, life; one's inner being, self

ὧδε (21) – here (in this place *or* to this place)

ὥρα, -ας, f. (8) – hour

ὡς (20) – that; (26) as, like; when

ὥσπερ (26) – as, just as

ὥστε (37) – that, so that, with the result that; therefore, thus; in order that

Vocabulary Supplement

This supplement to the text vocabulary covers the remaining words which occur thirty times or more in the Greek New Testament. Many of them occur in the examples and in the homework passages. Many should be easily learned on the basis of either other Greek words or English derivatives. Only the most basic meanings are given here; for additional meanings, consult a lexicon such as the one in the UBS text or Danker. Notice that in this list I have used the definite article to indicate gender.

ἄγγελος, -ου, ὁ – messenger; angel
ἀγρός, -οῦ, ὁ – field
ἀκάθαρτος, -ον – unclean
ἁμαρτωλός, -όν – sinful
ἀναγινώσκω – read
ἄνεμος, -ου, ὁ – wind
ἀπόστολος, -ου, ὁ – apostle
ἄρα – then, therefore
ἀρνέομαι – deny
ἀρνίον, -ου, τό – lamb
ἄρτι – just now
ἀσθενέω – be sick, be weak
ἀσπάζομαι – greet
ἄχρι / ἄχρις – *preposition with genitive*: until, as far as; *conjunction*: until
βλασφημέω – speak against God, blaspheme
γε – *enclitic particle used to focus attention on the word to which it is attached*
γενεά, -ᾶς, ἡ – generation
γλῶσσα, -ης, ἡ – tongue
γραφή, -ης, ἡ – Scripture
δεξιός, -ά, -όν – right
δεύτερος, -α, -ον – second
δέω – bind
διάβολος, -ον – slanderous; *mostly used as a substantive*: adversary, Devil
διαθήκη, -ης, ἡ – covenant; testament
διακονέω – serve
διακονία, -ας, ἡ – ministry, service
διδαχή, -ῆς, ἡ – teaching
διό – therefore
δοκέω – think; seem
δύνατος, -η, -ον – possible

δώδεκα – twelve

ἐγγύς – *adverb and preposition with genitive and occasionally dative*: near

ἐκκλησία, -ας, ἡ – church

ἐλεέω – have mercy

ἔμπροσθεν – *preposition with genitive*: before, *adverb*: ahead, in front of

ἐνώπιον – *preposition with genitive*: in the presence of, before

ἐξουσία, -ας, ἡ – authority

ἔξω – *adverb*: outside; *preposition with genitive*: out of, outside

ἐπαγγελία, -ας, ἡ – promise

ἐπερωτάω – ask

ἐπιγινώσκω – know

ἐπιθυμία, -ας, ἡ – desire

ἐπικαλέω – call; *middle*: call upon

ἐπιστρέφω – turn back

ἔσχατος, -η, -ον – last

εὐαγγελίζω – bring good news

εὐθέως – immediately

εὐθύς – immediately

εὐλογέω – bless

εὐχαριστέω – give thanks

ἐχθρός, -ή, -όν – hostile; *as a substantive*: enemy

ἕως – *conjunction*: until; *preposition with genitive*: as far as, until

ἤδη – already, now

θαυμάζω – wonder, be amazed

θεωρέω – see, look at

θηρίον, -ου, τό – animal, beast

θρόνος, -ου, ὁ – throne

ἴδιος, -α, -ον – one's own

ἰδού – *particle used to draw attention to what follows*: look, behold

ἱκανός, -ή, -όν – sufficient; fit

καθίζω – sit down

καινός, -ή, -όν – new

καλῶς – well

κατοικέω – live, live in

καυχάομαι – boast

κρατέω – hold fast; take hold of

λίθος, -ου, ὁ – stone

λογίζομαι – reckon; consider

λοιπός, -ή, -όν – rest, remaining
μᾶλλον – rather, more
μαρτυρία, -ας, ἡ – testimony
μέσος, -η, -ον – middle
μετανοέω – repent
μήτε – and not; neither, nor
μικρός, -ά, -όν – little
μνημεῖον, -ου, τό – grave, tomb
μόνος, -η, -ον – alone, only
ναί – yes
οἰκία, -ας, ἡ – house
οἰκοδομέω – build; edify
ὀλίγος, -η, -ον – few
ὅλος, -η, -ον – whole
ὅμοιος, -α, -ον – like
ὁμοίως – likewise
ὀπίσω – *preposition with genitive*: after; behind; *adverb*: back, behind
οὐαί – woe!
οὔτε – neither, nor
ὀφθαλμός, οῦ, ὁ – eye
παιδίον, -ου, τό – child
πάντοτε – always
παραβολή, -ῆς, ἡ – parable
παραγγέλω – command
παραγίνομαι – arrive
παρακαλέω – urge; encourage; comfort
παρίστημι – present: *intransitive*: be present
παρρησία, -ας, ἡ – openness; boldness
περί – *preposition with genitive*: concerning; for; *preposition with accusative*:
    around
περισσεύω – abound, overflow
περιτομή, -ῆς, ἡ – circumcision
πιστός, -ή, -όν – faithful; believing
πλήν – *conjunctive*: but, however; *preposition with genitive*: except
ποτήριον, -ου, τό – cup
πρεσβύτερος, -α, -ον – elder
πρόβατον, -ου, τό – sheep
προσευχή, -ῆς, ἡ – prayer

προσκυνέω – worship
πρῶτος, -η, -ον – first
πτωχός, ή, -όν – poor
σήμερον – today
σπείρω – sow
συναγωγή, -ῆς, ἡ – synagogue
συνείδησις, -εως, ἡ – conscience
σωτηρία, -ας, ἡ – salvation
τε – *enclitic particle*: and; and so
τιμή, -ῆς, ἡ – honor
τόπος, -ου, ὁ – place
τρίτος, -η, -ον – third
τυφλός, -ή, -όν – blind
ὑπάγω – go
ὑπάρχω – be
ὑπομονή, -ῆς, ἡ – patient endurance
ὑποστρέφω – return
φόβος, -ου, ὁ – fear
φυλακή, -ῆς, ἡ – prison; watch (of the night)
φυλή, -ῆς, ἡ – tribe
φωνέω – call
χαρά, ᾶς, ἡ – joy
χρεία, -ας, ἡ – need
χωρίς – *preposition with genitive*: without; *adverb*: separately

Index

Note: This is not meant to be a completely exhaustive index and does not include extensive cross referencing. Information can also be located by consulting the Table of Contents. [WB (1) = Workbook and Study Guide (Part 1)]

Accents
  acute, grave, and circumflex 16
  Appendix B 248
  change to grave when another
    word follows 21
  contract verbs 99
  enclitics 52
  first declension feminine 41, 43
  names of syllables 25
  noun accent (persistent) 25
  proclitics 21
  second declension masculine 25, 33
  second declension neuter 59
  third declension nouns 120
  verb accent (recessive) 28
Accusative case
  forms (See specific declension
    under Nouns.)
  introduction 23
  uses
    cognate accusative WB (1) 179
    direct object 23
    double accusative 102, WB (1) 31
    measure (extent of time) 232
    object of preposition 25
    subject of infinitive 226
Adjectives
  agreement 68
  attributive position 69
  comparative 143
  first and second declension 68
  in two forms / terminations 72
  participles used as 194
  predicate position 69
  relative 131
  substantive 70
  third declension 138
Adverbial καί 61
Adverbs
  indefinite 115

interrogative 114
  regular formation 110
Alphabet 16, 17
  miniscule letters 16
  uncial letters 16
Antecedent
  defined 129
  omitted 133
Anticipated answers 174
Aorist tense
  active indicative forms 46
  aspect 46
  first aorist 46
  introduction 46
  middle indicative forms 74
  passive indicative forms 159
  second aorist 47
  translation 46, 159
  unaugmented stems 177, 251
Apodosis 56
Article
  articular infinitive 226
  full paradigm 60
  translated as possessive WB (1) 13
  used to create substantive
    with adjective 70
    with participle 196
    with prepositional phrase
      or genitive 60
Aspect
  aorist tense 46
  future tense 36
  imperfect tense 27
  perfect, pluperfect tense 145, 152
  present tense 21
Assimilation (attraction) of
    relative pronoun 134
Attributive
  genitive bonus (2nd exam)
  position 69

Augment
    aorist   46
    imperfect   27
    pluperfect   150
Breathing Marks
    Appendix B   248
    introduction   16
Causal clause
    infinitive used as   236
    participle used as   199
    with ὅτι   74
Compound verbs   56
Conditions
    first class   57
    participle expressing   201
    second class   78
    third class   223
Conjugation   19
Conjunctions   21
    coordinating   56
    subordinating   56
Contract verbs
    alpha   108
    epsilon   99
    omicron   109
Crasis   107
Dative case
    forms (See specific declensions
        under Nouns.)
    introduction   32
    uses
        association   67
        destination   67
        direct object   39
        indirect object   32
        means (Instrument)   97
        object of preposition   34
        possession   WB (1) 125
        time   106
Declension of nouns   32
Dental consonants   36
Deponent verbs   63, 73
Diphthongs   17
Direct statement / quotation   101
Elision   38
Enclitics   52

Future tense
    active indicative forms   36
    aspect   36
    contract endings   175
    deponent futures   64
    introduction   36
    middle indicative forms   64
    passive indicative forms   161
    translation   36, 161
Gender of nouns   41
Genitive case
    forms (See specific declension
        under Nouns.)
    introduction   31
    uses
        absolute   204
        attributive   bonus (2nd exam)
        comparison   144
        direct object   39
        object of preposition   34
        objective   61
        partitive (of the whole)   116
        possession   31
        subjective   61
        time   123
Historical present   116
Imperative mood
    forms   237
    introduction   237
    tenses   237
    uses
        command   240
        prohibition   241
        request / entreaty   242
Imperfect tense
    active indicative forms   27
    aspect   27
    introduction   27
    M/P indicative forms   73, 82
    translation   27, 82
Indicative mood
    chart of endings   163
    defined   19
Indirect discourse
    infinitive   230
    question   126

statement   101
Infinitives
   forms   227
   introduction   226
   tenses   226
   uses
      cause   236
      complementary   230
      direct object   230
      epexegetical   233
      indirect discourse   230
      purpose   233
      result   235
      subject   229
      time   235
Intransitive verb   40
Iota subscript   22
Labial consonants   36
Liquid consonants   125
Liquid stem verbs   125
$-\mu\iota$ verbs (indicative)   165
Mood
   defined   19
   imperative   237
   indicative   19
   optative   253
   subjunctive   208
Nicene Creed   206
Nominative case
   forms (See specific declensions
      under Nouns.)
   introduction   23
   uses
      emphatic subject   92
      predicate nominative   53
      subject   23
Nouns
   contracted   77
   first declension feminine   41, 43
   first declension masculine   76
   second declension feminine   77
   second declension masculine   23, 33
   second declension neuter   59
   third declension masculine
      and feminine   118
   third declension neuter   136

Nu-movable   20
Number
   nouns   23
   third singular with neuter
      plural subject   60
   verbs   19
Numbers   61, 142
Optative mood (*Appendix* D)   253
Palatal consonants   36
Participles
   formation chart   192
   forms   155, 178
   introduction   176
   tenses   176
   uses
      adjectival proper   194
      adverbial   198
         cause   199
         concession   200
         condition   201
         manner   200
         means   200
         purpose   201
         result   201
         time   199
      attendant circumstance   202
      complementary   198
      genitive absolute   204
      periphrastic   155, 205
      redundant / pleonastic   203
      substantive   196
Particles   37
Perfect tense
   active indicative forms   147
   aspect   145, 152
   extensive / translation   145, 152
   intensive / translation   145, 152
   introduction   145
   M/P indicative forms   153
   with present force   146, 153
Person   19
Pluperfect tense
   active indicative forms   150
   aspect   145, 152
   extensive / translation   149, 152
   intensive / translation   150, 153

introduction 145, 149
M/P indicative forms 157
with simple past (or imperfect)
    force 150
Postpositives 29
Preposition (object of) 25
Present tense
    active indicative forms 19
    aspect 21
    historical present 116
    introduction 19
    M/P indicative forms 63, 82
    translation 19, 20, 82
Principal parts
    Appendix A 243
    introduction 37
Proclitics (See Accents.)
Pronouns
    demonstrative 104
    indefinite 115
    indefinite relative 130
    intensive 94
    interrogative 112, 114
    personal 92
    possessive 106
    reciprocal 106
    reflexive 95
    relative 129
Protasis 56
Punctuation 97
Subjunctive mood
    forms 209
    introduction 208
    tenses 208
    uses
        deliberative 221
        emphatic negation 222
        ἵνα clauses 216
            epexegetical 219
            purpose 216
            result 220
            substantival / noun clauses 217
                apposition 219
                direct object (content) 218
                predicate nominative 217
                subject 217

hortatory 221
indefinite relative clause 224
indefinite temporal clause 225
prohibition 223
third class condition 223
    future more probable 223
    present general 223
Subordinate clauses (indicative)
    causal 74
    conditional 56, 78
    indirect question 126
    indirect statement 101
    relative 129
Tense (See Aorist, Future, etc.)
    defined 19
Transitive verb 40
Type of action (See Aspect.)
Unaugmented aorist stems
        (*Appendix* C) 251
Verbs (See specific tense.)
Vocative case 122
Voice
    active 19
    defined 19
    middle 85
    passive 81